P
**COAL M**

"Few subjects are too difficult to deal with here, yet there is nothing sensationalistic... Those reading this can be assured they have met the real Loretta Lynn."

—*Billboard*

"The feisty, tell-it-like-it-is coal miner's daughter from Butcher Holler, Kentucky, talks about growing up dirt poor, hungry, and sexually ignorant... Since Loretta's education was, uh, haphazard, George Vecsey (who knows about miners—see his *One Sunset A Week*, 1974) wrote this down for her, but you'll hear her voice all right, that strong, high mountain twang, not chic, maybe, but real and earthy—like Loretta." —*Kirkus Reviews*

"This affecting and fascinating story will delight her fans and may even win her some converts... It's funny, sad, intense, but what makes it is Loretta herself—just folks, but a remarkable combination of innocence, strength, and country shrewdness." —*Publishers Weekly*

"[COAL MINER'S DAUGHTER] may introduce Lynn, a pioneer among female country music singers, to younger listeners who may only know her work through her recent recording with Jack White and/or tribute albums. Lynn tells her story in a straightforward manner, with great humor, no regrets, and a deeply embedded sense of dignity... [A] gentle, charming, and thoroughly engaging story of an American original, highly recommended for anyone interested in American music."

—*Library Journal*

# Coal
# Miner's
# Daughter

## ALSO BY LORETTA LYNN

*Me & Patsy Kickin' Up Dust: My Friendship
with Patsy Cline*

*Honky Tonk Girl: My Life in Lyrics*

*You're Cookin' It Country: My Favorite
Recipes and Memories*

*Still Woman Enough: A Memoir*

*Coal Miner's Daughter*

# Coal Miner's Daughter

## Loretta Lynn

WITH GEORGE VECSEY

**GRAND CENTRAL**
**PUBLISHING**

New York  Boston

Grand Central Publishing
Hachette Book Group
1290 Avenue of the Americas, New York, NY 10104
grandcentralpublishing.com
twitter.com/grandcentralpub

Originally published by Henry Regnery Co. in 1976.

First Grand Central Publishing edition: February 2021
First Grand Central Publishing mass market edition: September 2022

Grand Central Publishing is a division of Hachette Book Group, Inc. The Grand Central Publishing name and logo is a trademark of Hachette Book Group, Inc.

The publisher is not responsible for websites (or their content) that are not owned by the publisher.

The Hachette Speakers Bureau provides a wide range of authors for speaking events. To find out more, go to www.hachettespeakersbureau.com or call (866) 376-6591.

All photographs in insert 1 are from the personal collection of Loretta Lynn, except where otherwise noted (copyright Loretta Lynn).

All photos in insert 2 are courtesy of the Coal Miner's Daughter Museum, except where otherwise noted.

Library of Congress Cataloging-in-Publication Data
Names: Lynn, Loretta, author.
Title: Coal miner's daughter / Loretta Lynn.
Description: First Grand Central Publishing Edition. | New York: Grand Central Publishing, 2021. | Summary: "Reissued for the 40th Anniversary of the Oscar-winning, Sissy Spacek-starring film of the same name, COAL MINER'S DAUGHTER recounts Loretta Lynn's astonishing journey to become one of the original queens of country music. Loretta grew up dirt poor in the mountains of Kentucky, she was married at fifteen years old, and became a mother soon after. At the age of twenty-four, her husband, Doo, gave her a guitar as an anniversary present. Soon, she began penning songs and singing in front of honky-tonk audiences, and, through years of hard work, talent, and true grit, eventually made her way to Nashville, the Grand Ole Opry, eventually securing her place in country music history. Loretta's prolific and influential songwriting made her the first woman to receive a gold record in country music, and got her named the first female Entertainer of the Year by the Country Music Association. This riveting memoir introduces readers to all the highs and lows on her road to success and the tough, smart, funny, and fascinating woman behind the legend"-- Provided by publisher.
Identifiers: LCCN 2020030170 | ISBN 9781538701713 (trade paperback) | ISBN 9781538701690 (ebook)
Subjects: LCSH: Lynn, Loretta. | Country musicians--United States--Biography. | LCGFT: Autobiographies.
Classification: LCC ML420.L947 A3 2021 | DDC 782.421642092 [B]--dc23
LC record available at https://lccn.loc.gov/2020030170

ISBNs: 9781538701706 (mass market), 9781538701690 (ebook)

Printed in the United States of America

OPM

10  9  8  7  6  5  4  3  2  1

*To My Husband, Doo. Always.*

# Contents

*Preface to the New Edition*   *xiii*

*About Me and This Book*   *xvii*

1   Butcher Holler   1

2   Daddy   10

3   Mommy   19

4   Family Style   27

5   School Days   35

6   The Pie Social   46

7   Doolittle   53

8   Hey, You Ain't Supposed to Wear Clothes under Your Nightgown   60

9   Doo Kicks Me Out   68

10   Two Thousand Miles from Home   73

11  A Death in the Family     84

12  Beginner's Luck     93

13  An Honest-to-Goodness Record     101

14  Fans     106

15  The Education of a Country Singer     114

16  Music City, U.S.A.     123

17  Patsy     129

18  My Kids     135

19  Performer     143

20  Songwriter     150

21  We Bought the Whole Town     156

22  Me and Doo     170

23  The Hyden Widows     177

24  The Truth about My Health     186

25  Mexico     195

26  Entertainer of the Year     199

27  Death Threats     213

28  Baptized at Last     218

29  Confessions of a Bug                         227

30  On the Road                                 232

31  What's Next?                                251

What Came Next: Forty More Years
with Loretta Lynn                              255

32  The View from the Mountain Top              257

33  Locking Horns                               260

34  My Work Husband (Conway Twitty)             262

35  True Love                                   266

36  Angels                                      269

37  Sloe Gin Fizz (Jack White)                  271

38  Fake News                                   275

*Acknowledgments*                              279

*Reading Group Guide*                          283

# Preface to the New Edition

It's been over forty years since the book you hold in your hands was released. First it was a best-selling book; then it was an Oscar-winning movie. Forty years.

To me, that feels like yesterday.

Today I'm eighty-eight years old. Who'd have thought I'd live to be this old? I sure didn't. My daddy had a stroke when he was just fifty-one—and I got kids older than that!

Lately I think a lot about the past. My memories are as real to me as the minute I'm living in now. When I think about people I've loved who have already passed, my heart fills up and the memories just start to pour. That's the way I felt when me and my daughter decided to write about my good friend Patsy Cline here lately. I'd been talking about Patsy a lot and my daughter said, "Momma, we've got to write some of this down." I knew she was right. Patsy was my best friend. If it weren't for her, I don't know what I'd have done. Me and her made a great team.

While we were writing the book that became *Me & Patsy Kickin' Up Dust*, our editor asked me questions like, "Did that happen in kindergarten or third grade?" or "What color was that couch?" I told her, "Honey, I don't know. When you've lived as long as I have, you just try and remember back that far!" Some things you just know and some things, well, who cares?

Fortunately, a lot of my memories have been preserved. Lord knows I've done thousands of interviews over the years, so there's plenty of articles, videos, and even books where I've told a lot about my life. Plus, I keep near about everything. My kids accuse me of being a hoarder, whatever that means. Growing up poor, in the Depression, I learned to hold on to things. So, all my life I've been saving things from my fans, from my travels, and from my career. Clothes, letters, cards, furniture, awards, little presents from all over the world—you name it, I got it.

About twenty years ago we got serious and built a big, beautiful museum out near my house so fans who visit have somewhere to go and learn about my life and career. Tim Cobb designed it. We call it the Coal Miner's Daughter Museum. It's out on my property in Hurricane Mills, right across from the replica of the house I grew up in that they built for the *Coal Miner's Daughter* movie. You can go inside and walk around. It's fully furnished and looks just like it did when I was growing up, right down to the cup of tea sitting there on the kitchen table where my momma used to read tea leaves. You can walk from there over to my museum. It's big—18,000 square feet! Inside I've got a bunch of my stage outfits—from the very first stage dress I ever made to my ball gowns, all my awards, and every single one of my records. The whole place is real interactive, so you can walk onto my first tour bus and see a replica of the one-room schoolhouse I used to go to back in Kentucky. I've featured special friends and family, like Conway Twitty, my sister Crystal Gayle, and of course, Patsy Cline. There's always something new to see 'cause Tim keeps the displays fresh. People say it rivals Graceland—it's just farther out in the country, just like me.

Even in a place this size, we still don't have room to show everything. Tim went back into storage the other day to find a dress Barbra Streisand gave me. He's got everything cataloged and real orderly and knows where everything is. He hauled out a bunch of big old scrapbooks. Boy, those things just took me back to 1975. They'd been in a closet in the big house for years, but then we had a house fire when a candle tipped over on the porch. I burned my hand trying to put that thing out with a pillow. Anyway, I guess somebody'd rescued them and moved them and I never even paid much attention. I pulled back the cover of one and I could smell the smoke. The pages stuck together, singed around the edges. Inside were hundreds of clippings—interviews and articles about me. I'd forgotten most all of them, to tell the truth. But what about took my breath away were the odds and ends that I had tucked in there, too, like a handwritten note from my dear friend, country music legend Ernest Tubb, a program from a White House dinner, and an invitation to the Oscars. Those little mementos took me right back.

So, I got to thinking we might take a look back at *Coal Miner's Daughter*, maybe give it an update. After you read this new edition, you'll find some new materials we added there at the end. I hope you'll enjoy it as much as we enjoyed putting it together for you.

*Loretta Lynn*
*Hurricane Mills, Tennessee*
*April 2020*

# About Me and This Book

Well, I look out the window and what do I see?
The breeze is a-blowin' the leaves from the trees
Everything is free—everything but me...
—*"I Wanna Be Free," by Loretta Lynn*

I bloodied my husband's nose the other night. I didn't know I was doing it—I just woke up at three in the morning, and Doolittle was holding a towel to his nose. He told me I sat straight up, in my sleep, yelling, "Do you see this ring? Do you see this ring?" And I was a-throwing my hands around until my fingers dug into his nose.

"Loretta, what in the world were you talking about?" Doo asked me.

I said I was dreaming about some old guy that tried to make a date with me when I first started singing. I didn't have no ring at the time—we were too poor for that kind of stuff—but now in my dream I was showing that old buzzard I had a ring.

What does it mean when you carry on in your sleep like that? Somebody said it means you've got something on your mind. I said, "I *know* that." I ain't got much education, but I got some sense.

To me, this talking is almost like I've got things inside

me that never came out before. Usually, when something is bothering me, I write a song that tells my feelings, like, "Don't Come Home A-Drinkin' (with Lovin' on Your Mind)." That's really about me and my marriage.

I've still got things inside me—sad things, happy things—that people don't know about. I've had so many changes in my life, and I feel like there's more to come. I'm superstitious; I believe in reincarnation and extra-sensory perception; and I've got this feeling about more changes in my life. It's like a girl feels when her body starts to grow up, or a woman feels when a baby starts to grow inside her. You know it's there; you feel the stirrings, but it's deeper than words.

People know the basic facts about me—how I was married when I wasn't quite fourteen and had four babies by the time I was eighteen. Sometimes my husband tells me, "I raised you the way I wanted you to be." And it's true. I went from Daddy to Doo, and there's always been a man telling me what to do.

I was just a kid—didn't know nothing—picking strawberries in the fields with my babies on a blanket, under an umbrella. I'd change a few diapers, my fingers all rough and dirty, give 'em a few bottles, and go back to picking. So when I sing those country songs about women struggling to keep things going, you could say I've been there.

It's like that hit record I had in 1975, "The Pill," about this woman who's taking birth control pills so she won't have no more babies. Well, they didn't have none of them pills when I was younger, or I'd have been swallowing 'em like popcorn. See, the men who run some of the radio stations, they banned the record because they didn't like what I was saying. But the women knew. Like I say, I know what it's like to be pregnant and nervous and poor.

Now I've got this huge ranch in Tennessee, and I've been on the cover of *Newsweek* magazine, and I was the first woman ever named Entertainer of the Year in country music. I also got honorable mention in the Gallup poll as one of the "most admired women" in the United States. Lordy, I even got to meet Gregory Peck!

But some of my friends who know me best say they wouldn't trade places with me for a million dollars because of the pace I lead. I'm still a-traveling nearly two hundred nights a year to meet my fans who've given me everything I've got. In one way, I'm still working as hard as when I was working in the fields. But I'd have to admit the stakes are higher.

When I first came to Nashville, people called us "hillbilly singers" and hardly gave country music any respect. We lived in old cars and dirty hotels, and we ate when we could. Now country music is a big business. You go around the country, there's a thousand radio stations broadcasting our music. Why, they've even got a country station in New York City, where I played in that big building—what's it called, some kind of garden? Yeah, Madison Square Garden, that's right. So I've seen country music go uptown, like we say, and I'm proud I was there when it happened.

They've also made a movie called *Nashville* that people tell me was one of the biggest movies of 1975. Well, I ain't seen it, so I can't tell you whether it's any good or not. I don't follow the movies much, and I'd much rather see a Walt Disney movie if I do go.

But some of my friends told me there's two characters in there that resemble me and Doolittle—at least somewhat. Well, I met that girl who played the top country singer in the movie. She came to Nashville and talked to me and watched me perform for a few weeks. If she tried to imitate me in the movie, that's their problem. If they really wanted me, why didn't they just ask me?

But I ain't worrying about no movies. My records are still selling, and I get more offers for shows than I can handle. So if you're wondering whether that character in the movie is me, it ain't. This book is me. I've got my own life to lead.

And my life hasn't been easy, not even now. I've had chest surgery (nonmalignant, thank God) and blood poisoning, and sometimes I pass out on stage from migraine headaches. You hear all kinds of rumors about my sick spells, and also some rumors about me having trouble with aspirin pills. It wasn't what people thought—but I'll get to that later.

Also, I've had a bunch of death threats that we managed to keep secret. For a while, there was one or two people following me around until the police got 'em. Now I've got people protecting me all the time. Growing up in eastern Kentucky like I did, I'm used to having a few guns around to protect me (not that I'm crazy about waking up in the morning and seeing Doolittle's pistol right there on the dressing table).

You've heard my husband's name is "Mooney," right? Well, I call him "Doolittle" because that's his old Kentucky nickname. Everybody else calls him "Mooney," which is what they called him in Washington State when they found out he used to run moonshine.

You'll hear a lot of stories about Doolittle if you hang around Nashville long enough. Some of 'em are true and some of 'em ain't. Doo is a smart man in a lot of ways. We've been married for more than twenty-five years, but we've still got some problems that I don't know if we'll ever straighten out.

When we started on this book, me and Doolittle talked it over about how much we should tell about ourselves. Suppose I don't like the way he acts when he's drinking. Or suppose Doo thinks I'm meaner than a snake. Should we tell our troubles to other people in a book?

Well, Doo leaned back in his chair and thought about it for a minute. Then he said, "Hell's fire, Loretta, just tell the story the way it happened. I've always said you should never try to cover up things. Look, we're not perfect. Let's not pretend we are."

I agree with that. Nobody's perfect. The only one that ever was, was crucified. And sometimes I think our problems are made worse by the kind of business we're in.

Doo don't really like to be cooped up. He'd rather be out on the ranch, training his bird dogs, and I don't blame him. Heck, I don't like being cooped up either, only it seems that's what my life has become.

It's a strange deal. I'm supposed to be a country singer, writing songs about marriage and family and the way normal folks live. But mostly I'm living in motel rooms and traveling on my special bus with my private bedroom in the back. I don't even open the shades in my bus anymore. I've seen every highway in the United States by now, and they all look alike to me.

Playing these road shows is a weird experience. One minute I'm out on that stage, usually dressed in my long-sleeved, floor-length gowns, with my hair hanging down to my shoulders, smiling at my fans. There's such a feeling of love between me and those people. I know it shows on my face. Being onstage is the best part of my career. I just say whatever comes into my head, and I joke with my band, and we all have a good time. It's the only time when I really feel grown-up and in control of things.

As soon as that show is over, I sign autographs if

I'm not feeling sick, and then we pull away into the darkness and the fans just melt away. Then it's just me and Doolittle and the boys in my band rolling down the highway.

It's kind of lonely on the road. My first four kids are kind of grown-up now, but I still miss them and my eleven-year-old twins, who mostly stay home with the housekeeper. I've been trying to cut back on my road dates, but we still need the money because of some of the things we'd like to do. When you've got around fifty people on your payroll—heck, it used to be sixty-eight— the account books tell you to keep working.

It's getting so bad I don't even feel comfortable in my own house anymore. I get home for a day or two, and by the time I unpack my bags and see what's changed since I left, it's time to get moving again. Then all my family and fans come to visit, and I start getting so nervous in my own house that I sometimes even check into a motel in Nashville.

I was fighting with Doolittle one day about what kind of wallpaper we should put in our bedroom. We do the papering ourselves. When you're poor folks from eastern Kentucky, you don't lose the habit of doing things for yourself. Anyway, I wanted one color and Doo wanted another. Finally he said, "Hey, I spend more time in this house than you do." That hurt me, but it was the truth.

Being alone so much, I often get to thinking about my younger days. Things I'd like to tell somebody, if I had somebody to talk to. I can remember how poor we were—waiting to get new shoes in the fall, walking across the first frost in my bare feet, sometimes sharing shoes until your feet got bunions on 'em.

It's funny how most of the things I remember are about being poor. When I first started making money in Nashville, I was convinced I was gonna be poor again. Now I've sold millions of records, and my company tells me I've got a million dollars just sitting in the bank. But I could survive if we got poor again. In some ways, that was the best part of my life, learning how to survive.

Somebody said I should write all these memories down. But it ain't like writing a song. I mean, when I get a title for a song, I scribble it down on a napkin or an old paper bag—anything that's handy. Then when I get back to my room, I just start singing those words until I've got me a song.

People say I can't read or write because I've only got about a fourth-grade education. But I can read and write some. I'm not pretending I know how to write a book—not even a book about me. I'm too nervous to even sit in front of a tape recorder for long. I've always been full of nervous energy, and I've gotten used to clowning around onstage, and offstage, too.

But I'm not really as happy as I seem. I've known a lot of sad times in my life that don't square with that lady you see clowning up on the stage. You get used to sadness, growing up in the mountains, I guess. I was given up to die when I was a baby. I came close to drowning near my ranch a few years ago. And the doctors told me my heart stopped on the operating table when I had chest surgery in 1972. Ever since then, I've wanted to tell my life story.

The way I did it was this: The writers have always been really nice to me, and I've always enjoyed sitting and talking to 'em. But we finally got together with this one writer who used to live in Kentucky, name of George. He knows my part of the country real well; he's visited the coal mines, and he's been up to the hollers, so he speaks my language. Now for the past year he's been traveling with me and Doolittle. I've taken him to Butcher Holler and introduced him to my uncle Corman. I've taken him to the ranch and shown him all my scrapbooks. He's met my best friends, like the Johnson sisters. Him and his family took me to that itty-bitty Plymouth Rock up in Massachusetts. I couldn't believe how small it was. I got bigger rocks in my driveway.

Anyway, I told George, "We're gonna have us a hardback book. Doggone right, it's gonna be a good book. Anything I go at, I go at it hard, because I only do what I want. It's gonna be the best book about country music, because I don't take no seconds."

The only problem is how are we gonna spice this book up? I've heard about movie stars who had all kinds of marriages and adventures to reveal. But I've been married to the same man for all this time. The way we fight sometimes, you can tell. I'm trying to lead a good Christian life, especially since I got baptized two years ago. So there ain't too much spicy to tell about me—just the truth.

So I'm gonna start at the beginning and keep going, from Butcher Holler, where I was born, to Hurricane Mills, where I live now. By the time I get done, you're gonna know about the good times and the bad times in my life.

You can bet your last scrip penny I checked out every word before they sent it to the book company. And if I didn't think it was true, out it went.

The first thing I insisted was that it sound like me. When all those city folks try to fix up my talking, all they do is mess me up. Like the way I pronounce the word "holler." That's our word for the low space between two mountains. City people pronounce it "hollow" but that ain't the way I pronounce it. This is *my* book. Instead of

using *Webster's Dictionary*, we're using *Webb's Dictionary*—
Webb was my maiden name.

So when you're reading this book, just try to picture
me up onstage, singing my songs and clowning around,
and try to hear me saying "Butcher Holler." Then you'll
know it's me.

# CoaL
# Miner's
# Daughter

# 1

## Butcher Holler

Well, I was borned a coal miner's daughter,
In a cabin on a hill in Butcher Holler,
We were poor but we had love...
— *"Coal Miner's Daughter," by Loretta Lynn*

Most people know that much about me, because those are the first words of my biggest song. I open my show with it because I know people are gonna request it until I sing it. I wrote it myself, nine verses, and it broke my heart when I had to cut three verses out because it was too long. I could have written a thousand more verses, I've got so many memories of Butcher Holler.

To me, that place is the most important part of my life. My fans and writers are always making a big deal about me acting natural, right from the country. That's because I come from Butcher Holler, Kentucky, and I ain't never forgot it.

I'm always making Butcher Holler sound like the most backward part of the United States—and I think maybe it is. I've traveled all over this country, down South and out West, and I ain't never seen anything like it. And

I ain't making fun of it, because I'm the most backward person you ever saw. I never knew where babies came from until it happened to me.

This might give you an idea of how backward we are, but first, to appreciate this story, you've got to know that in eastern Kentucky we say the word "press" instead of "closet." Anyway, one of my best friends is Dr. John Turner, who took care of me when I was younger.

Doc swears he saw this patient standing in front of the hospital elevator, looking confused. Doc asked him what was the matter, and the patient said, "Doc, I just seen a nurse get into that press—and when the door opened, she was gone!" See, that patient lived in a holler all his life and never saw an elevator before. Myself, I never rode in an automobile until I was twelve.

Holler people are just different from anybody else. They live high up in the hills, one day at a time. There's probably a few who don't know who the president is, and there have been times when they were better off that way. Maybe things are changing now, with television and better roads and stuff, but I've got relatives living up in Butcher Holler who have never been further than Paintsville, ten miles away, in their lives. They're really beautiful people in their own way. Everybody else is worrying about the energy crisis, and talking about getting back to the simple things. My people are already there. If we run out of energy, my relatives know how to patch their houses and grow gardens, so they're gonna have the last laugh on everybody.

Let me explain where Butcher Holler is. You take any place in the United States today, and they've got an interstate highway, right? Well, you get on one of them interstates and drive to Huntington, West Virginia, which is already in pretty hilly country—but you ain't seen nothing yet. You get off Interstate 64 and head south along

Highway 23 into Kentucky. That's a good three-lane highway going past some nice farms and factories and mobile homes. You drive for about an hour and a half until you get to Paintsville, which has around four thousand people.

Paintsville may not look too big to outsiders, but in Johnson County it's the biggest thing going. That's the first place I ever saw a toilet with running water, just before I got married. I went into the bus station to go to the bathroom, but when I sat down on the seat, the toilet flushed automatically. I got so scared I was gonna get flushed down I ran out of there and waited until we found a good old outhouse.

When I was a little girl, my big city was Van Lear, which was five miles away, a coal camp for the Consolidation Coal Company, with rows of wooden houses they rented to the miners. There must have been ten thousand people living around Van Lear in the good times. The company had a post office and company stores where you paid for your things in scrip. If you went into debt, you owed your soul to the company store, just like the song says. The company also had a recreation hall where they showed movies. People make coal camps sound like slavery, but in a lot of ways it was the best thing ever happened to people—as long as the coal kept running.

Before I was born, Van Lear was a boomtown. The company kept their houses painted. The foremen had nice homes up on Silk Stocking Row, and the bosses had real beautiful homes. Off to one side was a row of houses called Black Man Holler where the black miners lived. They worked in the mines with the whites, but they had to live off by themselves. I'm sure there was prejudice in the coal camps, but my family grew up so high in the hollers we never knew about it.

My daddy was color-blind in two ways. About the

only color he could see real good was yellow, and I have trouble telling red from orange myself. But we were also color-blind about people. It's like in 1972, when I was up for the award for Best Female Singer on national television, and Charley Pride was going to present the award. People warned me not to kiss Charley in case I won, because it would hurt my popularity with country fans. I heard that one girl singer got canceled out down South after giving a little peck to a black friend on television. Well, Charley Pride is one of my favorite people in country music, and I got so mad that when I won, I made sure I gave him a big old hug and a kiss right on camera. You know what? Nobody canceled on me. If they had, fine, I'd have gone home to my babies and canned some string beans and the heck with them all.

But we didn't know about prejudice in Butcher Holler. We didn't know much about anything. Even Van Lear was another world to us. We would go down there about once a month and sometimes see a Tarzan movie or one of the Roy Rogers serials. We always went in the daytime, because coming back there weren't any cars, or roads, or electricity for lights in Butcher Holler. I remember going into Van Lear before Christmas when I was around twelve. It was at night, and their decorations were all lit up. It was the first time I really remember seeing electric lights. I sure was impressed.

My home was maybe five miles further up the mountains from Van Lear. The road was paved up to the mines; then it was topped with just coal slag—"red dog," we called it. That ran from the upper company store to the one-room schoolhouse. Then there was just a dirt path leading alongside the creek, in the narrow space between two ridges.

As you walked up the holler, the path got steeper and steeper, with trees growing on both sides of you. You had this feeling of being all wrapped up in the trees and hills, real secure-like. If you'd stop walking and just listen, you could hear a couple of kids playing outside, or maybe some birds in the trees. I used to love going out-of-doors at night and listening to the whippoorwills. Maybe it was the Cherokee in me, but I loved being outside. In the summertime, we'd hold lightning bugs (that's our word for fireflies) on our fingers and pretend they were diamond rings. Or we'd just sit there in the holler, and it would be perfectly quiet.

Holler kids were so bashful that they'd run and hide if they had company coming. I was still bashful after I was married and didn't make friends easily. The only way my husband could get me out of it was to tell me I was ignorant. See, he'd traveled outside the mountains. He'd been around.

We weren't really ignorant, just shy. If we'd see a stranger coming up the holler, somebody in the bottom house would shout up the hill, "Stranger coming up." If the stranger asked you questions, you'd just clam up until you knew his business. Lots of times they'd send revenue officers looking for a moonshine still up in the mountains. Us kids would look at him dumb-like and say, "Ain't nothing up here, mister." And all the time our uncles were making moonshine right up on the ridge.

Most of the people were Irish—not the Catholic kind, the other kind—from families that kept moving west until they finally settled in the hills. There wasn't nobody to take taxes from 'em or make 'em go to church if they didn't want to. So they grew into their own independent ways. They raised chickens and hogs, corn and berries. They didn't have no papers or listen to the news.

The biggest thing that ever happened in Butcher Holler was after World War II when a pilot bailed out of his army plane and it crashed up on the ridge. You could hear bullets going off in the fire for days. The first time a car ever came up the path was when Doolittle came a-courting in his jeep. Now they've got the dirt path widened so two-wheel-drive cars can get up. But it's about the same as ever. A few men work in the mines, and the women go into Paintsville for their food stamps and stuff. But it's still country.

I was up there last year, and my uncle Corman was telling me about the big shoot-out they just had. Seems one of his cousins fired at a hawk. Another cousin down the holler heard the shot, and just for meanness, he answered the shot. Suddenly there were two grown men, cousins to each other, shooting at their sounds. They were both behind trees, a-firing away, until they got tired of it and quit. Didn't hurt nothing, but they could have. That's just the way we are.

We still lend our old house out to relatives. They keep a guest book for my fans to sign. There's been people from almost every state in the nation, which ain't easy because there aren't any signs marking Butcher Holler. You've just got to ask directions, if you can find anybody to ask. The old house is falling apart now, the floor sagging and stuff. But they've still got my old bed and other furniture and someday I'm gonna put it all in the museum I'm building on the ranch.

My folks don't make a big fuss over me in Butcher Holler. They knew me when I was wearing flour sacks, so I ain't no big deal to them. I can go back there and we'll talk just the same way we always did—tell snake stories and ghost stories, believing about half of it.

Somebody wrote a story saying I should pay to have the road paved so people can drive up easier. I won't do it, and I'll tell you why. The only reason people ever heard of Butcher Holler was because I put it on the map. It's just a little place. If my daddy were alive today, he'd say

I shouldn't pave it. He'd know better. I waded out of the mud when I left Butcher Holler, and when I go back to visit, I wade through the mud again. They don't need no pavement.

We didn't even have cars when I was living there. When I was born, there was no sense in going to the hospital. We couldn't afford it anyway, not with the Depression going on. So we had this old woman, Old Aunt Harriet, around eighty years old, come to deliver me. She was almost blind, Mommy said, and she had to feel with her fingers where to cut the cord. Daddy had to sell our milk cow, Old Goldy, to pay thirty-five dollars to Old Aunt Harriet so she'd stay two weeks with Mommy.

After I was born, Mommy put me in the crib in the corner. We just had this one-room cabin they made from logs, with the cracks filled with moss and clay. The wind used to whistle in so bad Mommy would paper the walls with pages from her Sears and Roebuck catalog and movie magazines. I remember I could see pictures of Hitler, Clark Gable, and that Russian man—Stalin, is that his name?—and a picture of a beautiful woman with earphones on her head—a telephone operator. I never forgot how pretty she looked. Mommy never went to the movies, but she always liked pictures of Loretta Young and Claudette Colbert. Right over my crib she pasted pictures of them two stars. That's how I got my name. Lots of times I wonder if I would have made it in country music if I was named Claudette.

When I was born, Franklin Delano Roosevelt was the president for several years. That's the closest I'm gonna come to telling my age in this book, so don't go looking for it. I'm trying to make a living singing songs. I don't need nobody out there saying, "She don't look bad considering she's such-and-such years old."

One time on television, somebody asked my age and

I said it was none of his business unless he was selling insurance or taking the census. Then he asked me what year I was born in—and I told him! Afterward, my husband said I must be the dumbest person in the whole United States. Well, I may be dumb but I ain't stupid, at least not anymore. Now I've learned not to give away my age.

I was born on April 14, which I think is important because I believe in horoscopes. I was born under the sign of the Ram, which means I'm headstrong, don't like people telling me what to do. That's the truth. I listen to 'em, but if they're wrong, I just do what I think is right.

Mommy says I started to walk and talk around eleven months old, before I took sick. I had an ear infection called mastoiditis. The only way they could cure it was by drilling holes in my head to clean out the infection. They done this every day, then put cotton right into the holes. I had curly blond hair up until that time, but they cut off all of them curls so they could fix the infection. Mommy couldn't afford to keep me in the hospital overnight, so every day she'd walk with me the ten miles to Golden Rule Hospital in Paintsville, so they could scrape the infection. I've still got the scars from the drilling around my ears, which is why I wear my hair so long. It got so bad that people didn't think I was gonna live. Mommy got a letter from a woman a few years ago that said, "Whatever happened to that little girl that was gonna die?" Mommy wrote back and said that little girl is still alive today. But I didn't start walking again until I was four years old. I must have stayed in bed for years, but I don't remember none of it. I shut it all out, I guess.

I avoid going back through places where there's too much poverty. I wouldn't take nothing for the memories of what I went through—but I don't want to go back to it. I remember being hungry too much. I think maybe it's worse today, because people know they're poor from watching television news and stuff. Back then, we didn't know we were poor, and people were more proud then.

It bothers me to go back to Kentucky and see folks on welfare today because I know how hard my daddy worked to keep us alive during the Depression. Being poor really helped me. The country is making a big mistake by not teaching kids how to cook and raise a garden and build fires. It's like the Indian taught the white man how to survive. Do you think our kids could take an ear of corn and beat it up fine to make bread? I've done it. And I could do it again.

# 2

## Daddy

Daddy never took a handout,
We ate pinto beans and bacon,
But he worked to keep the wolf back from
the door...
—*"They Don't Make 'Em Like My Daddy,"*
*by Jerry Chesnut*

A few years ago, a fellow named Jerry Chesnut offered me a song called "They Don't Make 'Em Like My Daddy." All I heard was the title, and I just knew I had to make that record, because that's how I feel about my daddy, who died when he was a young man, around fifty-one years old. He had high blood pressure, and that worries me a lot because the doctors told me recently that I've got high blood pressure sometimes. Also, I have migraines, just like my daddy.

Even though he died before I ever got started singing, in 1959, I feel like Daddy's been the most important person in my life. I'm very close to Mommy, too, and though Doolittle has just about raised me since I was a girl, I had almost fourteen years of Daddy giving me love and security, the way a daddy should. He'd sit and hold me on his lap while he rocked by the fireplace. I think Daddy is the main reason why I always had respect for myself when times got rough between me and Doolittle—I knew my daddy loved me.

My worst feelings in my life were over leaving Daddy to go west. I didn't see him before he died, which makes me cry even today. I've often thought, if I could live my life over, I would tell him how much I loved him. Kids don't tell their parents. It's a shame, but it's true. My kids don't tell me that. I know they love me, but they don't put it into words. So that's what I try to do with some of my songs—to tell kids to love their parents while they're still around.

That song that Jerry Chesnut wrote tells about my daddy, even though it's about a great big man, and Daddy was only about five feet eight inches and weighed around 117 pounds.

We've got some pictures of Daddy, and he's usually got this straight face on him, not much emotion. Mountain people are like that. It's hard to read 'em if you don't know 'em. He was real shy, not like people from the coal camps who are used to talking with each other. But Butcher Holler was his kind of world. There, he was the greatest man you ever saw. He could fix anything with those wiry arms of his. He could hammer up a well box, or a fence for the hog, or a new outhouse. You had to do things for yourself in the hollers or you'd die.

Daddy's name was Melvin—Melvin Webb—but everybody called him "Ted." His daddy and mommy lived in Butcher Holler; she was a Butcher, from the first family that settled up there. One of Daddy's grandmothers was a full-blooded Cherokee squaw, and it's the same on my mother's side. So that means I'm one-quarter Cherokee—and proud of it. Other kids called me "half-breed" when I was a kid, but it didn't bother me. Being Indian was no big deal one way or the other. A lot of blood was mixed up in the hollers, if the truth be known. I was always proud of being Indian—and I've gotten more proud as the years go on.

Daddy didn't go to school much, but he could read and write some. He worked out-of-doors when he was young, farming and stuff. When he was about twenty, he met Mommy at the little church in the holler. They courted for around two years and then got married. They built their own little one-room wood cabin at the end of the holler. She would hold the boards and he would drive in the nails. Right after the Depression started, they began having kids—eight of them, four boys and four girls, in the next sixteen years. I was next to the oldest.

Daddy couldn't get much work during the Depression, and we didn't have money. I remember one Christmas when Daddy had only thirty-six cents for four children. Somehow, he managed to buy a little something for each of us down at the general store. He gave me a little plastic doll about three inches high, and I loved that like it was my own baby.

Daddy was more easygoing than Mommy. She did most of the correcting in the family. The only time Daddy would get mad was when someone would smart off at Mommy. Then he'd move right in there and settle it. He wasn't one of those men that's gone half the time, either—he didn't have no bad habits. He was always teasing Mommy, but in a nice way. If she got mad about something, he'd laugh and say, "The squaw's on the war-path tonight." I never forgot that line, and I wrote a song about it when I got older. But you know, the nice way he treated her gave me ideas about the way I wanted to be treated. I still feel there's better ways to handle a woman than whipping her into line. And I make that point clear in my songs, in case you hadn't noticed.

Daddy was upset when he couldn't find work in the lumber mills during the Depression. He was used to working hard. They didn't have stuff like welfare checks in those days, but Franklin Delano Roosevelt started the WPA (somebody told me that stands for Work Projects Administration), which gave men jobs. This is why you go into homes back in Kentucky today and you'll see pictures of FDR on the wall. Daddy would work a few days on the roads with a WPA crew and come home with a few dollars, as proud as could be. When he wasn't working on the roads, he worked on his big garden and patched the house to get us through the Depression.

The WPA took care of me, too. The agent came up the holler and gave me a real "store-boughten" dress when I was around seven years old. Up to that time, all I wore was flour sacks Mommy sewed up as dresses. I kept looking at pictures in the Sears and Roebuck catalog and thinking how pretty everyone looked—but I never figured I'd get a chance to look pretty, too.

But one day this agent brought this little blue dress with pink flowers and dainty little pockets. Mercy, how I loved it. Daddy kept saying, "Don't get your dress dirty." I took good care of it and put it in the laundry bag, but we let our family hog run loose and he snatched that dress and just chewed it to pieces. Ruined it, he did. I must have cried for days.

When the Depression got better, Daddy saved enough money to buy a house with four rooms in it. It was down the holler, next to his folks, in a big, broad clearing. This is the family house you see in the pictures, with the high porch facing the garden and the hill rearing up behind the house. We had a spring out back for fresh water and a well in front. We had a new outhouse in the back. In the winter, you'd wait too long because you didn't want to go outside in the cold. And then you'd have to run through the snow, hoping you'd make it to the outhouse. We still didn't have electricity, and our bunch of kids still had to sleep on pallets in the living room at night. But we had four rooms instead of one, and we really thought we'd arrived.

Finally, the mines got to working again, and Daddy decided to support his family as a coal miner. He never worked in the mines before, and it must have taken a lot of nerve to go into that terrible dark hole. But Daddy did it for us.

He worked at Consolidated Number Five, right down the holler. The seam of coal was only three feet high, and you can bet they didn't bother cutting the rock to give the men a place to stand up. That meant the miners had to crawl on their hands and knees and work on their sides or lying on their backs. Some of the miners wore knee pads, like the basketball players wear, but Daddy found that they raised him up so high that his back rubbed against the roof as he crawled into the mine. So he would come home every night with his knees all cut and sore, and he'd soak them in hot water before he could go to sleep. But the next morning he'd be out working in the garden again, until it was time to go to the mine.

Daddy worked the night shift. He left home around four o'clock every afternoon and walked down the holler. We kids, we hardly said good-bye to him. But looking back, I can see the worried look on Mommy's face. She would keep busy with the kids all afternoon and evening. She had her hands full. But after we were in bed, she would sit by the kerosene lamp and read her Bible or an old Western book until she heard Daddy coming up the steps. They'd lie in bed talking, but I never heard him complain about the mines. Coal miners are funny that way. They don't like to get their wives upset. I remember when that Hyden mine blew up in Kentucky on December 30, 1970, and I got myself in a big jam trying to raise money for those coal miners' kids' education—I'll tell more about that later on in this book. Some of those widows testified later that their husbands had warned them about the dangerous blasting they were doing in the mine. But the wives knew enough not to ask any questions, or else their husbands would have been laid off. I feel real proud of Daddy for working in the mines. He kept his family alive by breaking his own body down. That's the only way to look at it.

In the coal fields, you were never far from a disaster. When I was little, there was a big explosion in a mine above Van Lear that killed a lot of men. Other times, men would get killed in single accidents. I've walked past the mine when they were bringing out the men who were in a gas explosion. I remember all the women and children standing around, mostly crying. When I heard about the Hyden disaster, I could just picture those poor people huddled around a fire waiting for word about their men. That's what life is like whenever your man is a coal miner. I guess that's why I'm so soft on coal miners. I call my band "The Coal Miners," and whenever I meet a guy at one of my concerts who says he was a coal miner, why, my eyes just get full of tears because I know how those men suffer.

Like I said before, my daddy had high blood pressure and migraine headaches. I've seen him walk the floor many a night, crying from the pain. But when you're a kid, you don't think about it. One time they wrapped Daddy up in an old quilt Mommy made out of overalls and took him down the holler on an old wooden sled. Somebody said to me, "Your daddy won't be back." I didn't really understand what they meant. But after some time in the hospital, he came back. He couldn't catch a cold or he'd get real sick. He'd get up every morning and light a fire, so he wouldn't get sick. And when Daddy started getting that regular miner's paycheck again, he would drag home groceries on a wooden sled he built himself.

After he worked in the mines for a few years, he had trouble breathing. The doctors used to say that a miner was "nervous" or that he smoked too much. They didn't know about black lung in those days. Black lung is what you get when you breathe in too much coal dust. It never leaves your lungs—just stays there and clogs up your breathing, puts extra strain on your heart.

They used to tell the miners that coal dust was good for you, that it helped ward off colds. Or they'd tell a miner he would get sicker from dirty sheets than from working in a coal mine—lots of stupid things, but nobody knew any better then.

Sometimes Daddy didn't take a bath before he came home, and all you could see was the whites of his eyes. Well, if that coal dust could stick to his face like that, it must have gotten into his lungs, too. But it wasn't until some time after Daddy died that the miners just plumb refused to work unless the government paid them benefits. And all the time, England and other European countries were paying off their miners who had black lung. I've got relatives collecting black lung benefits today, but they came too late for Daddy. He got laid off when he couldn't work fast anymore. They just said, "Take your shovel and go home." No pension, no benefits, just "go home." This was after I moved away, but Mommy wrote me a letter. They tried running a grocery store, but that didn't work out because some people came down to get groceries but didn't pay him. He left the world owing nobody anything, but a lot of people owed him.

A few years later, the company closed down the entire mine where Daddy worked: bricked it right over. But after I got into show business, I asked them to find my daddy's old mining equipment. They had cemented all the old equipment inside the old bathhouse, but they broke in just for me and found an old carbide lamp and my cousin's safety helmet, which I'm going to put in the museum on my ranch. But they never found Daddy's old miner's cap or his identification tag. I'm pretty superstitious about things like that and curious about what could have happened to his stuff.

I remember after World War II Daddy saved up enough money for a battery-operated Philco radio. I'll never forget him pulling that radio up the holler on his sled and putting it in the corner of the living room, so proud of himself. It was the first radio we ever owned. I was eleven years old. Daddy didn't let us run it all the time because he wanted to save the batteries for Saturday night, when he was off from work. He would sit there by the grate, where it was warm, and turn on Lowell Thomas and the news. I still hear that great deep voice of Lowell Thomas today, and it makes me think of Daddy. Then we'd get our favorite radio program of all—the Grand Ole Opry, direct from Nashville, Tennessee.

Music was always big in our family. My grandfather, Daddy's father, played the banjo left-handed and we'd all sing. When he'd get drunk, he played it with his toes better than most people can with their fingers. But the Opry was something else. I'd sit on the floor and listen to Roy Acuff, Ernest Tubb, and Molly O'Day, who was the first woman singer I can remember. Mommy would do this little hoedown dance whenever Bill Monroe played his bluegrass music. I still do Mommy's dance on my shows, kicking up my heels, hopping up and down like a squaw. I call it the "hillbilly hoedown."

I can't say that I had big dreams of being a star at the Opry. It was another world to me. All I knew was Butcher Holler—didn't have no dreams that I knew about. But I'd curl up by Daddy and the radio and fall asleep, and on Sunday morning I'd find the radio still turned on, nothing playing, just some crackling noises. But inside my head I could still hear that music.

# 3

## Mommy

Mommy scrubbed our clothes on a washboard
every day.
Why I've seen her fingers bleed,
To complain, there was no need,
She'd smile in Mommy's understanding way...
— *"Coal Miner's Daughter," by Loretta Lynn*

The first time I sang "Coal Miner's Daughter" in public, I couldn't finish the song. I just broke down and cried because they sneaked my mommy into the wings of the theater. Just seeing her tore me all to pieces, because I've always felt like a little kid compared to her.

To me, my mother always was the most beautiful woman in the world. A redheaded Irish girl was her mother and a half Cherokee was her father. So Mommy's one-quarter Cherokee, with blue eyes and coal-black hair that's just now turning gray. Her skin gets dark if she just works in the garden for an hour. Her eyes look Irish, but her cheekbones look Indian. I always wanted to be as beautiful as Mommy, but I never made it. She and I have the same nose, but I've got these buck teeth that I've always hated. I tell our little twins that if they ever need braces, I'll find the money.

Mommy's name is Clara, but in Butcher Holler they called her "Clary." Me they called "Loretty." Everybody's name had to end with a y—that's a hillbilly way. Mommy still calls me "Loretty."

Mommy's father was named Nathaniel Ramey, which was changed from the old Indian name of Raney. He came from Jenny's Creek, named after Jenny Wiley, the white girl who was taken by the Indians, and now there's a state park named after her. I think she's kin to me somewhere back there.

Nathaniel Ramey used to stay with us sometimes— a quiet, proud man who never got a gray hair. He had twelve children by his first marriage and six by his second marriage, and he lived to be eighty-nine years old. We Cherokees are tough.

They didn't used to teach much about Indian history in grade school, but I managed to hear about the Trail of Tears, named after the time the U.S. government made most of the Cherokee Nation leave our mountains and go all the way out west somewhere. Lots of 'em died on the way. When I found out what they did to my ancestors, I had a fit.

I used to respect Andrew Jackson until I found out how he pushed the Indians around. Since I moved to Nashville, I went out to his home, The Hermitage, just one time—and I won't ever go back. He wasn't on my side—why should I be on his?

Near my house in Hurricane Mills is a place where the Cherokees had to ford the Tennessee River on their Trail of Tears. There are times when I can almost *feel* and *hear* them squaws and their babies crying from hunger.

The way I see it, the white man came over here and

said, "Look, we found us a new country." But it wasn't new. It belonged to the Indians, and it was taken away from them. From us. When I went to see that little Plymouth Rock in 1974, I read how the Indians taught the white man how to plant vegetables and build houses in that cold Massachusetts climate. If it wasn't for the Indians, them Pilgrims would have all starved.

I've always tried to help the Indians. My friends, the three Johnson sisters, are part Indian, just like me. In 1968 we got a campaign going for the Red Cloud Indian School at Pine Ridge, South Dakota. We took up six truckloads of clothing and school supplies and stuff. Then me and my band went up for a benefit show. They just about had to tie me down to keep me from taking an armful of those kids back home with me. I'd've done it, too.

At Christmastime, we still send candy and stuff up to the kids. They put my picture next to John F. Kennedy on the wall. The only thing that made me feel bad was when they had that uprising at Pine Ridge, because I didn't think that would help the people none. Still, the Indians have been treated bad—just about as bad as the blacks, really.

Nothing makes me madder than to hear people put Indians down. And if I hear some Indian complaining, I tell him to get smart and be proud of himself, because I am. In fact, I'm waiting for us to straighten this country out. Get everybody living in little tribes and fix his own medicine. We'd be a lot better off.

Mommy learned to doctor her whole family when she was still a baby. Her family got the fever during World War I. They were all lying around the cabin, talking out of their heads, and she was no more than five years old. Somehow she didn't get the fever, so she spent weeks fetching water and helping to cool them off.

Her daddy taught her how to put salve on the bad sores on her mother's legs, from blood vessels breaking. Her mother had twelve babies, but only five girls and a boy lived.

When Mommy was six, her mother died from the fever, and after that, she was on her own a lot. She'd go from one family to another. If somebody was having a baby, she would take care of the other kids. When she was staying with a family, Mommy would eat regularly. But other times she'd have to pick berries and sell 'em to get enough to eat. She also did washing and stuff like that, anything to help.

After Mommy got married, she used her Indian ways to raise us. She had her first seven kids at home, with an old midwife coming in to help. The last one, she went down to Paintsville Hospital to have. She figured she earned that. After Mommy had me, she was out setting onions on the hill only three days later. Mommy did everything the way they do it now—more natural. They get you up on your feet the first day now, and they let you go home after three days. Mommy was just ahead of her time. All eight children are alive today—so she must have been doing something right.

Whatever went wrong up on our holler, Mommy would take care of it. For burns, she'd make a salve of castor oil, flour, and sulphur. She'd cook it all together, then rub it on the wound and it would heal real fast. When you got a cold, Mommy would make a poultice from mustard seeds and rub it on your chest. It would take the cold right out of you. But it was so hot and smelly us kids would swear we'd rather have the cold than the poultice.

One time my brother Herman was cutting some weeds with a big scythe and he hit his foot, cutting an artery. That blood was pumping swoosh-swoosh-swoosh.

Mommy just ripped off her petticoat and twisted it around his leg in a tourniquet to stop the bleeding.

Mommy saved my life, too, when I was little. My dress caught fire when I was sitting too close to the fireplace. Mommy was supposed to be peeling potatoes for dinner but she decided to sit by the fire to get warm. She saw my dress on fire and she just pulled me off the floor and ripped that dress off my back. Then she beat out the fire with her bare hands. I didn't get burned at all, just a bloody nose from bumping against a chair. Mommy's hands were blistered for a week, even though she put them in cold water right away the way the Indians did.

Mommy had a special tea for every occasion. She'd make her teas out of roots and herbs, but she had to be real careful or they could kill you. Like one time she made a tea from the mayapple root, but instead of using the female mayapple she used the male. It gave one of the kids a stomachache for days. Mommy also made sassafras tea. Daddy drank that for his high blood pressure.

When I was little, I had a real bad case of black measles. I had 'em for nine days, but they wouldn't break out, and I was getting worse. Mommy told me she was gonna make a special tea out of sheep manure that was supposed to make the measles break out. Lordy, I watched her making that tea and I knew I was gonna die if I had to drink it. All of a sudden those measles started popping out all over me, and I was better in about two days. I never touched a drop of that tea. Maybe that was the way it really worked.

We also had a tea made from a weed called "life everlasting." It was good for colds and shivering. Sometimes we'd dry it out and smoke it a little. Some people think life everlasting is the same thing as marijuana, which also grows easily in the mountains, but I'm not sure about that. We never knew about marijuana when I was growing up, and I still haven't tried it to this day. I never did like smoking much, and I haven't touched tobacco since I was a girl.

Mommy smoked and she drank coffee, but she wouldn't let none of us kids do it. And we wouldn't complain about it, or she'd fix us good. One time we had company, and they asked me if I drank coffee. I was around eleven or so and I said, kind of smart, "No, Mommy won't let me drink coffee." Well, do you know that she made me drink a whole pot of coffee, just to teach me not to smart off? I was so sick my stomach was foundering for a day—that's a Kentucky word for "upset."

But I didn't learn my lesson about smarting off. We used to eat only two meals a day: breakfast and supper; we'd kind of snack on leftovers in between because we didn't have enough food. (Mommy even had to grind up an old plate during the winter to feed the chickens. Seemed like they must have liked it 'cause they gobbled it up real fast.) Anyway, Mommy would put sweet potatoes, apples, turnips, and cabbage heads in a hole under the floor and they'd keep all winter, wrapped in straw. She'd let us eat one sweet potato for supper and then another just before going to bed. Well, another time we had company, and they saw our leftover potatoes being warmed on the wood stove. The guest said, "Didn't you eat all your supper?" And I answered kind of smart, "No, my mommy only lets me have one sweet potato." Well, you guessed it. She made me eat every sweet potato in that pan. And this time I was so sick I thought I was really gonna die. That finally taught me a lesson about smarting off.

In spite of that, I still got into my share of trouble with Mommy. I hated to wash dishes, and I'd do anything to get out of it. I even hid the dirty dishes under the kitchen cabinet, and one time Mommy found out and cracked me over the head with a broomstick. Daddy saw this and said to her, "No wonder she don't have no sense!" At the time I thought, "Good old Daddy, always sticking up for his little girl." You won't believe this, but it wasn't until after I was married that I figured out Daddy wasn't exactly praising his little girl.

Mommy is still healing people. She now lives in Wabash, Indiana, where she married Daddy's first cousin, Tommy Butcher, and she works in a home for handicapped children. Her job is to make sure the kids get their medicines. She doesn't make the medicines herself—they're prescribed by a doctor—but she swears the medicines are the same as she made when she was raising us.

The home where she works is a beautiful place called Vernon Manor. You think of homes for handicapped people and you think of those big ugly buildings that the government puts up. But this is a private deal, and that's why it's so nice. It's laid out in a big H shape, all on the ground floor, and all the rooms are bright and sunny. The kids are from infants to nineteen years old, and most of 'em have physical problems, too.

They've got doctors and nurses, but I think Mommy knows just as much about curing them. She makes a salve out of soap and some other stuff and rubs it on those little children's sores. Her bosses say nobody can heal a child better than she can. They're always after her to teach them before she retires. Mommy says she's not much for writing things down; she's got a few secrets written down in a family Bible somewhere. I'd say that someday, that's gonna be valuable to medical science.

Her bosses call her "The Squaw," because she's got special powers. She can read the grounds in a coffee cup and tell your future. We've got some kind of extra-sensory perception in our family, too. Me and Mommy are on the same wavelength—I can always tell when she's sick. I'll call her up and say, "Mommy, what's wrong?" and she'll tell me she's got the virus. I'm the same way with my oldest daughter, Betty Sue. I think it has something to do with being Indian.

# 4

## Family Style

Hungry little baby on a cold hard floor,
Crying for milk but there ain't no more.
Can't get credit at the grocery store,
But that's how it is when you're poor...
—*"When You're Poor," by Tracey Lee*

I never asked Mommy and Daddy whether they wanted such a big family, but I do remember Mommy saying that as long as she was nursing, she couldn't have another baby. That's about the only kind of birth control they had in the mountains in those days. And the truth is that's the only method I knew until after I had my first four.

I remember Mommy nursing Jackie—we call him Jay Lee now—until he was four years old. When company came, he'd go behind the door and motion for Mommy to nurse him. He hates for me to remind him about that, but I do it just for meanness.

Mommy says I was always mischievous, fighting with my brothers all the time. She says I liked to draw attention to myself that way but that the kids never stayed mad at me for long.

I was the second child, right after Melvin—everybody calls him Junior. Herman came after me, followed by Jay Lee, then Peggy Sue, then Betty Ruth. Next was Donald Ray and finally Brenda. The oldest and the youngest were around fifteen years apart, so Mommy's nursing must have helped her with birth control just a little. Brenda was born after I got married. I told her to change her professional name to Crystal Gayle when she started her own singing career because we didn't want her to get confused with Brenda Lee. I didn't know Brenda too closely while she was growing up, but Peggy Sue was my first sister, and I claimed her right away. When she was born, I ran up and down Butcher Holler shouting, "I got a baby sister; I got the prettiest baby sister in the whole world!"

We were kind of isolated up on Butcher Holler. Sometimes I'd go down and help out my aunt, Nory Butcher, who had twelve kids of her own. She's always been there for me—giving me little knickknacks whenever I visit her. But lots of times in the winter, when the snows came, we'd go two or three weeks without seeing a soul. You got pretty close to your family that way. Everybody had their jobs to do. Mommy would never let me iron because I've got no patience for it. I'm like a bull in a china shop. I'm an Aries, wanting to ram my way through, and you can't do that with an old-fashioned iron on a wood stove.

They tried me at pouring coffee, but I wasn't even good at that. Daddy would say, "Here comes that heifer with the coffee," and I'd be going bump-bump-bump, spilling hot coffee over everybody. Oh, it was a mess. I tried being a waitress one time, and I was terrible. I'm just plain clumsy.

Mommy was the one who would spank us in the family. One time they made me sleep in the press—remember, that's our word for "closet." It was a dark place under the stairs, and I screamed and hollered because I was afraid of the dark. Even today, I never go to sleep without a light on in the bathroom.

I slept on the floor on a pallet until I was around nine years old. Then Mommy figured I shouldn't be sleeping with all my brothers, so they bought me a regular bed and put it in their room. Daddy was gone most of the night at the mine, so I slept in their room until I got married and moved out.

It was rough times back then. I can remember winters when all we ate for weeks was bread dipped in gravy made of brown flour and water, and that was supper. God only knows how we survived. Every now and then we'd have "coal miner's steak"—baloney.

We never had ice cream. We'd get snow in the winter and put milk and sugar on it. That was the closest we got. But we usually had good vegetables from the garden in the summer, plus all the greens Mommy would gather from the hillside. With her Indian ways, she could walk that ridge and come back with a potful of greens that she'd cook up. To this day, I prefer vegetables to meat.

Our main meat was from the hog. I never had beef until after I got married and was eating at Doolittle's place. I never saw red meat like that. I was afraid to eat it, but I got used to it. We also had chickens. Really, we'd eat whatever we could. Sometimes at night, while Daddy was at the mines, Mommy and Junior would go possum hunting. They'd hold a flashlight and draw the possum. Then the dog would chase the possum up a tree. Junior would climb the tree and shake the possum to the ground again and that dog would hold it, not tearing him up or nothing, until we put it in a sack. Possum meat has a real good taste. Squirrels, too. That was a real treat—squirrel meat with gravy and biscuits. Nowadays you don't hardly see a squirrel in the Appalachian Mountains. I think we ate 'em all during the Depression.

We never wasted anything in our household. When we had a chicken, Mommy would cut off the toenails and cut up the feet for the dumplings. The kids would fight over the head because the brains tasted good. The same thing for a hog. We'd cook the intestines, the feet—everything.

When we finished eating, Daddy would take part of the entrails and mix 'em with a can of lye and cook it all in a great pan on the outdoors fire. He'd make lye soap that way; it was the only soap we had. Mommy would take it and do the wash outdoors all day on Monday and hang our clothes on washlines strung across the holler.

The Depression wasn't our only problem. We also had to be careful about the big copperheads that live in the mountains. Whenever I go back to Butcher Holler, everybody's got their own story about going to the outhouse and stepping right on some big old copperhead. It was a fact of life.

I remember one time I was coming home from Aunt Tillie's after dark. Mommy used to borrow a Western book from her every night. I saw this thing on the porch, and I thought it was a broom that you sweep off the porch and garden with. I wondered why Mommy left it on the porch.

My brother Herman stepped over it, but I bent down to look at it. Copperheads have these diamond-shaped blocks, but it was so dark I couldn't see it. I yelled to Herman, "I don't know what it is, but it sure smells like cucumbers." At that, Mommy gave out a big yell from the other side of the house. I just fell backward. She came running out with a double-bladed ax and started whacking. Daddy came out with a light. She cut that copperhead into six or seven pieces. The head was about eight inches long—and it jumped for fifteen minutes. Daddy was so upset he kept yelling, "Get away from that head—it could still bite you."

But Daddy had his own pet—a black snake that used to crawl up from the cracks in the floor. Every time we had dinner, Daddy would feed it. When Jay Lee was born, that black snake crawled right into the crib and curled up with Jay Lee. Daddy said that black snakes are harmless, which they are, but when he went to the mines, Mommy killed it with an ax because she just couldn't stand the idea of a snake being in bed with Jay Lee. Daddy was mighty mad 'cause he missed his black snake.

We didn't have much to celebrate during the Depression, but we tried: Thanksgiving, Easter, Christmas. One of the biggest holidays for mountain people is called "May Meeting," which is really "Decoration Day" at the end of May, when everybody comes back to honor the dead. Today, with people moved up north to work in the factories, you get terrible traffic jams on "Hillbilly Highway"—Interstate 75—before Decoration Day. In those days, poor and with no cars or nothing, we'd get fifteen or twenty families in Butcher Holler to the little graveyard on the hill.

We would spend days fixing up the grounds, cutting the grass, cleaning the markers, putting in spring flowers. We're kind of sentimental about graveyards. We put them in high places, facing the eastern sun. Whenever I go back to Butcher Holler, Doolittle drives me up the steep hill to Daddy's grave. Usually, I bring plastic yellow flowers, because Daddy was color-blind and yellow was the only color he could tell. The plastic is so Daddy will have something nice that won't fade too fast.

The holidays were special times. Most of the time we just tried to stay alive and take care of the babies. That was my main job. I'd sit on the porch swing and rock them babies and sing at the top of my voice.

Daddy would say, "If you don't shut up, everyone in the holler will hear you." But I'd keep right on. I'd sing the old hymns like "Amazing Grace" or "This Little Light of Mine" and stuff like that, as loud as could be. I didn't care. And I'm still like that. I love to get up and sing at the top of my lungs. Just a show-off, I suppose.

That's how I got my first audience—singing on the porch. Daddy had two cousins who made moonshine up on the ridge, Willie Webb and Lee Dollarhyde. Sometimes they got in trouble with the law and got themselves sent away, but they always went back to moonshining again. I remember one time they were hiding out, living in our attic. That's when Mommy was about to have another baby. They heard the commotion and came down to see the new baby. When they saw it was a boy, they insisted we name it Willie Lee, one name for each of 'em. (He's the one we call Jay Lee nowadays.) He was just a little booger, around three pounds and four ounces, and he probably should have gone into one of those incubators down at the hospital. But Daddy made a tiny crib and rocking chair out of wood and Mommy nursed that baby until it survived. When he got bigger, I used to rock him on the porch and sing to him until Daddy said, "You're gonna ruin his ears if you sing so loud." But I didn't care.

One day I saw Lee Dollarhyde coming down off the hill. It was my thirteenth birthday—that's how I remember it. He pointed to a rocky ledge where he had his still hidden, and he said, "Loretta, you've got a real nice voice. I listen to you while I'm working up on the hill. You're gonna be a beautiful girl when you grow up." That made me so proud.

Lee was kind of strange. He was full grown but he

was like an eight-year-old, always nervous and drum-ming his fingers and tapping his feet. Sometimes he got into trouble just for meanness. Like one time, he heard about a store that couldn't be robbed because of a real vicious watchdog. Lee said, "That dog will be eating pork chops before this night is out." And that night he robbed the store while the dog was eating the pork-chop supper my uncle gave him.

Lee wasn't what you'd call a good robber. One time he robbed a clothing store to get himself new clothes, but he made one mistake. He changed clothes inside the store and left his old clothes behind. He even left his old hat—with his name inside of it. The sheriff was waiting for him the next morning.

Another time Lee stole a chicken and made tracks around the mines, to throw the police off his trail. But then he spilled chicken feed all the way to his own house. That's how they caught him. I think Lee was in jail eight or nine times.

He was a great guy at heart, like a Jesse James. He'd come in with some candy at Christmastime, and we'd just know he took it from somewhere. Then he'd come in at night with a fresh chicken, and Mommy wouldn't ask any questions—just fry her up, right away.

The law didn't like to mess with Lee too often because he had a bad temper. He hid stolen goods in caves and stuff all over our holler, but the law didn't come search-ing too often. When he met his end, it wasn't from the law. It happened on a Fourth of July, after I turned thirteen in April. Lee must have sold all his moonshine down in the coal camp and was going crazy knowing the miners wanted more. So Lee crossed the ridge behind us and went into the next holler, which was Greasy Creek.

I'm not too clear what happened next. Either Lee held a gun and robbed their moonshine, or else he just took it when they wasn't looking. Either way, he sold that batch to the miners. Then he went back for more. That was one time too many.

Nobody knows how he got shot, because whoever shot him carried his body on horseback up on the ridge and just left him there, with one jug still full of stolen moonshine alongside the body. The police never made much of a fuss about it. I guess they were glad he wouldn't be troubling them no more. My family never talked about getting revenge. This wasn't one of those feuds like the Hatfields and McCoys. Years later, somebody said one of Lee's kin fixed the man who killed Lee—but you never know what to believe.

All I can remember is Lee's mother, my grandmother, walking a path between her house and ours, just wailing at the top of her lungs. My parents didn't have a penny, but somehow they fixed up a coffin and a service for him. They sat up three nights with the body, praying and crying, like we do in the mountains. Lee had this old yellow dog named Charlie that used to sit with him while he was making the moonshine. Old Charlie sat outside for those three days, right under my window, howling and crying. It was pitiful.

After that, when I was minding the babies, I would still pretend my uncle Lee was up on the ridge. And I would sing a little louder, just for him.

# 5

## School Days

Our clothes were clean but faded, sometimes
our feet were bare
But no one noticed anything except the Lord
was there.
We'd come from all directions searchin' for
the way,
On my knees at school on Sunday, that's where
I learned to pray...
— *"Where I Learned to Pray," by Loretta Lynn*

If you want to make Mommy mad sometime, try telling her I don't have any education. She just might do
an Indian war dance on you. One of the papers ran a
story that made it sound like I never went to school, and
Mommy promised to send 'em my old report cards, just
to prove they were wrong.

The next time I saw Mommy at one of my perfor-
mances, I called her up onstage in front of something
like fourteen thousand fans and said, "This is that
Indian lady that told off them newspaper people."

Then I told her, "Sure, Mommy, my report cards have

all As on them—but you forget something. Remember how I used to help the teacher in that one-room schoolhouse? Part of my job was making out the report cards. I never told you this until just now—but I'm the one who used to give myself all them As."

The audience laughed, but I don't think Mommy saw the humor in it. She's real touchy about her children being as good as the next family's. And we are. She's proud because she was one of the few mothers in Butcher Holler that chased her kids out to school every day. But you've got to be honest about yourself, and I'll be the first to admit I don't have too much education.

For a long time, I never got my driver's license because I was scared of taking reading tests. But one public official knew I could drive a car and read all the signs and stuff, so he helped get me a license. Since Doo got me that beautiful Jaguar sports car for Christmas of 1974, sometimes I drive around the ranch, but I'm too nervous to drive in all that Nashville traffic.

I used to write out all my letters to my disc jockeys. They used to tease me about my handwriting and my words—they said I was inventing a new language of my own. I'd use words like "rememberize." But at least they got a letter from me. I get help on all my letters now. The lady who watches my children has two years of college, and she helps me type out the postcards to the disc jockeys and the fans.

I send out about six thousand postcards from Mexico every winter. There's not too many singers in country music who do that. My twins even lick the stamps. But I believe you've got to thank the fans if they take the trouble to write to you. Somebody got the idea I couldn't read one day on my bus because he saw some of my boys opening my mail for me. That's not because I can't read. That's because they screen out all the threats and the requests for money and that stuff. I read my letters from my good fans, and I try to answer 'em, too.

I write down the words to my songs, and I can read the Bible pretty well. I've also read some history books about my Indians to find out what the white man did. I've got white history books and red history books—and let me tell you, friends, they tell different stories about the same events.

I *ought* to be able to read a little, because Mommy made sure all us kids walked two miles down the holler to the one-room schoolhouse. There's a big difference between holler kids and coal-camp kids. The kids in Van Lear went to a regular school with one teacher for each grade, but we only had one teacher for all eight grades. Usually, we had six or seven different teachers a year. I guess they didn't get paid too good—or else we scared off those teachers who didn't know how to handle us.

One time the Social Security people said you could get more benefits if you had your kids enrolled in school. All over the hollers, there was fathers sending their fifteen-year-old sons back to school. Next thing you'd know, them big boys would be whipping the teacher. And then people would have to hire 'em a new teacher.

We were used to being out-of-doors, and we'd use any excuse to get out of the schoolhouse. Like going to the outhouse. There was a boys' outhouse on one side of the school and a girls' outhouse on the other side. Or, we'd say we needed a drink. Across the path was a spring that came down off the mountain. You'd bring your own cup and drink that water and it was delicious. One time my cousin Marie Castle and me went out for a drink and stayed a couple of hours. The teacher had to send her son to find us.

One time we got a new teacher that had only one arm, and we figured we'd test him out right away. But he made up for the arm he didn't have with a red paddle, and he just about wore us out. I don't know how he did it—but we never bothered him again.

Half the time I was fighting with my cousin Marie and the other girls. The other half I was fighting with the boys. People are always saying that the reason I got married before I was fourteen was because kids in the mountains get started with boys at an early age. Well, that wasn't true with me. I never had any boyfriends until Doolittle came along—I was too busy fighting with 'em to have boyfriends. One time I claimed a boyfriend, this little old boy named Granville Bolden. I used to sing out, "I love Granville Bolden," but I just did that out of meanness.

Fighting was how I got nine whippings in one day. We were playing "may-hide" out behind the school. (Most people call it "hide-and-seek" but we called it "may-hide." I told you—this is *Webb's Dictionary* here.) Anyway, this little cousin of mine, he tagged me, and I got mad and I said, "Why, you little turd, you."

The teacher heard it, and she gave me a whipping. I was a tough little kid. Mean? I'd die before I let on it hurt. Somebody asked me why I got whipped and I said, "Because I called my cousin a little turd." Well, that teacher heard me again, and she marched me right back in and whipped me again. That went on until I got whipped nine times in one afternoon. Finally, me and Junior went out the window and ran home. We got a new teacher soon after that, so I was saved.

When I got bigger, I got the job of walking to school early and starting the fire in the potbellied stove. I'd get paid a dollar a month for that. I also cleaned erasers and did little jobs. I was real proud because I was earning money and helping the teacher. I could add four and four and I could read the primer—"There goes Alice. Here comes Spot." So I'd start teaching the younger ones. We only had a few books and when we got new workbooks one year, we thought we were really something. I went to school clear through the eighth grade. I liked it so much I even repeated the eighth grade. Don't forget, there wasn't any ninth grade. But the way education used to be in one-room schoolhouses is about like fourth grade in a regular school.

Another reason I liked school was because we had this program on Friday where the kids performed. Mommy made me a ruffled, red crepe paper dress, and I wore it until it fell apart. And I'd get up in front of the class and sing for as long as they let me.

Sometimes people ask me what kind of music we sang back in eastern Kentucky in those days. Well, it was our own music. I know there's some kind of history to mountain music—like it came from Ireland or England or Scotland and we kept up the tradition, hidden off in the mountains. I know there are folk musicians who come down to the mountains to make tape recordings of the old people singing the old hymns and stuff. But I couldn't honestly say if we had that kind of music.

Some people even say we talk like people from England or Ireland. Like how I say *h* in front of some of my words. Like "hain't" instead of "ain't." Well, I just talk how I feel. And singing was the same way. If it was from the other side of the ocean, then that's the way it was. We didn't know, nor care very much.

Most of our songs told a story. You could tell me that's the old-fashioned way people had of telling the news, before newspapers and radio. All I know is most country songs are ballads. Like we'd sing true songs about somebody getting killed. Mommy taught me a song called "The Great Titanic," and she taught me how to make motions with my hands to help in telling the story.

Like when the ship went down, I'd curve my hands downward.

Another song I sang in my class was about a woman named Luly Barrs who got pregnant by this man, but he wouldn't marry her. He tied a piece of railroad steel around her neck and threw her into the Ohio River, and they found her three months later. You go back to Kentucky, and I'll bet you there's lots of old people still know the song about Luly Barrs.

Most of our songs we learned from our friends and our family. We didn't sing too much stuff from the radio when I was little because, like I said before, we didn't have a radio until I was eleven. The first song I remember on the radio was "I'm Walking the Floor over You," with Ernest Tubb singing. Nowadays, I can stand right on the stage and watch my friend Ernest Tubb singing that same song. Thrilled? That ain't the word for it.

These days, people learn their songs from the radio or records. You go up to the mountains and the kids all know the top country songs, even rock 'n' roll. But they don't know the old songs anymore.

When we weren't in school, we were still mean. We used to go around tipping outhouses over, or turning over corn shocks on Halloween. Anything to be mean.

Marie Castle was my cousin and my closest friend. She used to stay with us a lot, and we'd fight one minute and play together the next, but we always knew how the other one felt. Even today, when she pops into my bus in Columbus, Ohio, I know exactly what Marie is feeling. We'll just hug each other and start laughing and crying and telling stories about Butcher Holler. Ain't neither of us changed one bit. We're still mean.

The last time I was in Columbus, Marie reminded me about the Halloween when we saw a vision. We were rubbing soap on the windows of Tillie Dollarhyde, who lived just up the holler. I could see her working in the kitchen. Suddenly I looked down in the yard and saw that same woman walking by some rocks in her garden. Marie saw her, too. We just ran away and never went back to bother her. Doolittle says I'm crazy to believe in "haints"—that's our word for ghosts. But I've seen some things I can't explain at some séances we've held in the last couple of years. I'll get into that later.

Marie used to chew tobacco: Days Work, Beech-Nut—any brand she could find. Sometimes we both smoked rabbit tobacco, which grows wild in the hollers. That's the plant Mommy calls "life everlasting" and uses for tea.

Like I said before, Mommy smoked but she didn't want us to. She saw smoke coming out of the barn one time and accused Marie of smoking. Marie said I was smoking, too, so we both got whipped. The next day I whipped Marie on the way to school. She was heavier than me, but I was meaner.

One time me and Marie were supposed to be cleaning the kitchen but we got into some home-brewed beer my brother left around. We got dog drunk before we remembered we were supposed to be cleaning up. Well, we poured a whole can of lye into the tub of water. We put our brushes on the wet floor and went skating around, having a great time. I said, "Marie, this floor must really be dirty. Look at the dirt come up." But it wasn't dirt. It was the paint we were a-taking up. Mommy whipped us good when she got home. We were just lucky our skin was already used to the lye from doing the wash on Mondays. If it wasn't, we could have gotten burned bad, the more I think about it.

All of us kids had a starvation for candy. Oh, we'd eat anything with sugar in it. One time I drew a dollar on my daddy's credit at the company store and bought ten

PAYDAY candy bars and ten Fudgsicles. I hid the candy bars for later and ate the Fudgsicles before they melted, but I got so sick I thought I'd die. There I was, sick to my stomach, and to top it off, I caught my foot in some old wooden pilings down near the mine and they had to call Daddy out of work to set me free. I cut my foot and he made me walk home. I've still got that little scar to show for it. Years later, when I realized how hard Daddy worked to make that dollar, I felt sick all over again.

Another time me and Marie found this scrip penny from the Van Lear company store. We didn't feel like walking down to Van Lear so we went to the little grocery near the mine. The man who ran it was working his farm up on the hill. We called him down—him thinking our mothers wanted an order of food. When we handed him the scrip penny, he got so mad he threw it away—but he gave us the candy. We spent two hours trying to find that scrip penny again.

In one respect, things got better when I was growing up, because we got a doctor that would stick by us. It used to be we'd have to doctor ourselves. But while I was in school, we got this young doctor, John Turner, who was right from Johnson County. Not too many doctors wanted to work in the mountains; they can make more money in the big cities. But old Doc, he's got himself an airplane and a farm and a town house, so he hasn't done too bad himself. Plus, he was always there when you needed him.

Doc knows what kind of people we are. You can't fool him. He's always telling me stories about the country people who come to the hospital. He insists he had a woman tell him, "Doc, I'm worried about my daughter. She hasn't had her monthlies in about three months." So Doc asked the woman if her daughter ever had sexual intercourse. And the woman says, "I don't know, Doc, but if she needs it, give it to her, and put it on the medical card." See, we didn't know those big words in Butcher Holler.

Anyway, Doc was a good man for us. He'd go out and make house calls, even if he couldn't get there in his car. One of his earliest buddies was a fellow named Doolittle Lynn, who had this old mule that used to take Doc around during snowstorms. Doc didn't know it, but the mule was blind. One time Doolittle was taking Doc up to some sick family in a snowstorm, and Doc says, "The mule seems to be stumbling."

Doolittle replied, "Doc, you got to lift up his bridle every time you see a rough spot, so he'll know enough to raise his feet. Don't you know the mule is blind?"

Doc jumped down off that mule and swore he wouldn't ride no blind mule. But after a few feet in the snow, he got back on.

Doc used to come to school and give typhoid shots to all the kids. I used to volunteer to be the first and say, "See, it don't hurt." I didn't mind the shot—I guess I liked the attention.

Doc probably saved my life when I was about twelve. I got a blood infection in my leg, and I swear they gave me ninety-nine shots before I got better. That was in the days before penicillin. One night while I was in the hospital, my cousin Marie came to visit because I was lonesome. She slept in the bed with me all night. Early in the morning, while we were both asleep, the nurse came in to give me my shot. She grabbed the first leg she saw, which was Marie's, and she gave her the shot. Marie didn't appreciate it much. I swear I can remember 'em talking about amputating my leg, but Doc says he doesn't remember that.

Later Doc helped me with my first two babies, but then I didn't see him for a long time because we moved to Washington. After I started singing I came back to Paintsville and we got to be friends again. Nowadays whenever I get back to Johnson County I stay at his farm, along the Levisa Fork of the Big Sandy. Doc's second wife is named Gwen, and she likes to play country music herself. So Doc, just for fun, built this beautiful stage in his old airplane hangar. It's got a nicer dressing room and backstage than half the places we play. Doc holds a music jubilee every Saturday night and we play there once in the spring and once in the fall.

All my boys pile into Doc's house, and Gwen feeds us sausages and biscuits and eggs until we can't stand it. Doc and Doolittle like to drink and talk about that old blind mule until the two of them are about as blind as the mule.

I'll tell you, we hate to leave. People sit on haystacks and camp chairs, with swallows flying overhead and under the rafters, puffy clouds floating over the mountains, lightning bugs in the darkness. It's a real beautiful time. I wish we could play more in the country instead of them smoky, dirty places we go to. We're country musicians; I don't think we could play our kind of music if we didn't come from little places like Butcher Holler.

Most of us got started on the old-fashioned songs or in church, like me. We used our same school building for church every Sunday. We had different preachers sometimes, maybe a miner from one of the coal camps who had a calling to preach on Sundays. Sometimes a preacher would be waving his hands during the sermon and you'd see he had fingers missing, from some mining accident. Our regular preacher was named Elzie Banks, and I still see him when I go back home. We never had to pass the hat for Elzie—he preached 'cause he loved it. He could make that old building rock when he'd preach—holding one hand over his ear and shaking his other hand at the devil. I wrote about the old building in one of my hymns, "Where I Learned to Pray."

They don't hold school in that building anymore—the kids go down to Van Lear. But whenever I get home, I sneak through an open window and find my old blackboard. Then I take a piece of chalk and write:

LORETTA LYNN WAS HERE.

# 6

## The Pie Social

*I like my loving done country style,*
*And this little girl would walk a country mile,*
*To find me a good old slow-talking country*
*boy...*
—*"You're Looking at Country," by Loretta Lynn*

It was at that little school that I met my husband. I was just a little kid from Butcher Holler, didn't know nothing, and he was a grown man who already fought in World War II and worked in coal mines and traveled across the country.

That's why I get mad when people make remarks about my husband. If it wasn't for Doolittle, there would be no career. I wouldn't have started singing in the first place, and I wouldn't have had the inspiration for some of my best songs, in the second place. And I never could have run my business. So in a real sense, Doolittle is responsible for everything we've got. Let's get that straight right away.

Some people make jokes that he's called "Doolittle" because they think he doesn't do much. Actually, he got that nickname when he was just a baby around two years old. Nobody knows why—maybe because he was always a little feller. Today most people know him as "Mooney" because that's the nickname he picked up in Washington, like I told you, when they found out he used to run moonshine. But back home in Johnson County, everybody calls him "Doolittle," and I call him "Doo" for short.

Some people in Nashville like to make fun of Mooney Lynn. They see him wearing his old cowboy hat to town, even when we go out to dinner. Somebody once looked inside his hat and saw he wrote, "Like hell it's yours." But that's Doolittle: he fights for what's his, and he's smart.

In most ways, Doo has been a good husband. He's worked hard all his life to get things for me and the kids. I don't want to say he's never fooled around, or gotten drunk, or whipped me into line a little, because that ain't the truth. There were plenty of bad moments in our marriage, but I've always respected my husband's common sense. When he's traveling with me, I know things are going to work more smoothly because Doo is there, supervising things. I feel safe when he's around.

There was a time in Boston a few years ago when three kids threw whiskey bottles at our bus, which was brand-new at the time. Jim Webb, who's our driver, and some of the boys wanted to wipe them out. But Doolittle got up and said, "Boys, get back in the bus. We've got to stay overnight in this town tonight, and we don't want a riot." It was good he did that, or my boys might have really started something.

Of course, Doolittle ain't afraid of a fight himself. One time we were in Holland, in Europe, doing a show, and he walked out to get something to eat. There was this restaurant way down at the end of a long pier. Doo got sandwiches in a sack and was carrying them back. He was wearing his cowboy hat, which he always wears—it wouldn't be him without it—and there was this German guy walking right behind him saying, "Hey, cowboy." Maybe they were the only words he knew in English. Now Doo didn't bother with him for a long time, but the guy kept saying, "Hey, cowboy," real irritating-like, and brushing up against Doo. Well, Doo told him to stop but he didn't. Doo had enough of talking, so he transferred that sack to his left hand and came up with one punch right to the guy's chin. He hit the guy so hard the guy fell backward over the guardrail and down—about thirty feet into the ocean. This scared Doolittle because he was afraid the guy was knocked unconscious and would drown. But the salt water must have woke him up, because when Doo looked over the rail, he saw the guy swimming to shore. He decided to get out of there in a hurry. That night his hand was all swollen up, and when we asked him why, he told us what happened. Now whenever one of us wants to get Doo mad, we come up behind him and say, "Hey, cowboy." But I wouldn't advise any stranger doing it!

Everybody knows who's in charge when Doolittle is around. Like last summer, when we were playing in Ontelaunee Park, in Pennsylvania, and one of the fans wanted to buy a tape right in the middle of the show. Now, ordinarily we don't do this. We sell albums and tapes after the show is over but not during the performance. But Ken Riley, the drummer who's in charge of our sales, sold a tape during the show to a guy who walked up to the edge of the stage. He did it just for a joke, only Doolittle didn't think it was too funny. After the show he announced, "*That* won't happen again." He didn't say it real loud—but he made his point. Of course, we aim to do it again, just as soon as he's off the tour for a while. You can just bet I'll say to my boys, "Boys, get your tapes ready to sell. Doolittle ain't with us tonight." And we'll sell one—just to be mean.

But on important matters, we listen to my husband. That's why it drives me crazy when I hear somebody say, "Gee, Mooney, it must be great to be married to a rich singer so you don't have to work." That's the kind of person who doesn't know that Doo spends half a year running our ranch and the other half running our road show. He is *always* working. When someone says something like that, I can see the muscles get tight in Doo's neck, and I know he'd like to take a punch at that person.

Doolittle would like to be John Wayne, rough and tough, but really he's a softie. You should see him with our babies, the twins, and you'd know he's a good father. It's just that he doesn't like to show that part of himself to strangers. I guess that's the way men are supposed to behave. I don't know why. Me, I'm affectionate. I like to touch people and tell 'em I love 'em. I guess it isn't as easy for a man. Maybe that's why we've stayed married so long. They say opposites attract.

When I'm upset, I let loose with my tongue and everyone knows it. Or, when I'm nervous, which I am a lot of times, you can see me shaking a mile away. But when Doo is nervous, he holds it inside. He gets stomachaches and pains from not knowing how to let his feelings out. But bad or good, Doo is always the life of the party. Sometimes he pretends he's drunk so that everyone will loosen up and have a good time. That embarrasses me a lot, but he don't care. And when it comes to me, he won't allow me to embarrass him. He puts me down and I don't like it, but that's the way it is. We started off with almost a father-daughter relationship, and in some ways we've still got one.

In a lot of ways, it was good for me to marry someone

older than me, because I could learn from him. But, in another way, it wasn't so good because I went directly from Daddy to Doolittle without ever being on my own. Even today, men are telling me what to do. My husband, my lawyer, my accountant, my personal manager. In a sense, I still don't have complete control over myself. Maybe I never will. But if it wasn't for Doo, we wouldn't have what we have today. People ask if we would still be poor. My answer is no. Doo would have made sure that we had a good house and enough to eat, even if he had to work twenty-four hours a day.

I guess a lot of my fans have heard parts of how me and Doolittle met, but there's still a lot that I never told before. For example: it's true that I never met Doolittle until that night at the pie social. But I did see him during the war in his uniform—I remember shouting to my cousin, "Look at that boy! He looks like a little toy soldier." Doolittle says he saw me before he went into the service—I was only eleven at the time. When he came back from the army, I was getting close to fourteen. And things were different by then.

Since I was thirteen years old, the teacher let me help arrange the programs for the pie supper. I lined up all the talent, and I sang in the talent show. I was also in the beauty contest and in the cakewalk. I guess I was just about in everything because there weren't that many kids in the school.

One of the biggest events was the pie bidding. Whoever bought a girl's pie got to take her home. Well, I didn't know how to bake anything and I was sure nobody would buy my pie.

When it came to the beauty contest, there was only me and four other girls. It was a small school. The way it was judged was that the audience would bid money on the girl they thought was the prettiest. One of the bidders was this boy I thought was a little toy soldier. He looked young because he was only about five feet eight inches tall and weighed about 145 at the most, and he had this small face, like a cute boy. But actually, like I said, he'd already been in the war and everything. Well, he started bidding on me, and even though there was another girl I thought was prettier, I won the beauty contest.

Then it came to the pie bidding. I sat by my pie I'd somehow managed to bake. The fellow running this contest was the same little boy who helped me win the beauty contest. I knew I couldn't bake too good, but this old boy started bidding on my pie and this other boy named Flop Murphy started topping him. They were bidding against each other pretty heavy. Old Flop would bid three dollars, and this other boy would bid three and a quarter, and so on, like that. Finally Flop Murphy got to four fifty, and this other boy raps his hammer down real fast and says, "Five dollars and sold!" He bought it himself.

Well, the contest was over, and he won my pie. Now he had to try a piece of it. He should have known better because I got the salt can confused with the sugar can when I was baking it. Lord knows those cans looked alike. I cut the pie and took a piece for myself. My aunt was standing there and she was gonna try some, too. Well, the boy took a bite and looked like he was gonna start foundering. Then my aunt took a taste and said, "Loretta, you've used salt instead of sugar." That was all the pie we ate for five dollars, which was a heck of a lot of money in those days and in that town, even for a *good* pie.

Then it was time for everybody to go home. The way we usually went home at night was to light pieces of pine wood or pine roots and hold them in front of us like a torch so we wouldn't trip on the dirt path. But this boy, Doolittle, had this jeep he'd brought home from the army. He wanted me to ride in it, but I was scared to. I had ridden in the back of a pickup truck. But the jeep looked like something from Mars! So I said, "No, I ain't getting into that thing." He had to walk me up that path, holding one of those pine cones the way everybody did.

When we got to my house, he said, "Hey, come here, I'm gonna kiss you good night."

I was scared to death because I didn't know how to kiss. I never kissed a boy before. Should my lips be wet or dry? What if we bumped noses? That's the kind of thing that was going through my head. He kissed me right on the lips, and it was nice. The truth is I fell in love right there. I can't explain it, but it felt so nice to be kissed by this boy that I fell in love.

Well, he turned down the holler and said he'd see me soon. I didn't know it, but as soon as he got below the yard, he bumped his head on a big fence post and bloodied his nose. He forgot his pine torch and he had to crawl on his hands and knees until he got to the schoolhouse. I always thought it was my kiss that knocked him down. But he said it was the fence post.

Anyway, I saw him leave and I went into the house singing away. Mommy asked me how the social went, so I told her I won the beauty contest and my pie brought five dollars at the bidding. She said, "Well, who bid for your pie?"

And I said, "Doolittle Lynn."

She gave a kind of gasp and said, "Oooh, he's too old for you; and not only that, he's got a bad reputation. He's the wildest thing around here. You can't go with him."

I nodded my head. But meanwhile, all the time I was wondering when he'd come round again.

# 7

## Doolittle

Where I've been or where I'm goin' didn't
take a lot of knowin'
But I take a lot of pride in what I am…
    —*"I Take a Lot of Pride in What I Am,"*
        *by Merle Haggard*

Mommy didn't want me to have anything to do with Doolittle Lynn, but actually we had a lot in common. The Webbs and the Lynns had been living around Van Lear for a long time, and our ways were a lot the same. Besides, I was next-to-oldest of eight children and Doo was the oldest of ten, and we'd done our share of helping to raise kids. And both of us were familiar with coal mining.

Doo's father was a coal boss for a long time. If you think Doolittle is tough, you should see his old man. He must be over seventy now, but he's still got that cocky walk about him, like a bantam rooster. He's got these wild eyes—untamed, you know? And his hair is still red. His name is Oliver, but we call him "Red." I've always felt real close to Red. He helped me write one of my songs called "New Rainbow."

Red used to drink now and then, and there was no telling what he'd do. We used to see Red and Angie, that's Doo's mother, fussing sometimes. One time Doolittle had to tie Red up so he could come sparking— that's our way of saying "courting"—at my house without worrying about what Red was up to.

One night Doo's brother came running to my house saying that Angie had untied Red, and Red was chasing everybody around the yard. Doo had to rush home and wrestle his daddy to the ground. Even though Red had only about four teeth, he bit Doo until he was bleeding.

Everybody likes Red, but still, he does do some strange things. Doo says the worst thing his daddy ever did was on a Thanksgiving. Angie fixed up a beautiful turkey dinner with all the fixings and all ten kids were sitting around the table ready to eat. Red had this rule that none of the kids could eat until he himself was served—and one of the kids broke the rule. This made Red so mad that he picked up the table and dumped the whole dinner out the window. Luckily, most of the dinner slid right onto the tablecloth and didn't get ruined. The kids sneaked the food under the porch and had their Thanksgiving dinner in peace while Red raced around the house.

There's only one way to get along with Red—you can't pick on him. You just let him have a beer or two and don't nag him. But if he gets rough with you, get rough right back. He respects me and Doolittle, I think, because we're as mean as he is.

When we first got married, Red came out to live with us in Washington. Me and Red got along great. He taught me how to play pinochle while I was waiting for my third baby. I was too far along to pick vegetables, so me and Red would play pinochle all day. About ten minutes before Doo would be getting home, we'd rush around and straighten up the house. Red would sweep all the dirt under the rug, and I'd fix some supper. Then Doo would see all the pinochle scores written on a brown shopping bag and say, "I see you've been playing pinochle again."

And Red would say, "Just a few games."

Red never has been one to stay in one place for long. When Doo was just a boy in Kentucky, they heard rumors that coal was selling for twenty dollars a ton in Washington State. Red took off one day and nobody heard from him for a long time. That was rough on Doo's mommy. I've always loved Angie. Even today, she'll make me a big angel food cake whenever I visit. And she had her hands full in those days.

Meanwhile, Doo had to support his family by hoeing corn for fifty cents a day. Sometimes the grown men would help him finish his row so the boss wouldn't fire him. Even then, Doolittle wasn't satisfied with one job; he was always working. His aunt sold milk in the coal camp, so Doo delivered the milk on that old blind mule of his. They figured as long as he was hauling milk that way, maybe he could haul moonshine in the same jugs and the federal people wouldn't know the difference. They would pay him a nickel a gallon. He never actually made moonshine, but he hauled about an ocean of it.

Finally, Red came back from Washington and said he was prospecting for minerals. They packed up the family in an old 1933 Dodge and put their belongings in a two-wheel trailer they made. Every night, Angie would find a creek and cook dinner. Around St. Louis, the motor bearings tore loose. That meant they had to drive slowly one day, then spend the next day fixing the bearings. They did this all the way to Washington.

Doo told me he got so thirsty in Utah that when he saw this lake, he begged to get out and take a sip. His daddy told him it was salty, but Doo wouldn't believe it. He found out the hard way that his daddy was right. It was the Great Salt Lake.

It took them twenty days to get across the country. They finally broke down thirty miles from their town, and Red's boss had to tow 'em the rest of the way. They settled down, but it was the middle of the Depression and there wasn't much money going around. The kids got put back two years, every one of 'em, because of their Kentucky education. One day Red took off again—didn't say a word to anybody—and Doolittle was left responsible for his mother and the nine kids.

Doo was in the first year of high school when he finally quit. He says he did pretty good, and I believe him. He had to walk four miles to the school bus every morning. He also had to get food for the family. He saved up for a shotgun and a few shells, and he used to sneak up on the pheasants so as to not waste shells. He'd go to the potato farms after the farmers picked what they wanted. Anything they didn't grade, he could take—and there were plenty of good ones left.

Some guy made Doo a deal that if he would clean out the chicken houses, he'd give Doo an old Ford that was hardly used. And another time Doo used someone's bull-dozer to clear a road to a creek, and then he'd go after salmon. You ain't supposed to get salmon when they're swimming upstream to spawn. But if you're hungry, you do. So Doo would take a pitchfork and watch for small-sized salmon, because the big ones were all bruised up from swimming in that tiny creek. He'd get a whole load of 'em, and his mom would smoke enough for the win-ter. One day the game warden caught Doo and said by law he should run him in. But he knew Doo's folks were hungry, so he told him to take those fish straight home to his mom. Once when a deer got hit by a car, the game warden was supposed to take it to the hospital to get it fixed—but he brought it to Doo instead to kill and clean.

Doo was still out west when the war started. He and other men helped make lookout towers because they figured the Japanese would attack from the Pacific Ocean. Doo wanted to join the service real bad, but his mom was so scared about a war breaking out on the West Coast that she decided to go back home to Kentucky. She didn't drive, so Doo got what was called a "hardship driver's license," which they gave to kids who were underage.

By this time they were driving a '34 Chevrolet, and Doo built a two-wheel trailer out of an old car frame so he could haul his mom's old Maytag washer back to Kentucky. He wasn't full grown yet, maybe around five feet two inches, so he had to put wooden blocks on the pedals of the car and an apple box on the seat to raise him up some. He loaded his mother and brothers and sisters in the old car and they took off. All they had was sixty-eight dollars and some ration stamps for gas.

But it was the same deal coming back as it was going out there. The rear end fell apart in Iowa City, and the whole family had to camp outdoors again while Doolittle tried to fix the car. He finally talked his way into working in a car shop, where they taught him to use one of those flame-throwers that cuts cars. He worked for four days, and then a guy in the shop fixed the rear end for him. By this time they had used too many gas stamps and were down to twelve dollars in cash, so they didn't dare leave Iowa City. Doo's mother was getting nervous they'd never get back to Kentucky alive, with them camping out and such.

Doo told me once he couldn't sleep at night just worrying about what was gonna happen to his family. One night he got an idea, and he was so afraid he'd forget it that he stayed up all night. The next morning he told his family to follow him down to the welfare office and nobody say a word, just obey his orders. So he lined up his family in the welfare office and asked for gas stamps. The man said it was impossible to give extra stamps. So Doolittle says, "All right, if we have to stay in Iowa City, there's eleven of us, and we're gonna have to go on welfare. Let's see, we'll need food and clothing and welfare checks..."

Doo says that man told him, "Don't move. Don't go away. I'll see what I can do." And in about five minutes, that man had a huge handful of stamps that he gave to Doolittle. That's how they got back to Kentucky. Doo even had enough gas stamps left to sell for cash.

When he got his family settled, Doo tried to join the service. But he was underage and underweight. The army told him to join the navy. The marines told him to join the coast guard. Nobody wanted him. But finally the army took him in 1944, even though he was still too young. In sixteen weeks he was in Europe. Doo don't talk too much about the war, not even to me. But he was in Germany, France, and Italy for the last year of the war. Sometimes when people talk about the bad things that went on in Vietnam, Doo will say, "Aw, that's always happened in wars." But he don't tell too many details.

I know that when he got home after the war, he couldn't adjust to being home again. He couldn't sleep at night because he had nightmares about snakes and stuff. The only time he could sleep was during the day. That's how he met me, actually. He was trying to sleep around the house, and his mother was talking to the school-teacher about that pie social. The teacher was complaining to Angie that she couldn't get no one to auction off the pies, and she started to cry. This woke Doo up and he said, "Lady, if you stop crying, I'll auction off your damn pies for you." Angie got mad at Doo because he talked rough to a schoolteacher, but he didn't care. I think there were two little Banks girls he wanted to meet at the school anyway and play post office and spin-the-bottle with. But he says, "As soon as I saw Loretta, I knew I wanted to get ahold of her."

Well, he did. He gave me that great big kiss on our first night that made me fall in love with him. Then he got that bloody nose from walking into that fence post. But that didn't discourage him. The next evening our family was sitting on the porch after supper and we heard this terrible noise coming up the holler. We looked and there was this jeep blasting up the dirt path. You can ask Mommy. It was the first automobile that ever came up Butcher Holler in history. And Doolittle pulled into our yard as pleased as could be and said, "From now on, we're gonna take my jeep."

# 8

## Hey, You Ain't Supposed to Wear Clothes under Your Nightgown

You can feel my body tremble
As I wonder what this moment holds in store.
And as you put your arms around me,
You can tell I've never been this far before...
　　—*"I've Never Been This Far Before," Carroll
　　　Baker's version of Conway Twitty's song*

I was glad to see Doo, but I was afraid my daddy was going to say something. I knew they didn't want me to see Doolittle, but you know how kids are—they're going to do what they want anyhow.

I still wouldn't go in that jeep with him, not at first, so we courted at my house. It was cold—we met on December 10—and we had to stay indoors. We would sit in the front room and talk, with all my sisters and brothers saying things about when he was gonna kiss me and stuff like that. And my mommy walking in saying, "Would you like a soda?" or talking about the weather. Just to keep an eye on us, you know.

We didn't have much to talk about. I was just a bashful kid, never been anywhere. He told me a little about the army, and he talked a lot about Washington State and said he wanted to move back there someday. I didn't have nothing to tell him about what I'd done. Kind of a one-sided affair, wasn't it? But that was how we spent December 11. The next day he talked me into riding in his jeep. But I didn't go with him just because he had a car. It was almost the opposite. I was scared to death to drive in it, even though he was very confident. He would try anything in a jeep—drive up the side of a mountain, if you dared him. He wasn't afraid of nothing.

He kept hanging around my house. Just a-hanging around. At Christmastime he bought me a doll and said we were gonna get married and that next Christmas we'd have a real live doll. I didn't know what he was talking about. I never thought about getting married and having babies. And all the time my mommy and my daddy were telling me it was just puppy love.

But it was more than that. When we were working on this book, Doo told the writer, "I was attracted to Loretta at first by her looks. She was real mature with a full woman's figure. I didn't know she was only thirteen until I was at her house a few times. But it didn't change my mind. When you're in love, it don't make no difference. I was fresh out of the service and I had done my share of chasing around. I knew what I was looking for to marry—and Loretta was it."

Mommy and Daddy started getting real nervous. Doo had this reputation for being wild because he drove too fast and had gone out with other girls. You know how country people are. Actually, he wasn't as wild as our own two boys are today, but he seemed pretty wild then. Mommy and Daddy were afraid I was getting serious so Mommy decided to send me to her sister's house, just across the Big Sandy into West Virginia. She packed my clothes and had me driven over there.

I didn't know what was going on. Mommy's sister was trying to get me to forget about Doolittle, because she fixed me up with this other boy who was as old as Doolittle, maybe even older. She got this boy to visit me at her house one night while she and her husband went up to their room. This boy got fresh with me and scared me half to death. He was a-grabbing and I was a-running all around the living room. Finally he gave up. Too tired from running, I guess. The next day Doolittle found out what the deal was. I don't know how he knew where I was staying, but he showed up in his jeep and told me, "Get your stuff. We're leaving here." I even left my clothes behind and never told Mommy what happened at her sister's house. I just came home like nothing happened.

Then me and Doo started going out on dates, right after New Year's. We were talking about getting married in April or June or sometime. One night we went to a skating rink over near Prestonsburg with my brother and his girlfriend. Daddy warned us not to go there because they sold moonshine and it was kind of a rough place. But we went anyway. When I got home, Daddy whipped my butt. It was the first time he spanked me in years. But it didn't change things.

I kept telling Mommy, "We're gonna get married," and she kept saying, "You're too young." But I kept telling her.

We were talking now about waiting until February, but one Friday night Doolittle came over and said he had a big paycheck that day from working in the mines. He said we might as well get married the next day since he had the money. I thought if he asked me, I might as well get married. So I said yes.

Me and Doo had this discussion in the living room at my house. Daddy knew something was up. He was standing on the outside porch, even though it was cold out. He liked to stand out there at night, where it was dark and quiet. So I told Doo, "You'd better tell Daddy." But when Doo went out on the porch, Daddy said, "You'd better tell Clary."

Doo found Mommy in the bedroom and tried to tell her, but she said, "You'd better tell Ted about it."

But when Doo went back to Daddy, he said, "You'd better tell Clary."

I could see they was gonna run Doo back and forth all night, and they still weren't gonna go for it. So I told Doo, "Wait until they get tired and decide to go to bed. Then they'll be together and they'll have to listen together." So we waited and finally Doo told 'em he wanted to marry me.

Daddy said that I was awful young to be thinking about getting married. Doo said he knew that, but he'd take real good care of me. They didn't exactly say yes, but I knew we were gonna do it. After Doo went home, Mommy and Daddy cried all night and didn't hardly talk to me.

Daddy did make Doo promise not to whip me, and not to take me too far from home. And Mommy told me, "This is something you'll regret for the rest of your life."

Well, there have been times when I thought Mommy was right, and there's been times when I knew she was wrong. But on that particular day, I was just gonna go ahead and get married. Mommy told me later that the reason she let me get married was she knew if it was her, she'd have gone out and gotten married anyway. She said I always looked older and acted older than my age. So she knew there was no sense arguing.

We got married Saturday, January 10. I remember Mommy's Cherokee father, Nathaniel Ramey, rocking on the front porch. He never said much, but he looked at Doolittle and said, "You be good to my little girl, or I'll kill you." Doolittle seemed impressed, because he knew that Indians never make promises they don't keep.

I was wearing my aunt's dress and my mother's shoes. The dress hung down below my knees. I had to be the ugliest bride you ever saw. We just went down to the county courthouse in Paintsville to the judge and got it done. We didn't have a ring. I didn't know nothing about rings. In fact, I never had a ring until after I started singing and the guys would come around and try to date me. They'd say, "Well, you don't have no ring on." So Doo went out and bought a ring just to let them know I was married.

But on our wedding night we weren't that organized. We got there at eight o'clock, but Daddy didn't come down until eleven o'clock to give me away. He stood in the back of the room and didn't say a word. Mommy didn't even come down. She's never been to any weddings except my sister Brenda's, and I haven't gone to any of my kids' weddings, either. It just makes me nervous— I don't know why.

At our wedding, Doo wrote down his name as Oliver Vanetta Lynn, and I said, "Who's that?" See, I thought his real name was Doolittle.

We were taking our honeymoon at Chandler's Cabins, about seventeen miles from Paintsville. But before we could leave, Marie's daddy got in Doo's jeep and said he was coming with us on our honeymoon. I didn't know what we were gonna do, but Doo gave him a pint of Fat Messer's best moonshine and let him off on the highway somewhere. Then we went on our honeymoon.

Before we get any further along, let me say that I didn't have much of an idea what a honeymoon was all about. Doo was the first boy I ever went with, and

I didn't go with him long enough to know what was going on. My parents never told me nothing. Now, I was different with my girls. I told 'em the facts straight off. My daddy used to tell me they got me by turning over a cabbage leaf—and I believed it. I'm sure my little twins know more than I did when I got married. I think a mother should talk to her girls about it. But that was a different time back then.

So, we drove to these cabins, which were nothing fancy, just a little bunch of cabins side by side. But I thought it was the end of the world. I guess I was a little nervous. We got into that little cabin, and I was shaking like I was freezing. Doolittle turned on the radiator and I sat right down on it, wrapped in my little red teddy bear coat, the only coat I owned. I just kept shivering, even when the heat went up. My husband, he went to bed. He was wearing shorts and one of them undershirts with no sleeves. I was embarrassed just to look at him. He said, "Can't you come to bed?"

I said, "I'm freezing to death!" But I know it was nerves. His mother had bought me a nightgown. I had never worn any kind of gown because we always used to sleep in our underclothes. So he said, "Go ahead, get your gown and go in the bathroom."

I took out this gown; it was white with raised white flowers and leaves on it, thinner than flannel, and to me it was beautiful because I never saw anything like it. It was long and straight and I thought you wore it over everything. I was in bad shape—scared to death, I suppose. So I put the gown over my clothes and came back out.

Doo said, "Hey, you ain't supposed to wear clothes under your nightgown."

Well, I went back and took off my dress and left all my underclothes on. He sent me back again. By this time it was three o'clock in the morning. It was getting late,

I guess you'd say. So I took off my slip and went back. I guess he didn't think that was too smart. He really had a time with this little girl he married. He finally more or less had to rip off my panties. The rest of it was kind of a blur. I guess I went into a fit and didn't know what he was doing. He didn't tell me nothing, so I just lay there.

The next day we were getting hungry and Doo said we should go to this little restaurant next door. But I said I couldn't go to the restaurant and face all these people who would know what we were doing in the cabin. So for three days I stayed inside while Doo brought me the food. I didn't know nothing. I could tell you things but they probably couldn't be printed. I was just so young.

I still think about it every time we go back to Johnson County and we pass that old motel. It's changed its name but last summer they gave me and Doolittle the key to our old room. Everybody thought that was funny but I said they better be careful or we just might show up sometime and use the room. Things might be better this time around.

They couldn't be much worse. Looking back, I'd say that sex didn't mean that much to me for a long time. I think I picked up the old woman's attitude that sex was fun for men—but not for women. Doo even got some sex books for me to read, but it wasn't until I was older that I started to enjoy it a little more. I didn't even know that much about my body—having a climax and stuff. It was all a mystery for a long time. When I was in my late twenties, this doctor told me about having a climax— how you could help yourself. I didn't even know women could do that. But it would be better if men knew more about what pleases women. Being patient, being gentle... I'd have welcomed that.

I can't say I recommend getting married at thirteen or fourteen. Most of the girls from Kentucky didn't get married until they were eighteen or nineteen. But today you see younger kids getting married—or just living together. I used to tell people it was "just plain wrong" for kids to sleep together before they got married. But nowadays I don't want to go telling other people how to live their lives. Maybe living together is a better idea than getting married when you're so young. It seems like some people don't start having fights until they get married. Marriage puts pressure on you sometimes, knowing it's a lifetime deal.

It also helps to know the facts of life when you do get married. I was only married four months when I started getting sick in the morning. I didn't know what was wrong, so I went down to Doc Turner and told him my symptoms. Doc told me to get undressed and he put this big sheet over me. But I was so embarrassed I just pulled the sheet over my head, like an ostrich. When he was done, Doc told me I could get dressed again. After that, he put his arm around my waist and he said, "Honey, your trouble is you're pregnant."

"What's that?" I asked. 'Cause I didn't know what the word meant.

"You're gonna have a baby," Doc said.

"Oh my gosh!" I said. "I can't have no babies yet."

And Doc said, "Well, you're married, aren't you? And you sleep with your man, don't you? So you're pregnant."

I couldn't believe it. Here I used to tell Mommy I didn't want to rock her babies no more, and now I was gonna have one of my own. All I could think about was Doolittle telling me I was gonna have my own doll by next Christmas.

# 9

## Doo Kicks Me Out

I'm tired of asking you where you've been,
Tired of all this misery I'm in,
Two steps forward and six steps back again...
—*"Two Steps Forward," by Loretta Lynn*

It was bad enough being fourteen and pregnant. But it was even worse when Doolittle kicked me out. When I was about two months pregnant, Doo told me to go home to my parents. What else could I do when I was only fourteen? I went home.

When we were doing this book, my writer asked, "Mooney, how could you kick her out when she was so young?"

And Doo kind of hid his face and said, "Aw, her and my sister used to sit around yapping when I came home from work." Actually, Doo knows it was a bad thing to do—now. But then it didn't seem so bad to him.

Sometimes Doo says he kicked me out because of my cooking, but I know better. He met this girl named Pearl who lived in one of the coal camps. He insists he never touched her, just talking on the street and stuff. But he was leading up to it. Plus, there was this other woman who had been with every man in Johnson County just about. Doo had been with her before we got married, and he went back to her again.

I can see where having such a young wife would give a man ideas about straying. But still, at the time, it hurt me bad. I could tell Doo wasn't happy with me. I didn't know what sex was all about. I think even if I had been handled real gentle, it might not have made any difference. I was too young to be living with a man. It's that simple.

There were other problems, too. They say the quickest way to a man's heart is through his stomach. Well, I didn't get to Doo's heart that way, either.

I never had been too good in the kitchen because my mommy was so good at it. When I got married, all I knew was beans and potatoes and corn bread, while Doolittle was used to pot roast and stuff like that.

He knew right away he was in for bad cooking when he asked me to make pancakes and I didn't know how. I never did get it right. We were living with his family for a while until we got our own little shack, and Angie showed me a few things. But after we moved into the camp in Van Lear, I still couldn't cook. Every night Doo would come home from the mines, and if he didn't like what I cooked, he'd just throw it over the porch. We had a dog named Drive who was getting fat eating all the stuff Doo throwed out. But sometimes Drive wasn't hungry and Doo would point to the mess of food and say, "You see? Even the dog won't eat your cooking."

One time I had two of my girl friends do the cooking, and they were pretty good cooks. But when Doo got home, he didn't know who cooked it, and out of habit he just dumped it over the porch. He said I couldn't cook and he told his brother to take me home.

Doo was starting to visit this Pearl after I went back to Mommy and Daddy. I was feeling really low, being fourteen and pregnant and getting kicked out already. My brothers started to tease me, and I'd fight with 'em, chasing Junior or Herman through the cornfields, slapping 'em if I could catch 'em.

Mommy, the practical one, suggested I should start getting out with my friends again. She told me to take the bus to Paintsville to see a picture show. The movie was called *I Wonder Who's Kissing Her Now*—which was a pretty good title for my situation. Doolittle saw me downtown and kept cracking funny little jokes to flirt with me, but I wouldn't talk to him. I was mad at him for the way he treated me.

After the movies, when I was walking up Butcher Holler, Doolittle was following me. I had these new shoes that were giving me blisters and he said, "Hey, you're walking funny. Take off your shoes." I still didn't talk to him, but I took off my shoes. Finally, he said he wanted to talk to me about ordering clothes for the baby. So I let him talk to me, and we decided to get together again. Later I found that Doo's uncle Jake told him, "That's a real good girl you got there. You ought to make up with her."

When I moved back, I found that Doolittle's girlfriend was still writing letters to him. I'm not supposed to be able to read and write too good—but I managed to make my point in a little letter I wrote to her. I said she better get it straight that Doolittle Lynn is married to me. And I mailed it.

On Saturday morning I went down to the Paintsville post office and watched that hussy pick up her mail. When she came out, you could tell she was furious. Just then, along comes Doolittle, walking down the street. I could see her jaws a-moving, telling him to give back her picture, which he still had. Then she took off down the street, still mad. I don't think Doolittle ever heard from her again—and good riddance.

Now, the reason I'm telling the story is this: We've been married for a long time, in a business with a lot of traveling involved. I'm not the backward little country girl I was then. I was just learning that there's a lot of women who like to move in on other women's husbands, and I don't go for it. I made my point in "Fist City," which is a song about a real woman in Tennessee who was making eyes at Doolittle while I was a-singing on the stage.

I let her know she was gonna get a mouthful of knuckles if she kept it up. And I'd have done it. I've always had a bad temper when it came to seeing women making eyes at my man. Let 'em go get their own if they're so good.

It wasn't until much later that men started making moves on me—I'll get into that later. But here I was, fourteen years old and learning the facts of life the hard way. Sure, I've heard people say men are bound to run around a little bit. It's their nature. Well, shoot, I don't believe in double standards, where men can get away with things that women can't. In God's eyes, there's no double standard. That's one of the things I've been trying to say in my songs. Lots of country songs are about people trying to get along—falling in love, quarreling, having affairs, messing up their lives. That's life, and we've got to face it.

But life works both ways. There's plenty of songs about how women should stand by their men and give them plenty of loving when they walk through the door, and that's fine. But what about the man's responsibility? A man is supposed to give his wife a good time, too. Let him be tender with her once in a while. And it's even more important for two people to respect each other—you don't save a marriage just by putting on some sexy nightgown when your old man comes home from the factory. But maybe the old man could save the marriage by asking his wife, "What do you think we should do about this situation?" No woman likes to be told, "Here's the deal."

I'm not a big fan of women's liberation, but maybe it will help women stand up for the respect they're due. And maybe they won't be cutting each other up so much. I don't like seeing women act so jealous about other women. You hear it backstage at the Opry; you hear it when women get together for coffee. They should talk about the things they have in common—families, cooking, jobs, whatever. If they can't talk to their husbands, because their husbands don't care what they think, well, at least they should talk with other women. But it don't work out that way. Women are too jealous. I know women who get upset if they see me hug their husbands and tell 'em I love 'em. I've gotten in trouble just for being friendly with people. The men get the wrong idea and so do their wives.

Anyway, I think it's about time people were more respectful of each other. I know how I wanted to be treated when I got married.

# 10

## Two Thousand Miles from Home

But here in Topeka, the rain is a-fallin',
The faucet is a-drippin' and the kids are a-bawlin'
One of 'em's a-toddlin' and one is a-crawlin',
And... one's on the way...
— *"One's on the Way," by Shel Silverstein*

One of the reasons we were able to talk my parents into letting me get married was because Doo promised not to take me far from home. But a year after we got married, I found myself two thousand miles from home.

It was probably a good idea anyway. When a young couple gets married, they should move away from their families so they can't run home every minute. This way, we were either going to get along, or not. And there wasn't going to be any family to interfere.

The move started when Doo had troubles at the mine. He never really liked mining that much, but he figured he should give it a try since his daddy was a boss for so long. But it was bad work—underground, dangerous, not a great future. Doo was the boss of a five-man crew for Consolidated. He'd supervise them mining the coal;

then he'd drive the coal over to the tipple, where it would be weighed. They were rough days in mining; if the guy at the tipple didn't like you, he could really hurt you.

One day the man wrote up a slip that said Doo had dirty coal. Doo got out of the cab and argued that the coal didn't have no slate, no dirt, no red dog. But the man must have had it in for Doo, because they went around on it for a while. Doo didn't want to drive around trying to sell the coal somewhere else, so he got back into the cab and dumped the coal on the loading platform. Then he drove off, with the guy cussing him.

It didn't end there. They sent the sheriff after Doo and put him in the county jail for a few hours until it got straightened out. But Doo knew he was done at the tipple and done as a boss. He didn't care much anyway. Coal was going downhill; the union was telling miners their medical cards were no good, ruining everything they had worked for all their lives. Doo could see it was getting worse and worse. He wasn't middle-aged like my daddy; he had seen other parts of the country and knew he could make a living at something else. So he talked my oldest brother, Junior, into hitching out to Washington State with him, and the next thing I knew, I was back living with my family again, with that little baby kicking inside of me.

It was only a month before I got word from Doo. He had gotten hired by these two farmers, Bob and Clyde Green, and they gave him enough money for me to ride the train all the way to Washington. I had never been outside the mountains before, never rode a train. Daddy didn't want me to go. He tried to scare me, telling me how sometimes those trains crash. But we bought the ticket because I wanted to be with Doo. I was still only fourteen, but I was a married woman and my place was with my husband.

Mommy fixed me up a basket of food, a big brown paper sack of chicken, moon pies, biscuits, and hog meat. I didn't know they had a dining room on the train, but I couldn't afford it anyway. And besides, I was too bashful to go in there, even if I could. Fortunately, Junior's wife, Bonnie, was making the trip with me.

We went down the next day to meet the train, with Daddy crying. It was at the old Van Lear Junction that ain't there anymore. But back in those days you'd have a passenger train stopping at least once a day. It was a real swinging time for the railroads. I remember me and Daddy weighing ourselves on the scale in the depot— me seven months pregnant, but both of us weighing the same: 117 pounds.

I was scared to death. Mommy wrote a note to the conductor in her beautiful handwriting, asking him to take care of me. She was afraid I'd get sick and have the baby right on the train. I wish I knew the name of that conductor because he was one of the finest men I have met in my life. I was so bashful I didn't want anybody to know I was pregnant, so I sat by the bathroom with my raincoat wrapped around me. But this conductor would give me a pillow every night, and he would turn the coach seat around and let me lie down. Then he would get me fresh food from the dining car—cold milk and fresh fruit and stuff—and never made me pay.

That man sat and talked to me for three days, knowing I was nervous about getting to Washington. After two days I heard him yell, "WASHINGTON!" the way conductors yell. I got all excited and started jumping up and down, and he said, "Honey, you're still a long way from Custer—Washington's a big state." He said it was another day on the train before Bellingham, which is up near the Canadian border.

Finally, he told us we could get off. I looked around

for Doo, but I couldn't find him. Then I saw Junior with another man, who turned out to be Clyde Green. They said Doo was out hunting for our supper. We drove out to the Green ranch near Custer, a little town of around 325 people, and there was Doolittle. He had shot a duck and wanted me to taste it for the first time. Doo has always been real good about providing for his family.

We were living in the Greens' farmhouse—Doolittle working on the ranch and me scrubbing clothes and ironing and cleaning and cooking, seven days a week. Bob and Clyde were real good to me, treated me like a sister. They would include us in their Christmas dinner. And after their mother died, their aunt, Blanche Smith, came to live with 'em. And that's where I learned to cook.

Blanche Smith was an old, old lady but she was what Doolittle calls an "expensive" cook—she didn't mind spending money on good meat and vegetables. Bob and Clyde used to drive Doo crazy by killing a cow and then grinding it all down into hamburger. See, they were just bachelors and didn't care about fancy cooking. But one day Doo asked the butcher to save him just one good steak. That night, he fried it up with potatoes and put it down in front of 'em and said, "See, that's the way you can eat if you don't grind it down into hamburger."

After that, Blanche gave Doo a shopping order and the bill came to sixty-eight dollars, but it was fresh food and things they never had in the house before. They liked it better than anybody. After that, we ate good even when I cooked, because Blanche taught me how.

After I got settled, it was time to have the baby. I knew how to change 'em but I didn't know how to have 'em. I was afraid I'd have the baby in the middle of the night and wouldn't know it, and the baby would smother to death.

I went into labor at 11:30 at night and went to the hospital an hour later. But it was a total of twenty-seven hours before I had the baby. There was no way I could have had it without knowing. When I started delivering, I thought I'd die. I was just too small in my bones to deliver a nine-month baby, and I had to take time to stretch. Finally, they put this mask over my head and it was like falling down a well. I didn't know what happened until I heard the crying. But even then, I didn't know what it was.

I knew Doo wanted a boy, so we had the name already picked out—Jack. I was under gas and I didn't know what the nurse was telling me. I kept saying it was a boy and she kept saying it was a girl. When I realized she knew better than me, I started crying. I always thought you got what you wanted. Doolittle came in and said he was glad it was a girl, but I knew he wasn't. Finally, the nurses told me that since I wanted a boy, they would keep that little girl for themselves. I was so young I almost believed them.

We called her Betty Sue. She was only five pounds and sixteen inches, the shortest baby that hospital ever had, they told me. Her head was like an egg, all out of shape and bruised. They said I was lucky to have a nine-month baby.

They kept me in the hospital for a week. I was trying to nurse Betty, but I never had any milk for my babies, so they put her on the bottle and let me go home. Having that first baby was like having a doll and playing house. I really loved bathing and diapering her. I never felt like it was a lifetime deal—not with one baby. That didn't strike me until I had the second baby a year later. We went back home to have that one because we were homesick, and that's where I had the boy.

I remember that one because Doo's mommy kept

telling me there was a full moon and I was gonna have the baby that night. I told her I wasn't ready yet. So that day I helped her do the wash for thirteen people, hanging it all over the holler. Then the clothesline broke, and we had to do it all over again. Took us all day, till dark. Then the moon came up and Angie said, "See, you're gonna have the baby tonight." But I didn't believe her until the pains came.

Then it started snowing and it got real cold and Doo had trouble starting up the car. Angie gave me a bath and made me comfortable. She was a real help to me. And we started down out of Butcher Holler, with me in such pain. The car stalled out down by the schoolhouse, and I said all I wanted to do was lay down in the schoolhouse and rest. The pains were getting closer together. But of course, if I'd've done that, I'd've froze to death. So Angie made me stay in the car and they got me to the hospital. It was Pearl Harbor Day, December 7—that's how I remember my first son.

We couldn't afford to stay overnight in the hospital, so I went home five hours after having the baby. We drove back up the holler again, like I'd hardly been away. I rested for a while, then had to wash out diapers and draw water from the well, less than twenty-four hours after delivering the boy.

We called him Jack Benny—not just because Jack Benny was my favorite comedian, but because we liked the two names. He doesn't like for people to know his middle name, but you know how Southern people like to use two names instead of one. So when I want to get him mad, I call him Jack Benny.

After I had that second baby, I had two miscarriages, both times after only a month or two being pregnant. Somebody told me if the baby isn't going to be healthy, that's how Mother Nature takes care of things. But I almost died of blood poisoning after the second mis-carriage, which is not exactly the care I expected from Mother Nature. I didn't go to the hospital after the second miscarriage because we didn't have the money—and when they discovered I had blood poisoning, it was almost too late.

I kept on getting pregnant, though. I carried a baby almost full term and the doctors said I needed a caesarean operation. But I was still a minor and I couldn't sign my own consent, even though I already had two babies. They needed Doo's signature, but he was off in the woods on a logging job. They put me in the hospital for three days and kept me under medicine. They'd wake me up and say, "Mrs. Lynn, isn't there any way we can reach your husband?"

And I'd say, "He's in the woods." We were back in Washington by this time. Then they'd put me back to sleep again. But finally I had the baby the regular way, and Doo called in from some logging camp and they kept teasing him. First they said it was a boy, then a girl, then a boy again. But it was a boy, and we named him Ernest Ray.

That's when the doctors told me I've got Rh-negative blood, which meant I would have trouble having more babies. But we didn't do anything about not getting pregnant, so eleven months after the boy, I had my second girl, with no real problems.

We didn't name the girl until she was four years old; the nurses told Doolittle we had to give her a name before she left the hospital, and he got mad and took her home and didn't name her Clara Marie for four years. That's how stubborn he is. We called her "Cissy," which is still what everybody calls her.

By that time, I was nineteen years old and had four babies. After one miscarriage, I went to the doctor to ask how to stop having babies and he said, "Honey, you should be thinking about having your first baby, not your last." Then he gave me a diaphragm, which I used for a while—when I remembered.

Sometimes in my show I make a joke about how I stopped having babies every year: "I keep my legs crossed now instead of my fingers." But it wasn't funny back then. I was so ignorant, and women didn't have what they do today. I love my kids, but I wish they had the pill when I was first married. I didn't get to enjoy the first four kids; I had 'em so fast. I was too busy trying to feed 'em and put clothes on 'em.

That's why I was so proud of my song "The Pill"—that was my biggest-selling record early in 1975. I really believe in those words. It's all about how the man keeps the woman barefoot and pregnant over the years. I think it's great that women have a way of protecting themselves now, without worrying about the man.

You know, we recorded that song three years ago, but we held it out, figuring people weren't ready to accept it. When we released it, the people loved it. I mean the *women* loved it. But the men who run the radio stations were scared to death. It's like a challenge to the man's way of thinking. See, they'll play a song about making love in a field because that's sexy, from a man's point of view. But something that's really important to women, like birth control, they don't want no part of, leastways not on the air. Well, my fans played the record and bought so many copies they forced most of the radio stations to play it. Some preachers criticized it in church—but that just did me a favor by making the people more curious.

But you know something funny? I never really took the pill for birth control in my life. The only time I took it was to regulate my periods. That was after Doo got

himself clipped—what's that they call it, a vasectomy?—
after my twins came along.

I'm glad I had six kids because I couldn't imagine my
life without 'em. But I think a woman needs control over
her own life, and the pill is what helps her do it.

That's also why I won't ever say anything against the
abortion laws they made easier a few years ago. Personally, I think you should prevent unwanted pregnancy
rather than get an abortion. I don't think I could have
an abortion. It would be wrong for me. But I'm thinking
of all the poor girls who get pregnant when they don't
want to be, and how they should have a choice instead of
leaving it up to some politician or doctor who don't have
to raise the baby. I believe they should be able to have an
abortion. I told that to this Atlanta newspaper, *The Great
Speckled Bird*, which is supposed to be for hippies and
people like that. Some of my country friends got upset
when I kept a copy of that newspaper in my office, but
I said it was one of the best articles ever done about me
because they printed exactly what I said.

Somehow I managed to get through those years with
all those babies. I don't know how I did it. When you're
young, you think everything is exciting. When you get
older, you say, "How in the world did I do that?"

I was learning something all the time in those days,
back in Washington. A woman named Edna Brann
taught me how to can meat and vegetables, and we never
ate any store-canned food after that.

Edna used to enter the Northwest Washington Fair
over in Lynden, the biggest town near us. The next year
she talked me into entering the fair. We put our stuff
in her pickup truck and drove it over. We were hoping
that she'd win a first prize, which she'd never done. The
next day we went back to see the results and found blue
ribbons hanging all over *my* stuff. I couldn't believe it!

I counted seventeen blue ribbons, thirteen seconds, and seven third prizes, plus a pair of dishes, a whole barrel of Crisco, all kinds of spices, ten dozen fruit jars, and twenty-five dollars in cash.

Edna seemed as thrilled as me. I felt so good that I started jumping up and down, shaking the whole fair building. They took a picture of me, three feet off the ground, and the next day they enlarged it to life-size and hung it outside the fairgrounds.

They still have that picture. In 1974, me and my band played the Lynden fair, and hundreds of my old friends came out that I hadn't seen in years. They still remembered me jumping in the air and screaming when I won. Doolittle said I yelled so loud I startled him in the quarter-horse contest and made him finish second. And all I could think about were those mean things he'd said about my cooking.

Except for winning that contest, there wasn't much excitement in those years. I worked hard around the ranch, me and Blanche, caring for thirty-six people during peak seasons. When the fruits and vegetables were ripe, they needed every hand they could get. My nails were always broken, and my hands were rough and chapped. The only clothes I owned, just about, were blue jeans and a checked shirt. I went barefoot most of the time.

After a while, Doolittle went into the logging business with another man. He learned to climb those tall trees and chop 'em down to size. He was good enough to keep us going for five or six years. We had our own house on the Green ranch by this time, though it wasn't nothing fancy. When we left, they just knocked it clear to the ground. But we were making it in Washington. I didn't have any fancy dreams, but I knew the day would come when we'd have our own house, a real house, and I'd be able to buy things for the babies from the

Sears and Roebuck catalog. That was the big thing in my dreams.

We didn't have much money for entertainment. I never went out much because we couldn't afford a babysitter. Besides, Doo liked to go out with the boys and have a few beers. It was them days that gave me the idea for the song "Don't Come Home A-Drinkin' (with Lovin' on Your Mind)," which I wrote with my sister Peggy Sue.

My entertainment was staying home and singing along with the radio when I could find country music. It wasn't too big out in Washington, but once in a while you could find Ernest Tubb and Hank Williams. Betty Sue says she can remember being a little girl and hearing me imitate all the Kitty Wells records and asking her, "How did that sound?"

But that was my only fun. I was so far away from Mommy and Daddy that I'd sing to myself for hours, more out of homesickness than anything else.

# 11

## A Death in the Family

Now Daddy talked with the Lord every day,
And Daddy and God were real close.
So let's just say it seems that God
Takes the ones He loves the most . . .
      —*"Mama, Why?," by Loretta Lynn*

When we lived in Washington, I only saw my family a few times. When it was time for my second baby to be born, we got just plain homesick, me and Doo, and went back to Kentucky, where Doc Turner delivered my first boy. But after I had the baby, we went back to Washington.

The next thing I heard, Daddy had a stroke and was let out of his job at the mines. We weren't in any position to send money. We hardly had enough to get by on. So Daddy went north to Indiana to try and find work. That's what a lot of us mountain people do. You can see 'em in all the big cities up north—Detroit, Indianapolis, Chicago. I'll see 'em standing around, kind of bashful, the men more bashful than the women.

So Daddy moved to Wabash, where we had some

friends and relatives, and put in his application at the factory. But they wouldn't take him because all he knew was mining, and because of his black lung and high blood pressure. He was still only in his forties, but he couldn't find a job by himself. He was so bashful; it must have been hard looking for a job and hearing the boss say they wouldn't hire him.

After Daddy got home to Kentucky again, Mommy said she'd give it a try. See, the men are supposed to be the head of the household in the country. But the women lots of times find it easier to get along with office work and stores. Mommy went back to Wabash and found a job at the Penguin Point drive-in restaurant for sixty-five cents an hour. But after a while they gave her a raise because she was so good. Mommy already had eight kids by this time. Brenda—Crystal, she's called now—was just a baby. But Mommy was so beautiful and young-looking that her boss didn't know that she had any kids. One day Mommy told him that her family was coming up to live in Wabash. The man couldn't believe it. He said, "I didn't even know you were married." She was even paying taxes as a single person. But Mommy didn't think it was anybody's business. She still kept a job after the family came up. Most of the kids went right into public schools in Wabash and Daddy got a job at Spencer-Karnel, the only factory that didn't give medical examinations. They settled down and became more like Indiana people than Kentucky. I think about 25 percent of Wabash is from the mountains. Some of Doo's family settled there, too.

After Mommy and Daddy settled in Indiana, we visited 'em twice. One time there I got a job in a restaurant, sometimes waiting on tables, but mostly washing dishes. I wasn't any good at it because I was so clumsy. I was always dropping something. Doolittle worked in a

General Electric factory, but he was itchy to get back to the West Coast, so after about six months we left.

Four years later we spent two months in Indiana, and that was the last time I seen Daddy alive. He sent me cards on my birthdays, with presents when they could afford it—fake pearls on my nineteenth birthday, a shirt on my twentieth or twenty-first.

I would think about Daddy a lot, out in Washington, and later I even began to dream about him. One night in 1959 I dreamed, as clear as anything, I saw him wearing a blue suit and lying in a wine-colored coffin. I was terribly upset by the dream, so I woke Doolittle up and told him about it. He said I shouldn't pay no attention to it. Yet when I went back to sleep, I had the exact same dream all over again, only this time I could see myself wringing my hands.

I was still dreaming when Clyde Green knocked on the door and said there was a phone call for me. People didn't usually call me that early. Sure enough, it was Mommy, telling me Daddy was gone. That was February 23, 1959, the day after George Washington's birthday.

Later I learned how pitiful Daddy's last days were. They just had this big flood in Wabash, the worst they ever had. The river went right through their home, putting them without food or beds for a while. Daddy went down to the Red Cross to ask for help, but everybody was pushing their way to the front of the line, even people that wasn't in the flood. So Daddy just turned and went out. That night he got a migraine headache and was walking the floor all night, Mommy said. That was about the time I was having my dreams, you see? Do you think that I could have been feeling Daddy's pain more than two thousand miles away? That morning he got a lift to the factory, where he just fell over around eight thirty and died a little later. When I got the call, I wasn't surprised. They said he died of a stroke, but I figure the coal mines done it.

Me and Doolittle just got in the car and headed east for the funeral. They held it in the big brick church in Van Lear—mountain people may move away to find work, but we get buried in our mountains. I always wished it had been held in the little white church in Butcher Holler. That was more natural to Daddy.

They had this big, fat undertaker from Wabash bring the body down from Indiana to Kentucky. That man couldn't believe how steep the hills were in Kentucky, him trying to move that coffin. We put Daddy up at Mommy's sister's house, where we sat up three nights a-praying.

When me and Doo got there, we saw Daddy dressed in a blue suit and lying in a wine-colored coffin—just like I dreamed it!

We buried Daddy in the family plot on the high ridge over Butcher Holler, and I left yellow flowers. For six months afterward, I'd have these nightmares of trying to get to Daddy to tell him I loved him, of being caught in huckleberry vines, or climbing the mountain, afraid I'd get home too late...

Later I wrote the song called "Mama, Why?" It asks the question, "Why did God take my daddy?" I know we're not supposed to question God, but I just felt that he died so young—only fifty-one years old. Daddy never did know what success was like in his life. His times were hard, and he never had anything nice. I wish I could have been a singer when he was alive, so I could have helped him. But he never did know me when I was singing—though I feel like Daddy *has* helped me.

See, I still feel like Daddy is with me. I can feel his presence. Whenever I go back to Johnson County, I know he's there. There's this old bridge from Paintsville to Van Lear that goes over the Levisa Fork of the Big

Sandy. When I was little, I always hated to walk that bridge because it was so shaky and high. Now whenever we drive over that bridge I know that Daddy is watching over me.

When we go back to our house in Butcher Holler, I can see the grate where Daddy used to sit and rock me in his arms, him spitting in the fire. I can still feel his arms around me.

And I'm not the only one who feels this way. My writer, George, told me that the first minute he visited my house in Butcher Holler, he could sense Daddy on the porch, just like the night when I said I was getting married, and Daddy just paced back and forth on that porch, purely busting with emotion. I really believe that people take different forms, and death doesn't end things.

That's the way we mountain people are. Daddy's younger brother Corman still lives in an old cabin up the holler. Corman was a real quiet boy, about twelve years younger than Daddy was. He's real shy. He's one of us who never could adjust to life outside Butcher Holler.

Sometimes Corman is so shy that he won't even look me in the face, or talk one word to me. But if I threaten to whup him, Corman gets as nice as can be. The last time I was there, Corman told me he knew Daddy was going to die the night before he did. Corman said he was walking in the darkness, when he saw something yellow in the woods, like a spaceship almost, but not moving. Corman said when they brought Daddy back for the funeral, he knew then that it was no spaceship, but rather it was Daddy's coffin—with the yellow flowers. Like I said, we've got a kind of extrasensory perception, ESP, in my family, but it also goes along with being mountain people. Maybe it's from not being so busy with books and television and other people. We can feel things going around in the air.

You can say that's crazy if you want. But I know *I've* got ESP. It's like I can always tell how my oldest daughter Betty is feeling. If I dream that I'm whipping Betty, I know she's in trouble. Or I'll see her crying and call her on the telephone and say, "Betty Sue, what's the matter—aren't you taking your medicine?" And it'll turn out she's feeling sick.

Now Doolittle says I'm crazy to believe these things, but I believe 'em. I believe in reincarnation, too. I once read that you could feel your past lives if you concentrated real hard. So I tried it in my hotel room. I wasn't asleep but kind of in a trance. I lay down quiet and let my mind drift.

All of a sudden I was an Indian woman wearing moccasins and a long buckskin dress and I had my hair in pigtails. Even the sounds and smells were vivid to me. All around me there was a huge field with Indians riding horseback. I was standing next to a mounted Indian—I sensed he was the chief and that he was my husband. I knew he was about to go off into battle, and I was saying good-bye to him. Then a shot rang out, and my husband fell off his horse. I started screaming, and that woke me out of my trance. That's all I can remember.

In the second such experience, I saw myself dressed up in an Irish costume, doing an Irish dance down a country lane in front of a big white house. But then the telephone rang and the trance ended.

But I know I've always had a strong feeling for Indian things, and Irish music has always made me respond in a deep-down way. I know my church doesn't believe in reincarnation, but sometimes I'm positive I was really an Indian and an Irish girl in times before this one.

Anyway, after Daddy's funeral, me and Doo went back to Washington State. The next summer, Mommy brought the family to stay with us. It was good to spend some time with them because I'd been away from home almost ten years, and I didn't hardly know the little ones. This is when I found out that Jack was singing in a hotel club in Wabash. He used to sing on the radio station in Paintsville and now he was singing in public. Peggy and Brenda, the baby, were singing, too. And me, I hadn't even started yet. But I don't think that really gave me the idea to start singing. That came later. They stayed with us the summer, and then Mommy went back to her job in Wabash and took the kids with her.

A little later was when Mommy married Daddy's first cousin, Tommy Butcher. She knew him in Butcher Holler about as long as she knew Daddy. Tommy's been real good with us. To me, he's one in a million, and I love him very much. Tommy used to be pretty wild when he was younger, but he's reformed now and he works in a factory. The only time he's wild is behind the wheel of a car. Mommy won't drive with him from Wabash to Nashville because he goes practically a hundred miles an hour the whole way.

Three of the boys live near Mommy and work in the factories around there. Herman, my second brother, sings with a country group in a tavern in Wabash. He's pretty good, and one of his daughters, named Hermalee, is coming along as a singer, too. Betty Ruth is the only one of my family who lives apart from everybody. She lives in Scranton, Pennsylvania, where her husband is thinking of going into church work.

Four of us, of course, live around Nashville and work in show business. This is a difficult business to make it in, and I've tried to encourage 'em and open doors for 'em, but it leads to a lot of problems. There's only so many who can make it big in show business. Mommy gets caught in the middle because she wants all her kids to get ahead, like any mother, I guess, and she don't treat me any different from the rest, which is good. The only difference is that I've been able to really make it big in Nashville.

Peggy Sue has had some good records and has written some nice songs. Now she's married to Sonny Wright, who used to be my front man. When they perform together, they're a good duet.

Jay Lee was my front man when I first started to sing out in Washington. I brought him to Nashville with me after I moved there, and he's making it on his own. He plays a real good fiddle, and he plays dates on the road.

And Brenda, of course, changed her name to Crystal Gayle and is making it on her own. She used to travel around with me when she was younger, but you've got to go on your own sooner or later. Otherwise, people are always comparing you to your big sister, and nobody likes that.

It's a problem, being related to another performer. We knew this son of a famous man singer—not Hank Williams Junior, by the way—who told a disc jockey, "I'm strictly on my own. I don't want anybody to judge me by my father." He said some other things, and he was so nasty about it that, as soon as that boy left the studio, the disc jockey said, "The next sound you hear will be the record breaking." And he broke it, right on the air. It's a rough deal all around, them trying to make it when there's bound to be comparisons.

I know it's hard on Crystal Gayle, because I can see how she reacts to it. I remember one time, she and I went on the radio together and the disc jockey said to her, "Well, I guess you're a coal miner's daughter, too." He was just trying to make conversation, you know. And Crystal said, "No, I'm not."

The disc jockey sounded confused and said, well, if we had the same parents, she must be a coal miner's daughter.

But Crystal said, no, she was raised in the city, in Indiana. And it's the truth. She don't remember her early days in Kentucky; her ways are different from mine. She married a boy from Wabash named Bill Gatzimos who had long hair. He about scared my family half to death, them thinking Crystal was going with a hippie. But long hair didn't bother me—I could tell he was a real nice boy from a good family. He was on the honor roll at Indiana University Bloomington. When they got married, he put off his career in psychology to help Crystal with her career.

I've tried to do all I could for the three of 'em. I had 'em on Decca Records—now MCA—for a long time, but they couldn't come up with hit songs regular. I've had 'em in my talent agency. But if you help 'em, they feel guilty. If you don't help 'em, *you* feel guilty. And me being so close, it's just natural to want to help.

It must be tough on them. Everywhere they go, people judge them as "Loretta Lynn's family." I wouldn't want that to happen to me. I think probably the best thing is to tell everybody in Nashville that I ain't opening no doors for my family. That way, when they make it big, they'll be more proud of themselves. See, even if a singer opens doors for her family, she can't guarantee they'll be nice to the fans, or work hard, or show up on time, or write hit songs. One thing Doolittle taught me, which I never forgot, was in the long run you make your own luck— good, bad, or indifferent.

# 12

## Beginner's Luck

As I sit here tonight, the jukebox playing,
Just a tune about the wild side of life...
—*"It Wasn't God Who Made Honky Tonk
Angels," by J. D. Miller*

As you can tell, I've always liked to sing. But the singing career was Doolittle's idea. I was sitting home on our anniversary. I was already twenty-four years old. My oldest girl was ten. I was embroidering pheasants and bird dogs. Doolittle had something on his mind. I could tell because his face gets kind of drawn in when he's thinking. He had got me this seventeen-dollar Harmony guitar at Sears and Roebuck for my eighteenth birthday, and I had started to learn to play the thing. This was the first guitar I ever owned—before, all I'd ever done was hold my brother's guitar sometimes. Now a few years later, Doo said I had a good voice and he wanted me to sing. What did I think? Well, I was surprised. Stunned, you could say. I didn't know Doolittle thought that much about my singing. I was proud to be noticed, to tell you the truth, so I went right to work on it. When the kids were in school or asleep at night, I'd sit in my front room, learning how to play the guitar better. I never took no lessons or nothing—I just played. After a while, I got where I could play a pretty good tune on it. First I was singing Kitty Wells's songs on it, but after a while I started making up my own.

I used to think up songs when I was around nine, but now I started again. My first song was "The Doggone Blues," a real slow country waltz about a woman whose boyfriend left her. It went:

"I'm so lonely and blue, no one to tell my troubles to…"

I never got that one published. And it's a good thing. I look back and I know those darling little songs were pitiful. But at the time I thought they were beautiful.

I think I practiced about two months on that guitar. Then Doolittle started telling me I had to sing in public. It was a big step, because I didn't think I was ready to face an audience. I was so bashful that if strangers even talked to me, I'd turn away, so I sure didn't want to go singing in public. But he said it was a chance for us to make some extra money, so I kept practicing. He said I could do it, and he said he'd set me up at some club. So I did it—because he said I could. He made all the decisions in those days.

Now that's what I mean when I say my husband is responsible for my career. It wasn't my idea: he told me I could do it. I'd still be a housewife today if he didn't bring that guitar home and then encourage me to be a singer.

Why deny it? Doolittle is a brilliant man, always looking to do something different or better. If we're off in Kentucky and somebody says the road to Daddy's graveyard is washed out, Doolittle don't just grumble about it. He borrows somebody's bulldozer and goes up and fixes the road. He's a good worker and a good businessman, too. I've always had faith in his judgment that way. When he told me something, I was pretty sure it would probably work out.

So, early in 1960, me and Doo went out to this Delta Grange Hall on a Saturday night to hear some country music. We were with two other couples, friends of ours. The boys like to have a few beers and get a little loud. You know how it is. Anyway, this night, Doo had him a few beers until he went up to the bandleader and said, "Hey, I got a girl here tonight who's the best country singer there is, next to Kitty Wells, and I ain't kidding."

Course, they didn't believe him, you know. They just figured he was some crazy drunk. But he kept pestering them. Me? I was standing near the door, ready to run in case they said yes. But they didn't—not that night. They said he should bring me over to their house on the next Wednesday and they'd give me a tryout. I was so relieved you couldn't believe it. I figured Wednesday would never come. But it did, and on Wednesday night Doo brought home a babysitter and said, "You ain't forgotten? You're singing tonight." Lord, I could have died. But he just walked me over there, so I had no choice.

It was the house of John and Marshall Penn, two guys in the group called the Westerneers. They opened the door and saw Doolittle, and you could tell by their faces they were thinking, "Oh, it's you again." But they let us in. They had this taping equipment for a radio show they did. They asked me what song I knew. I was barely able to say the words. The only song I knew clear through was "There He Goes," which was a big hit at the time.

The leader asked me, "In what key?"

I didn't know what a key was and don't hardly know now. They kept pecking at the keys until I hit one I liked. Then I took off, and they sort of took off after me. I sang the one song and went home. I sure figured, well, that's that and good riddance.

But the next morning they was a-pecking at my door, and at seven o'clock if you can believe it, asking me if I would sing at the Grange Hall that Saturday night. The Penn brothers said they would pay me five dollars for the show, and they would use the tape on their radio show. I just couldn't believe it! And then I got scared, real scared. Doolittle told me I was going to sing, scared or not. He told me I was stupid. That made me so mad I made up my mind to sing. I've often wondered if that was a psychology trick he played on me.

Saturday came around, and it was a special party at the Grange Hall. The governor of Washington was there in person. We were all supposed to dress in old clothes, like in olden times. I got a dress from a friend of mine—a long white dress that her aunt got married in. It was so old it was turning to yellow. Everybody was waiting on tables before the music began. You know how clumsy I am. Remember, like I told you, my father used to call me "that heifer" when I'd go spilling the coffee. Would you believe they actually made me pour coffee for the governor? My hands were shaking so bad I dropped the cup right at his feet. It broke into a thousand pieces. I've been a mess all my life. It's a wonder I'm still going.

But after the dinner came the music part. They introduced me, and I got on the stage. I turned my back to the audience, just like a lady, and bent over to get the pick for my guitar. But I tripped on the long dress and nearly fell off the stage. Oh, it was something! The governor said later it was the best part of the show. I also sang "Tennessee Waltz." I hadn't ever been on a stage in my life, and I'm sure I was terrible. But the Penn brothers invited me back the next Saturday night, paying me another five dollars. I thought I was a millionaire.

There wasn't too much call for country music in Washington in those days. You had more fans for Perry Como and Doris Day than you did for Ernest Tubb and Kitty Wells. People were kind of ashamed of country. When I'd tell people I liked country music, they'd get this look on their faces. In Nashville, we've got this saying, "closet country," meaning you've got to enjoy it in secret. That's almost the way it was back in those days. But the Penn brothers, with Howard Rodell as the front man, got to be popular and were invited to sing on Friday nights, too. We'd get ourselves a babysitter and go wherever they told us.

One time they were playing in the Club Palace in Blaine, Washington. The folks in that tavern were a real tough bunch and they had to sneak me in the back door because I didn't look old enough to sing in a tavern. I already had four kids, but I acted like a baby; I was so bashful it was pitiful. If Doolittle didn't keep telling me I was a stupid hillbilly, I never would've made it.

After three or four months, me and Doolittle split off from the Penn brothers and we formed our own group, playing in Bill's Tavern on weekends. I played rhythm guitar, which is something I always liked to do. My brother Jack was the lead man, and Roland Smiley played the steel guitar. We called him "Smiley O'Steel." We were in the big time now, we thought—stage names and everything. We got this big coffee pot and painted a picture of a cat on it. That was the kitty, see? If somebody wanted a certain song, they'd drop a nickel or a dime in the kitty and make their request.

We called the group "Loretta's Trail Blazers," though Jack said we should have been called "Loretta's Tail Riders" because I used to ride their tails to do better. But Doolittle was behind the whole thing. He was still working days as a heavy-duty auto mechanic, but he'd come over to Bill's every night and keep an eye on everything.

Just getting up in front of the audience was a terror. I'd look in their faces and just about freeze up. The announcer would say something to me and I'd be scared of saying a word. When I got established more, I met Little Jimmy Dickens, who taught me this trick of not looking at them as individual faces but rather looking at them as a crowd. That way you wouldn't worry about why somebody was yawning or looking at their wristwatch. When I first started and I'd see them yawning, I'd just go to pieces.

Before long we were playing six nights for Bill Hofstron, who owned the tavern. There wasn't any slack time but it was very enjoyable to me because I'd been a housewife since I was thirteen. Now it seemed like I was getting out, the way I would have if I'd gone to high school or not gotten married and stuff. I was learning things and going places I'd never been before.

On Sundays we used to play mental hospitals and air force bases and things like that. In one mental hospital, there was this boy around sixteen or seventeen years old who just stared off into space the first time we sang there. The second time, he asked for a cigarette, and one of the boys gave him one. But one of the other patients squashed that lit cigarette right on this boy's hand, and I felt so bad for him that I went over to talk to him. I could see he was starting to listen a little bit. When I asked him about the hospital, he said, "They bring us here and forget about us. This is a world of forgotten people."

I never forgot those words. When I got home, I wrote a song called "The World of Forgotten People." Only I made it a love song about myself. I didn't think country music fans would want to hear a song about a lonely mental patient cooped up in a hospital. People came to our shows and they wanted songs about love. But these days it seems there are songs about other aspects of life.

You hear songs that Kris Kristofferson and Tom T. Hall and Merle Haggard write and they're more about people's problems. Sometimes I think I could get away with writing "The World of Forgotten People" and make it about mental hospitals. But then look at all the trouble I got into for singing "The Pill." So maybe people aren't ready for real life.

I sang at the fair in Lynden where I won the canning contest a few years before. During the singing contest, there was a horse-pulling contest underway nearby, and some of the crowd started drifting over to it. I started singing, and they started drifting back. I sang "Gone," which at the time was a big recording for Ferlin Husky, and I got such a big hand from the audience that I encored with "A Fallen Star," which was the B side of his recording. I got paid twenty-five dollars as a first prize, and me and Doo were so excited we made up our minds then and there to head for Nashville. But believe me, it wasn't as easy as it might sound.

Doolittle decided to get me on the Buck Owens television show up in Tacoma, Washington. Buck was just starting singing in those days and he wasn't the big name he is today. But his show was pretty important in that part of the country. He was playing in a rough place, the Pantania Club, on weekends, and we drove up there and Doolittle started telling him how good I was. Buck kept saying I should come back for amateur night the next night but Doolittle kept saying, "Man, I can't afford to stay over. This is our only night in Tacoma." So Buck let me sing one song, and he must have liked it because he let me sing another. Finally he came over and sat down with us and said we should really stay over for his amateur television show on Saturday night. Doolittle decided maybe we'd better manage it somehow.

The next day I was one of thirty competitors on

amateur night. It was my birthday, I remember that, and I wore my cowboy outfit. It was a fluffy black-and-white dress and I wore white cowboy boots. I looked like Annie Oakley or something, but I thought I was the prettiest thing that ever was.

I sang "My Shoes Keep Walking Back to You." And you know what? I won the contest. The winner was supposed to be an amateur, which meant they didn't give a money prize, just a wristwatch. I had a choice—men's or women's. I chose one for Doolittle, but it stopped the next day and I started crying and took it back to Buck. He explained the watch only cost a couple of dollars and he didn't have the money to get it fixed. I didn't complain. Poor Buck was as broke as we were. He couldn't afford a coat and it was cold in Tacoma. He was nice to us, and I'm still his biggest fan. I'll guarantee you, Buck made it the hard way and he deserves every good thing he gets.

One other lucky thing came out of that television show. It was broadcast up in Canada—Vancouver, British Columbia—where a man named Norm Burley heard me. He had been in the lumber business and was real wealthy. But he lost his wife and he was lonely. Doo and I were just like a couple of kids, and Norm Burley kind of adopted us. He said he wanted to help us by giving us a contract to make a record. He didn't wear any red suit or black boots, but that man sure looked like Santa Claus to us.

# 13

## An Honest-to-Goodness Record

Ever since you left me, I've done nothing but
wrong.
Many nights I've laid awake and cried.
We once were happy, my heart was in a whirl,
But now I'm a honky tonk girl...
—*"I'm a Honky Tonk Girl," by Loretta Lynn*

Mr. Burley wanted to help but he didn't know any
more about the recording business than we did. He
left it up to us what song we would record. I'd written
this song called "Honky Tonk Girl." It was mostly about
a girl I used to see in Bill's Tavern drinking beer and crying. I don't think she recognized that song was about her.

The way I started writing those songs, I went down
to the candy store and bought a copy of *Country Song
Roundup*, the magazine with the words to the hit songs.
I figured it looked so simple in these books that, since
everyone else was writing songs, I might as well, too.
There was nothing to it, really. I'd think up a title first,
then write some words, then pick out a tune on my little
old rhythm guitar. Mr. Burley liked "Honky Tonk Girl,"

and he gave us the money to take it to Los Angeles. That was the biggest city to go to on the West Coast to get a record made.

Me and Doo left the kids with my brother and his wife, and we drove down to Los Angeles. A couple of studios wouldn't even let Doo past the front secretary, even though he had money from Mr. Burley. See, Mr. Burley had different companies, so it was no trick for him to start a new record company. We called it Zero Records. But none of us knew anything about the record business. There was one fellow named Don Grashey who had some business sense, and he ran the record company for Mr. Burley.

We didn't have any studio or a band, so we went to these studios in Los Angeles. I'd sit outside and wait for Doo to come out. Each time he'd get this sad look on his face and I figured, "We can't *even pay* to get me on a record. Nobody will even take our money." But then Doo went up to this studio where Speedy West worked. He was well-known in country music. Somehow they agreed to let me make my record.

I went inside to this little studio about half the size of a motel room. But I saw these men and machines and a few musicians, and I got all scared. I still didn't know about notes or anything, but I showed 'em the words and hummed the tune and they started to fiddle around. After I sang a few lines, Speedy West said, "Hey, let's hold it up a few hours and get a few more pickers."

What he did, really, was to get better pickers. He must've heard something he liked, because he brought in some good musicians from around town and they picked up on my song real well. By the end of the day we had both sides recorded—"Whispering Sea" was the other side. And a few weeks later they sent us a shipment of records with the Zero label.

The record was fine, but we were pitiful. We didn't know anything about releasing a record, but we tried our best. Doolittle had a hobby of photography at the time, so he made up a picture of me. We mailed out 3,500 copies of the record and my picture and sent them to every radio station we could find. We had a list of all the country stations—I don't know how we got that. We even wrote a little bit about my life.

We'd call up the disc jockeys and ask 'em to play the record, and most of 'em did. Those boys have always been on our side. But we couldn't get the records to the stores fast enough. Someone would hear the record on the jukebox or the radio, then go into a store and ask to buy it—and the owner wouldn't have it. It was a big mess, but we really tried to get those records out. And all that time, Doolittle was still working at his full-time auto mechanic job in the garage, paying our bills and keeping us alive.

One day in the summer, our steel-guitar man came over to the house and said, "Hey, your record is on the charts." We were so stupid we didn't know what the charts meant. But it meant we were in the top ten in some places, based on jukebox plays. The July 25, 1960, *Billboard* listed us as number fourteen on the national country music charts.

Mr. Burley was pleased with our success and said he would pay for us to go on a promotion trip across the country, all the way to Nashville. And then Mr. Burley said one of the kindest things I've ever heard. He said he thought I had a lot of talent and he wanted me to learn as much about the business as I could. And he said that if I ever got a chance to go with a major recording company, he would release me from our contract. He said he never wanted to stand in our way. But I didn't believe it would ever come to that.

So we took off in our old Mercury, trying to promote the record. We went down the West Coast, too poor to stay in motels, sleeping in the car and eating baloney-and-cheese sandwiches. To this day I can't stand any sandwiches for that reason. I ate too many of 'em when I was young. I only had one good dress. When we were driving, I'd just wear jeans or something. We had this list of radio stations and we'd keep turning the dial as we drove. When we got near a station, I'd hop in the back of the car and change into my dress. Then we'd go inside the radio station.

We didn't care if it was a 500-watt local station or a 50,000-watt clear channel station—we'd hit 'em all. The little stations were better for us. When you're little, you appreciate someone else who's little. I was just a nobody. I'd walk into the station and introduce myself. That was hard at first, because I was so bashful. But those disc jockeys were nice to me everywhere. I looked like a kid—my hair was curly back in those days and Doolittle never let me wear any makeup.

At one place I asked if they had my record, and they said no. I looked out of the corner of my eye and spotted it in the garbage can. I asked politely if I could give 'em a copy. They said all right. I walked over to the garbage can and handed 'em the record. They smiled kind of sheepish-like, but ever since then, this studio has been behind me all the way.

I'd stay in those radio stations as long as they let me talk on the air—and there was Doolittle sitting out in the car, listening to me on the radio, getting burned up if I said something dumb. But you know something? I was starting to enjoy myself, meeting all those boys. It was more exciting then than it is now. Nowadays I never stop at country stations anymore because of our tight schedule. And besides, my bus wouldn't fit in the driveway. It's such a different deal now.

I remember going into a station in Tucson, Arizona, where the disc jockey was a little boy, same age as me, pimples on his face, greasy hair. He was so nice to me that we used to write letters back and forth until he got into singing, too. Waylon Jennings, that's who it was. One disc jockey who remembers me is Hugh Cherry. He was working an all-night show on KFOX in Long Beach, California. One evening I rang his buzzer and said to him, "A disc jockey in Seattle said if someone wants to get a hillbilly record to break in California, you are the man to see. Well, I've got one here, 'Honky Tonk Girl.' It's mine."

He played it and liked it. We told him we were distributing it ourselves to every disc jockey on our way to Nashville to get on the Grand Ole Opry. He couldn't believe it when I said Doo was waiting in the car. He said, "But, honey, don't you know it takes three or four years to get on the Opry?" I told him, "Maybe so, but I can't wait that long."

Well, we got to the Opry that same year, the year we started singing. And in that same year, I was listed right behind Jan Howard, Margie Bowes, and Connie Hall as Most Promising Female Singer. The next time I saw Hugh Cherry he said, "Well, you made it—lots sooner than I expected!"

# 14

## Fans

I listen to you singing to me on the radio;
I hear you every Saturday on the Grand Ole
Opry show;
They put your records on the jukebox at the
Truck Stop Inn,
And I spend a dollar on you every night,
Loretta Lynn...
        —"I Love You, Loretta Lynn,"
                    by Johnny Durham

The disc jockeys were important to my career, but there's one bunch of people that was even more important—my fans. They've heard me say this a million times, I'm sure, but I wouldn't have nothing if it wasn't for my fans.

They started noticing me when I made my first record, "Honky Tonk Girl," and then they started pestering the stores and the radio stations to get more of my records. Only there wasn't more at the time. Even before I got established in Nashville, I had loyal fans like the three Johnson sisters from Wild Horse, Colorado. If I hadn't met these three girls, there's no telling what would have happened—or maybe I mean what wouldn't have happened.

You can't believe how loyal country fans are. They're just not like any other music fans. Country fans like a singer on personality and on voice and not because of a short-lived fad. They'll buy anything you put out as long as you give them good quality. They're fans for life. My manager, David Skepner, used to work for some of the pop and rock musicians for the Music Corporation of America, and he really knows the record business. He says that rock fans may buy a million copies of an album by some rock group. But if they think a rock group puts out a bad album, the fans will forget 'em forever. Well, that's not the way it is in country music. Once they like you, it's for life.

A good country musician can figure on selling three albums a year at three hundred thousand sales per album—and doing it for fifteen or twenty years. There's dozens of country musicians who've done that, with some luck and some talent. But the secret is getting loyal fans; they'll write letters and send out fan-club bulletins just pestering each other to buy your albums. I know it sounds strange for a lot of hardworking folks to be out bugging each other to "help Loretta out," but that's how loyal they are.

I've got so many fans that I recognize all around the country. If I go to the West Coast, there're the same faces from last year. If I'm up north somewhere, there're my same fans. I'd list all of 'em, but I know I can't. Most of my fan club is women, which is how I want it. The men have enough things going for 'em in this life. We women have got to stick together. My shows are really geared to women fans, if you think about it—to the hardworking housewife who's afraid some girl down at the factory is going to steal her husband, or wishing she could bust out of her shell a little bit. Those are things most women feel, and that's who I'm thinking about and singing to during my shows. And the girls know it.

A lot of people believe that fan clubs are a bunch of hussies who go around sleeping with the male performers or making spectacles of themselves. Well, there's a few like that in country music, I guess, but most of my fans are real ladies. We joke around and call the fans "bugs" because of the way they cluster around my bus. But those "bugs" don't bug me. I'm proud of my fans, and I hope that they'll always be proud of me.

I've got one of the biggest fan clubs in the country. They pay dues of a few dollars a year, and they help run the activities. There is also the International Fan Club Association, run by those three Johnson girls. There's around twenty thousand members in that club, and most of them really root for me, and I appreciate it.

Let me show you what the fans have done for my career. I was just trying to get established, making a trip to Colorado on my own, without Doolittle. The Johnson girls had heard my record and they had pestered some club in Aurora, Colorado, to hire me for one night for fifteen dollars. I didn't know them from the Rocky Mountains, but I got on the bus and went.

That bus driver was the meanest man, telling me how great George Jones was and how he never heard of me. I didn't mind that, but I kept telling him that I was supposed to get off the bus in Aurora and he insisted I had to go to downtown Denver. All of a sudden, looking out the window, I saw the club I was supposed to play in, the Four Seasons, and a road sign that said Aurora. I hollered for him to let me off. He finally did and I had to walk back to the club with my guitar, my purse, and my overnight bag. That was Loretta Lynn, making it in the big time.

I got to this club and I was so nervous, just pacing around and stuff, and I was looking for a friendly face. I kept saying, "They ain't here, they ain't here." But then a disc jockey pointed out these three girls standing around backstage. And they were so friendly, you could have sworn we knew each other all our lives.

Loudilla is the oldest. She's very smart and well-spoken, and she's a writer, too. Then there's Loretta. You've got to look out for her—she's kind of unpredictable. She'll say whatever she feels like. But she's a very warm girl who'll do anything for you—she just likes to act crazy. And then there's Kay, the youngest. She's kind of quiet, but she's a big help to her sisters with all the details and hard work, and she's always quick with a kind word to people. They adopted me as a sister in that first meeting. Besides, we had a lot in common.

Just standing there backstage, we discovered they are part Indian, just like me. And they came from a poor background, too. They moved from Oklahoma because their daddy was trying to get a better farm and they used to get snubbed when they arrived in Colorado.

People used to call them "sodbusters" and "suitcase farmers" and "trailer trash." But their daddy, Mack Johnson, worked hard and built up his farm in Wild Horse. He used to listen to Roy Acuff on the radio, just like my daddy used to listen to Ernest Tubb. They remember sitting around the old farmhouse on Saturday night, eating popcorn and listening to the Grand Ole Opry. So you'd have to say we had a lot in common. Loretta, she's crazy like me. She'd say, "How come whenever the white man won it was called a victory, but whenever the Indians won it was called a massacre?" Even though I was supposed to be the one in show business, those girls were more worldly than me.

They asked me if I was going to get made up for the

show. Patsy Cline, the leading woman singer, had just played the club the week before, and I guess she knew how to dress herself. Doolittle always thought I looked more natural without makeup, but he wasn't on this trip, so the girls put a little eye makeup on me for the first time in my life. I thought I looked nice.

The show was a big success. When it was over, I slept at the motel, and in the morning they even drove me to my next place. I felt so good about having friends that I told 'em they were my friends for life. And that's the way it's worked out. I get to see 'em about four times a year. I just love to go to their ranch and go riding around in a farm truck. They've got antelopes running wild. It helps me a lot just to spend a day there. I can just giggle and talk with those girls. They don't demand anything from me. They're not fans anymore—they're friends.

When I'm around them girls, we just sit around and tease each other something fierce. Loretta sings in shows sometimes, and I'll swear she acts more like she was in show business than I do. She'll dress up with sexy halters and tight clothes and stuff—things I won't do. They're always trying to talk me into wearing more modern clothes. I know what they mean by "modern." They'd poke fun at those long dresses I used to wear, with their high necklines. Loretta bought me a short skirt one time. She still makes fun of the way I looked in the mirror and said, "Oh my God, you can see my kneecaps!"

Loretta just does whatever comes into her mind. My writer, George, won't ever forget the first time he met her at my ranch. She brought some homemade pecan pie from Colorado and asked him if he wanted some. He said he did. She made him hold out his hand—no plate, no napkin, just sticky pecan pie. She laughed for an hour.

Those girls have done everything for me. Sometimes

I love to travel with 'em in their car, just like in the old days. Just them and their daddy. We'll follow my bus from one place to another. We'll even go into a restaurant, just the five of us, and maybe nobody will even recognize me. Then we'll have a good time just drinking Coke and eating cheeseburgers and talking about the old days when I was breaking in. And if someone comes over for an autograph, Loretta will say, "Hey, can't you see we're eating?" Or maybe Loudilla and Kay will talk to that person, so I can finish eating. They are very protective of me. I wish I could take 'em with me full-time. But they have their own lives, running the ranch for their daddy. I call him "Daddy" myself.

After they met me, those little country girls would travel around their area, asking for my records on the jukeboxes. If my records weren't on the jukeboxes, they put 'em there. And when I signed at Decca, they started this fan club for me. There was an early fan club run by Mary Ann Cooper, but that didn't work out too good. So the Johnson sisters organized one, and they had the right touch. They ran it for four years, spending their own money before they finally had to ask for help, which I gave 'em. Mack Johnson bought a typewriter and a mimeograph machine worth over $450. Now they put out a bulletin a few times a year, giving my schedule and running a letter from me, plus all kinds of gossip about the show and other people in the business. And they're always plugging my records.

We have a get-together of fans every year in a different place, with them traveling from all over the country just to attend. We're real close—wherever I go, the fan presidents visit me. I get a chance to say thank you just before the Fan Fair—a convention for over ten thousand fans—every year in June. My fan club presidents and Conway Twitty's are invited to a banquet at one of the big hotels in Nashville. Jimmy Jay from my booking agency cooks a pig for two days, getting that thick barbecue sauce all over it. Everybody helps themselves to potato salad and coleslaw and all the soda they can drink, and I just sit there and get barbecue sauce all over my face from kissing everybody for all the help they've been. By the time we go home, we're all full of sauce, just a bunch of country bumpkins. And that's the way we like it.

You never know what's going to happen the week of Fan Fair. Last year, at about eight o'clock on Sunday morning, we got a phone call from Joyce Perkins, the president of our club in Westwego, Louisiana. She said she had just driven up from Louisiana with a load of stuffed crab—she cooks Cajun style—and she asked if she could bring it out to the ranch. Well, Doolittle could never refuse an offer like that. Joyce brought out these huge trays of food—better than anything you could buy in a restaurant—and Doo and George, my writer, ate all of it that night.

Sometimes the fans get to be a little too much during that week of Fan Fair. They just pop into the kitchen while we're sitting around. It sounds terrible—but I can't relax in my own home. So the Johnson girls drive me to the motel where I make my headquarters during Fan Fair.

The Johnsons understand my moods, but it's hard to explain to somebody who's driven five hundred miles to see you that you're tired and you've got company and you can't squeeze anyone else around the kitchen table. Other times I'll be on the road somewhere and someone'll say they've been waiting five years to see me. Last year I was feeling sick until I saw this old man, about eighty, near my bus. All I could think about was sleeping in my bus, when his daughter said he was going to die soon, but he wanted to meet me first. I gave him a hug and signed an autograph, and he said, "Take me home, boys, I'm ready to die now." I got back in the bus and told my boys, "Boys, I ain't sick. I just learned what courage is."

I don't care what anyone says, it helps an artist to know that people love you. When I hear people cheering for my hit songs, even though I've sung them a thousand times, I want to put everything I have into the songs. I know that sometimes we goof off, just play for ourselves, but those fans have saved up their money and you've got to give them your very best.

There are some things you can't do for the fans. For one thing, I can't have all of them on the bus because the insurance company won't allow it. But the fans don't understand that. They get this hurt look if you don't come out and sign an autograph. Maybe there's a poor gal who's driven a hundred miles and she doesn't have a ticket for my show; all she wants to do is to give me a little sewing kit as a present or something. And I'm too tired to get off my couch. It happens. I've done it. And it breaks my heart. But there has got to be a limit sometimes. These are things I learned the hard way. When I started out in show business, I didn't know what to expect. The next chapter may give you some idea of how much I had to learn.

# 15

# The Education of a Country Singer

The women all look at you like you're bad,
The men all hope you are.
But if you go too far, you're gonna wear the scar,
Of a woman that's rated "X"…
— *"Rated 'X,' " by Loretta Lynn*

It's a good thing I had my husband and the Johnson girls because I never would have survived without them. I wasn't innocent like when I got married. Me and Doo had enough problems by then, so I knew that men and women didn't always get along. But now I was out every night in these clubs, and I couldn't believe what I saw.

One time out in Colorado, just after I met the Johnsons, I got a call to my motel room from a man who asked me if I would like to make some money. I said, "Oh yeah!" I was thinking I could go home and show Doo I made some money on my own. What did the man want me to sing? In this little sneaky voice, he says, "Forget about the singing; there's a bunch of guys who want to be entertained."

I didn't know much, so I yelled across the room to

the Johnson girls, "Hey, there's this guy on the phone, and he wants me to entertain 'em, but he don't want me to sing. What's he want me to do?" Loudilla took the phone from my hand and hung it up real hard. Then she slowly explained to me what he wanted. All I could say was, "Is that right?"

But it wasn't just telephone calls. I'd get offers right in the clubs. I'd be up on the stage singing, and guys would be writing their room numbers on slips of paper or asking me to have a drink with 'em after the show. I didn't have a wedding ring, and besides, people told me men liked your singing better if they didn't know you were married. Later I started wearing a ring, but that didn't slow 'em down any.

Another time we were working a club in Chicago for twenty-five dollars a night. It was the roughest place I ever worked. They had no stage, just this poor little two-man band, and you had to stand up on the bar to sing. Fortunately, Doo was traveling with me. He came into the bar and saw what was happening, and he grabbed one guy and walked him outside. I hope Doo didn't hurt him.

At first, I had to work clubs to sell for the jukeboxes, to get known. You'd have to work three or four shows a night to make any money, and that was hard work. Also, you'd get guys who'd been drinking and think that gave 'em the right to grab you and hug you. I don't mind some old boy if he's with his family or something. But the way some guys in those drinking clubs grab you—now, that's not family!

I don't have anything against people drinking, as long as they don't mess up other people's lives. But I've got to be honest and say I don't like playing clubs because of the hard work and the way a few guys carry on.

I was still kind of backward when I got to Nashville

for the first time. Doo had to stay back with the babies, so Mr. Burley hired me a girl to travel with. She was a big redhead—I think her name was Mack—and she was something else. She was supposed to promote me and my record, but she had other ideas about how to attract attention.

The first thing she did was to hire convertibles and get us bikini bathing suits. I never had one in my life and I wouldn't wear it. She said you had to show off what you got. I said I wouldn't have it. That's not the way my mommy and my daddy raised me, and my husband would die if he found out, after killing me first.

"That's the way everybody does it," the redhead said.

"If it is, I better get out right now," I replied. But I didn't get out, and things were getting worse.

We were in some towns where she would go out on a date with some disc jockey. I didn't know what was going on. Then she said, "You better go out on dates with disc jockeys, too. That's the way it's done." I said I was married and didn't go out on dates with nobody. It was a shaky situation.

We got to Nashville and this redhead had me on a radio station. I'm not gonna mention the station, but it wasn't WSM. I figured we were done with the town, but Mack said if we stayed around until Tuesday, they'd play my record.

I told her I didn't have to do that. Then I asked her, "What do they expect from us if we stay?" She shrugged her shoulders, and I knew what she meant—if you want to make it in this business, you've got to sleep with those men.

I got real scared. I was over my head with this girl. I picked up the phone and started calling my husband. Mack got mad and started throwing ashtrays around the room, yelling, "Do that and I'll tear up your contract."

My life has run from misery to happiness—and sometimes back to misery. This was one of the best times. I had just come to Nashville, had been on the Grand Ole Opry, and my first record had hit number one on the charts. The photographer told me to burst out of the Opry door and hug Doolittle and look happy. That wasn't hard to do right then. (The reason I look so tall is that I'm standing on a higher step than Doolittle.)

Me and my cousin Marie Castle were closer than sisters—and we still are. This was taken when I was around four years old. We were so poor, I had to borrow the dress from Marie so I'd look nicer.

Right before I got married, they took this picture of me. It was along the railroad tracks up in Butcher Holler, right where they hauled the coal down from the mines. Those tracks ain't there anymore—and neither is that thirteen-year-old girl you see. What ever became of her?

Marshall News Prints, Inc. (Paintsville *Herald*)

Doolittle looked just like a little toy soldier the first time I ever saw him. The army took this picture, and they ran it in the Paintsville *Herald*. He was around seventeen at the time—but he looks younger, doesn't he? Right after this, he got shipped to Europe for the last part of the war.

*Above:* Sometime during the war, Mommy and Daddy posed outside Daddy's father's house, right up the holler from our place. You can see the rough logs from the house, right above Daddy's head, and you can see the hills slanting off to the side. That's real Kentucky mountain country. *Below:* On the night I announced I was getting married, Daddy paced for hours on the porch you see here. He and Mommy told me it was the worst decision I could ever make. Whenever I visit the old home now, I can feel Daddy's presence very strongly on that porch—and other people have told me the same thing.

Bob Parker from Straus Printers, Lithographers, Madison, Wis.

Daddy was real gentle with kids. That's why I expected so much out of marriage, figuring that all men should be steady and pleasant, like my daddy. He sure looks big and strong, don't he? But actually he was only around 117 pounds and five feet eight inches tall.

I bought my first stage outfit when I was making five dollars a night at Bill's Tavern in Washington State. Doolittle gave me that Gibson guitar—that got me started—for my birthday. I used to wear cowboy hats in those days. I was real country.

That cute little guy I'm cuddling up with is my husband, folks. I sure look different myself, don't I? Well, I was around twenty-one years old and was taking care of four kids and didn't have much time or money for myself. Heck, I had just about figured out what was causing all them kids.

Right after Daddy died, Mommy drove out with the family to visit us in Washington. That's Brenda (now called Crystal Gayle), Betty Ruth, Peggy Sue, me, Mommy, and Jay Lee.

*Herald* Staff Photo, Bellingham, Washington

The Bellingham newspaper sent out a photographer after I won all the blue ribbons for canning at the state fair. If I knew how I'd done it, I would have told 'em.

Who did you expect Doolittle would name his boat after? He hadn't seen Dolly Parton yet! We used to go fishing along the coast of Washington. Jack and Ernest Ray helped hold up the fish, while Betty Sue kind of watched.

Doolittle took this picture of me and developed it himself. Then we passed out a copy to every disc jockey from Washington to Nashville. I didn't know nothing about makeup in those days—Doo wouldn't even let me use it.

That's history being made on October 15, 1960—my first time on the Grand Ole Opry. Everybody else was so casual, playing for that audience, but I was scared to death. The fans cheered so hard, I got invited back, week after week, and that was how I got to stay in Nashville.

We really thought we had it made in 1962. We rented this little house in Madison, Tennessee, for $100 a month, and we sent for our four kids up in Indiana. I was getting $50 a date then, and we saved up $600 to buy this car. We thought we were flying high—and we were very grateful.

*Above:* Here I am with Doyle and Teddy Wilburn, back in 1963, when I was starting to travel with 'em. I made that little white outfit myself, and they were trying to get me to wear high heels. *Below:* Two of the greatest people I have ever met, Owen Bradley and Ernest Tubb, join me during a recording session in 1964. I don't remember what song I was singing, but it wasn't "One's on the Way." In fact, as it turned out, two were on the way. I was eight months pregnant with my twins.

Once in a while I'd get inspired to finish my act with the "hillbilly hoedown." That's how Mommy used to dance while listening to the radio back home. I guess nobody's gonna make me an offer to dance in the ballet, but it's fun.

I brought my gang to the Walter Reed army hospital in Washington, D.C. This one soldier joined me and Kenny Starr in a little tune. I try to visit people in hospitals when I can, smiling and joking around while I'm there. But when I leave, I just start crying.

Never mind those pictures of me laughing—somebody caught me sitting
around backstage, thinking about my life. This is the way I really am inside.

*Above:* We do most of our traveling in our special bus. My private bedroom is in the back, and the boys sleep in bunks in the middle. Jim Webb is the driver. You look at the size of that boy, and you know why I feel safe on that bus. *Below:* Pretty fancy bunch of coal miners, don't you think? These are my boys: (front row, left to right) Bob Hempker, steel guitar; Don Ballinger, front man; Dave Thornhill, lead guitar; Gene Dunlap, piano; (back row) Chuck Flynn, bass; Ken Riley, drums.

*Left:* They held "Loretta Lynn Day" in Georgia on February 21, 1974. They asked me to address the state legislature and I told 'em: "I don't know what you-all are doing, but I sure hope it comes out all right!" *Right:* Three of the best friends anybody could have, Loudilla, Kay, and Loretta Johnson (left to right), are the presidents of my fan club. They are three different personalities, and I love 'em all.

At a quiet moment during rehearsal, David Skepner and I trade words of wisdom. David is my manager. He's from Beverly Hills, California, but I think we're making a little bit of a country boy out of him.

Me and Eddy Arnold posed with Charley Pride when Charley won the Grammy Award as the best country singer. I think Charley has been one of the best things to happen to country music, to prove it belongs to everybody. He knows that I'm his biggest fan.

This was my birthday present on April 14, 1973. They marched me into this office—and there was my biggest hero, Gregory Peck. He gave me a big hug when I met him, but mostly I just sat and stared at him, while him and Doolittle talked like old friends.

Me and my partner, Conway Twitty, cleaned up at the 1972 Country Music Association Awards. We won the Vocal Duo of the Year, and I got the Female Vocalist of the Year Award. Then I was the first woman ever named Entertainer of the Year.

Hope Powell

Of all the television shows I've been on, Dinah Shore's is where I feel most comfortable. We talk so easy together, and she gives me good advice about show business. I just hope she don't mind when I mess up her kitchen like I do.

Doolittle is real close to the twins, Patsy and Peggy. This was taken when they were around five years old. It makes them mad if I make a mistake over which is which. But Doolittle can always tell them apart, because he's taken care of them while I was working on the road.

When I visited the Red Cloud Indian School in Pine Ridge, South Dakota, I was all ready to take about a dozen of those children home with me. I'm proud of being part Cherokee, and I think it's time all us Indians felt the same way.

*Above:* The only thing missing in this picture from Hurricane Mills is a couple of fans tiptoeing up the front lawn. Usually, there's some stranger asking for an autograph or taking pictures. Now that we opened the dude ranch down the road, we've had to post a security man, because the crowds got so big. *Below, left:* We're just a couple of the Webb girls, trying to get ahead in Nashville. My sister Crystal Gayle has had a couple of hit records and is gonna have more. I've been wearing more of these denim and sequin outfits lately—it's the "new me." *Below, right:* This is how Doolittle looks 364 days a year—whether he's backstage at the Opry, out on the ranch, or traveling with me. Somebody once looked inside Doolittle's hat and saw the words: "Like hell it's yours." He's very protective of what he thinks belongs to him.

Finally I got Doo on the phone, and I was crying. He told me if I didn't quit crying, he was gonna make me quit the business. I started telling him what was going on. Doo said I shouldn't do nothing, just move on to the next town, which was Cincinnati, and he'd join me. So I told Mack I wasn't gonna sleep with no disc jockeys this time or any time, and we should go to Cincinnati. When Doo arrived, he told me Mr. Burley said, "You tell that redheaded bitch Loretta doesn't have to sleep with anybody." And they fired the redhead. I've tried to forget about her. I don't like to remember bad situations.

That kind of thing never happened to me again, I'm glad to say. My husband stayed closer to me after that, and other people like the Johnsons watched out for me, too. But I was getting some kind of education in the ways of the world.

I guess growing up in Butcher Holler just didn't prepare me for the facts of life, just like I didn't know anything about sex when I got married. In fact, I was still pretty ignorant even with four kids. I didn't even know there was such a thing as a lesbian until my daughter came home from *grade* school and told me. I couldn't believe it then—but now I can.

I think there's a few of my fans who are lesbians— maybe more than a few. But they're my fans, and they visit me, just like anybody else, and it don't bother me. I've even got one friend who tells me about her personal life, and she'll even fix my hair or something. But she would never do anything that would upset me. It's not your friends who are the problem anyway. I've had a couple of women I didn't know proposition me, or even try something. That's why I've gotten more careful about seeing a lot of strangers.

Working in those clubs I got to see it all. I'd see a husband coming in with someone else's wife. A wife coming in with someone else's husband. It was all the same, the public and the musicians. It started to seem like the whole world was like that. Then I got to worrying if Doo was doing the same thing, see, because everyone else was. It was a bad time for me in that respect, because of what I saw.

The only good thing was I started writing more songs. Everyone says all my songs are about myself. That's not completely true, because if I did all the things I write about, I wouldn't be here—I'd be all worn out in some old people's home. But I've seen things, and that's *almost* the same as doing 'em.

Like one of my songs was "You Ain't Woman Enough to Take My Man." This one I didn't really write about myself. There was a little girl, she was a bit on the plump side, not much. She came backstage one night, crying, and she said, "Loretta, my husband is going with another woman, so he brought her here tonight. See that guy sitting out there? See that girl sitting beside him?"

I looked at that other girl and I thought, "My God, don't tell me you're going to let something like that take your husband away from you!" 'Cause, to me, she was twice the woman that other gal was. So I looked back at her and said, "Why, she ain't woman enough to take your man!" Just like that, as soon as I said it, I knew I had a hit song. She was all prepared to take a back seat because her husband fell for another woman. But that's not something I'd let myself do. By the way, that girl fought for her man, and a few months later she wrote to me and said they were back together again. I still see her, and she's still married to that same guy.

That's the same way I wrote "Fist City." There was a gal in Tennessee who was after my man, like I said before. I was up singing every night and she'd come around to the clubs and she'd hang around him. So finally I wrote this song that said, "You better lay off my man...or I'll grab you by the hair of your head and lift you off of the ground."

And I would. I've been in a couple of fights in my life. I fight like a woman. I scratch and kick and bite and punch. Women are much meaner than men. So I warned any girl making eyes at Doo then, and I'm still jealous enough to warn 'em today—if you see this cute little old boy near me wearing his cowboy hat, you'd better walk a circle around us if you don't want to go to Fist City. (Although I guess I'd better be careful what I say. For all I know, there might be a dozen gals out there ready to take me on.)

Doolittle knows he don't have to worry about me, even if we're not together on the road all the time. Once in a while he'll pick up some rumor, but Nashville is famous for rumors. After twenty-five years of being married, I ain't cheated on him.

People ask me sometimes, "Doesn't it get lonely on the road? Don't you ever meet a man you'd like to spend some time with?" Usually I just answer a flat-out no. But that's really too simple an answer. The truth is everybody finds themselves attracted to different people at different times. Anybody who says that ain't true is just a liar. I'm normal in that respect. I've met men I *could* like—but I haven't ever seen one yet who could take the place of my family. So I stay out of trouble.

I wrote a song about that once called "I'm Dynamite," and in it was a line, "Please don't light the fuse." See, the way I look at it, it's up to the woman to keep out of trouble. Maybe if I was the type who liked to go to parties and drink, I'd get in trouble. That's why I don't condemn Doo for what he's done. As long as you keep up with this traveling life, with all the people and parties, there're bound to be temptations. As for what Doo has done, it's not anything I haven't thought about doing myself.

But I've seen what happened to women when they started messing around. They lost their families and they went downhill in a hurry. I've had friends like that. I'd rather write a song about it—that's my way of staying out of trouble. My marriage means too much to take a chance.

Besides, if I wasn't married, I couldn't do the same things I do now. I couldn't be friendly with a lot of men, hug 'em and tell 'em I love 'em. They might take it the wrong way, and that would spoil things for me.

But sometimes men take your personality wrong. They see me up on the stage and they think I'm just waiting for their telephone call. Like this doctor from Texas who followed me around whenever I played that part of the country. He wouldn't take no for an answer. He'd be calling up and wanting to meet me. One night I was taking a bath and he called me from the lobby and said, "Well, I've found you." I didn't know how he got my room number, but he did. He said he wanted to watch TV in my room. I said it was too late, the TV was off.

He said he wanted to talk, so I said he could talk on the phone. Then he started telling me about his troubles with his wife, which is about the worst approach a man can use. I said, "Why don't you write to Dear Abby?" He hung up, and I haven't heard from him since. But he knows who he is.

But just because you don't go for that kind of stuff doesn't mean it's not there. You just look around you. That's why I think country music is so popular with ordinary people. Because not everybody can appreciate poetry or classical music, and they don't like words that say one thing and mean another thing. Country music is real. Country music tells the story the way things are. People fall in love and then one of 'em starts cheating around, or both of 'em sometimes. And usually there's somebody who gets hurt. Our country songs are nothing but the truth. That's why they're so popular.

It's like that song Conway Twitty and I did in 1974, "As Soon as I Hang Up the Phone." It starts with the phone ringing and Conway, in a choking kind of voice, tries to tell me good-bye. Now, for a while, I don't pay any attention to what he's saying, but he keeps bringing the subject back to him leaving. Finally he says it's true, and I sing, "Ohhhh noooo..."

Now, how many people have gotten bad news on the phone about their man or woman? Lots. And I bet most of 'em react the way I do in that song. Well, that song started being played on the jukeboxes over and over again because it was real.

You just look around at the problems that people keep having. Divorces and split-ups and extra boyfriends and girlfriends all over the place. I don't know how they find the time for it. And another reason country songs are so popular: some of the songs are about ourselves, really. We ain't no better than anybody else.

As for me, I ain't slept with nobody except my husband. I'm always getting letters from Conway's fans who say I was responsible for breaking up his marriage. Those fans hear Conway and me singing on our records, or they know that we're partners in a talent agency. But that's the *only* way we're partners. I've heard rumors about me and every singer in country music. There were even rumors about me and Ernest Tubb, and he's like a father to me. As far as I'm concerned, Ernest Tubb hung the moon. But my friends know me better than that. I also know you don't have to sleep with anybody to make it in this business. If I do sleep with anybody, it will be for my own accord. Like I told that redhead back in 1961, that ain't the way my mommy and my daddy raised me.

# 16

# Music City, U.S.A.

I'll dress up like a movie star,
And pretty up my hair
And no one here is gonna know,
What I'll be doing there...
— *"Hey, Loretta," by Shel Silverstein*

That experience with the redhead taught us to be more careful about our contacts, but it didn't stop us from trying to make it in Nashville. I guess I went at it like a bull in a china shop, the same way I am about everything—all energy. I'd be on people's doorsteps at eight in the morning, holding copies of my first record and of new songs I'd written.

People started calling me "Colonel Parker" because that was the name of the man who promoted Elvis Presley. Well, I was no Colonel Parker, but I sure could have used one. I was wearing a ninety-nine-cent dress from the Salvation Army, and me and Doolittle spent more than one night sleeping in the car to save money.

I went over to the Opry and pestered Ott Devine, the manager, until he let me on the show. My first appearance was on October 15, 1960; the Opry paid guests fifteen dollars in those days, and we were sure glad to have the money.

I was nervous when they took me backstage. It was kind of crowded and informal, with all sorts of people hanging around. You'd see some picker you never heard of standing right next to some great star like Roy Acuff. It seemed disorganized, but it was a radio show and only the studio audience could see people milling around backstage. On the radio, it was the most exciting thing in the world to hear. In person, you'd see those people, how exhausted they were from driving all day. But they'd come alive if they liked you. I sang "Honky Tonk Girl" and they really cheered me, and Ott Devine invited me back again.

Somebody hinted that when you went on the stage of the Grand Ole Opry, you should wear high-heeled shoes and look a little more stylish. But I was used to low-heeled boots and didn't want to look too fancy.

Out of those first Opry appearances, I got an invitation to tour Alaska with Johnny Horton. Before I could, he was on his way back to Nashville when he got killed in a car wreck. Then they talked about matching me with Jim Reeves, but he, too, died before we got together.

Me and Doo realized that we needed good advice if we were going to make it. We decided to try the Wilburn Brothers, who were a big act in country music at that time. I met them once before when I asked for their autographs. Now I looked 'em up and asked what they could do for me.

Of course, I already had my first record on the charts and was on my way to being included in the Most Promising Female Singer category, so they didn't have anything to do with that, or with getting me on the Opry. Plus, I was already considered for a television show, which later turned out to be their show.

We sat around and talked for a few hours in their

office. There were four brothers from Arkansas—Doyle, Teddy, Leslie, and Lester. I remember Doyle liked my voice, and Teddy thought I sounded like Kitty Wells. Doyle did most of the business, and Teddy was a songwriter. They also ran a talent agency.

They asked me if I was under contract to anybody else. I remember Mr. Burley had promised to let me out of the contract if I moved to Nashville. I called him and he said, "Go ahead and sign. I'm tearing up your contract with me." He was a sweet old man and I think he was as happy as we were about the Wilburn deal.

That was the start of a relationship that brought me a lot of happiness—but ended in a lot of pain. I really got close to the Wilburns and their mother—I still call her "Mom" today. For a long time, they managed my career and were also my song publishers. But around 1970, I got the feeling they weren't growing with me anymore. So I went out and formed my own company. There's a big court case still going on, so my lawyers have told me I can't make any comments about the Wilburns, or why I left them.

It isn't easy for me to hold back on my feelings, but when your lawyer talks, you'd better listen. But I've got to say this much: the Wilburns were good for me, when I was getting started. In my house in Hurricane Mills, I've got a portrait of the Wilburns where everybody can see it. If you'll notice in my fan booklets and stuff, there is usually a picture of those two boys entitled simply "Doyle and Teddy." You can't ever go back to what used to be, but you can be honest and remember it.

Anyway, the way it started, Doyle and Teddy took me to their recording studio, called Sure-Fire, where I recorded a song called "Fool Number One." They figured I might as well start at the top, so they took the "demo" record to Owen Bradley at Decca Records.

Owen Bradley is one of the biggest men in the business. He was named to the Country Music Hall of Fame in 1974. He talks like an easygoing country man, but he's been responsible for more country music hits than anybody. He was polite to the Wilburns when they brought in my record, but he said I sounded too much like Kitty Wells, which I probably did. Since he already had Kitty herself and Patsy Cline and Brenda Lee at Decca, he didn't need me.

But Owen said he wanted that song for Brenda Lee, who was just a kid at the time. And Doyle said, "Owen, I'm not pitching you a song, I'm pitching you an artist." So Owen agreed to give me a six-month contract if Doyle would let Brenda record the song. It got to be a big hit for her, and things worked out for me, too.

Decca started to call me "The Decca Doll from Kentucky." I remember my first recording session for them. I was gonna record "The Girl That I Am Now" and "I Walked Away from the Wreck." I was so scared I just stood in the background and was even afraid to speak to the musicians. I'd see those fabulous side musicians like Grady Martin and Floyd Cramer, guys the public doesn't know but who are really superstars for making a singer sound good. I'd get so choked up I couldn't sing.

But Owen would put up a screen, so I couldn't see nobody; I'd just sing to myself. He said he did the same thing for Brenda Lee and it helped.

I always felt like Owen was a father to me. He could see I was just a scared little country girl, and he made me relax. I remember one time, after we signed, we didn't have any money. I started crying in his office, and he gave me a thousand dollars out of his pocket, not from the company, to pay my rent and the back bills. The next year we were making some money, and we paid Owen back. But I ain't never forgotten that man helping me like he did.

Owen gave me good advice lots of times. Doyle and Teddy were trying to polish me up, make me a "performer," while Owen felt I should stay more natural. They were both right, in their own ways, but it was nice to have somebody say, "Just pronounce the words the way you want, Loretta." That's what Owen told me. He never made me feel like I was a dumb hillbilly just because I said "ain't" or "holler." Owen said people would always understand me, so long as I was myself.

Once we had the contracts with the Wilburns and Decca, we knew we could make it in Nashville. I wouldn't have stayed if I didn't think I was going to make it. You've got to go all the way. Doolittle had already closed up our house in Washington State, and we moved the four kids to Indiana, where both of our mothers were living.

It was tough leaving Washington. Blanche Smith was upset because she said my four kids kept her young. She said, "I'm not going to live if you take away my babies." She was an old lady at the time, and sure enough, she died about six months after we moved. I still miss Bob and Clyde Green. Every holiday, I start crying just thinking about those eleven years when Blanche and those two boys were as close as family. I see the Greens once in a while, and we talk over the old days.

Another bad thing was saying good-bye to my musicians. My brother Jay Lee was going to move to Nashville with us, but I couldn't bring those other boys down. There was no way I could pay 'em a salary. I think it just about broke the heart of my steel man, Smiley, because I don't believe he ever played in a band again.

It was the fall of 1961 when we settled in Nashville. Me and Doolittle were staying with a woman named Faye Walton, who lives around Indianapolis now. I once got a letter from her, bawling me out for not giving her enough credit. Well, it was true—she used to help us out a lot. So if you've bought a copy of this book, Faye, thanks a lot.

Doolittle went to work in a shop, but he was only taking cars he could fix in his spare time. He was starting to travel with me and was taking an interest in the business. Before the year was out, I was named Most Promising Female Singer, and Decca was talking about lengthening my contract.

It looked like we were gonna have it easy in Nashville. But then I learned not everybody was on my side.

# 17

# Patsy

Someone said that time heals sorrow
But I can't help but dread tomorrow,
When I miss you more today than yesterday . . .
—*"I Miss You More Today," by Loretta Lynn*
*and Lorene Allen*

Once we were living in Nashville, we began to get regular dates, and I found myself being invited back to the Opry week after week. But then I ran into some jealousy, and if it wasn't for Patsy Cline, I don't think I would have lasted.

It seems there were a lot of girl singers who were trying to get to the top at the same time. When I came along, they got jealous and started complaining at the Opry because I got invited back so much. Then they started telephoning me and saying I ought to go back to the West Coast.

One girl asked me who I was sleeping with to get on the Opry so fast. It hurt so much that I cried day and night. My husband said, "If you don't quit this crying, I'm gonna take you back to the West Coast and forget it." And he would have.

But that's when I met Patsy. She was around twenty-seven, and she'd known plenty of hard times trying to make it. Just after I got to Nashville, she was in a car accident that almost killed her. I was on the Ernest Tubb Record Shop radio show that they do every Saturday night, and I said, "Patsy has the number one record, 'I Fall to Pieces,' and she's in the hospital." Patsy heard it and asked her husband, Charlie Dick, to bring me to the hospital. She was all bandaged up. We talked a good while and became close friends right away. From then on, if she had a fight with her husband, she'd call me. If I had a fight with Doolittle, I'd call her.

The main reason we became good friends was we were both struggling. Patsy had gotten cut out of a lot of money on a couple of her hit songs, and now she was in the hospital all banged up. We both felt we wouldn't try to hurt each other.

I guess the other girls didn't know about me and Patsy being friends. They called a party at one of their homes to discuss how to stop me from being on the Opry, and they invited Patsy! There were about six of them, younger ones just coming up. I'm not saying who they were, but they know it themselves. The only thing I will say is that Kitty Wells wasn't one of them. She's always been my idol, and she was on the road at the time. Plus, she's too good and religious a person to do what the others did. Anyway, inviting Patsy was their mistake. She called me up and told me what the deal was and said we both should go to that meeting. I said I didn't have anything to wear, and besides the meeting was about me. She said going was the best thing to do. She told me to get my hair done, and she came over to my house with a new outfit she had bought for me and she made me go.

When we got to the house, there were all these Cadillacs belonging to the top women singers in the country.

We went in there, and they didn't say a word. That ended their plan. Patsy put the stamp of approval on me, and I never had any problems with them again. In fact, they are all my friends now. But I made a point of it when new girls came along to give 'em all a chance, because I wouldn't treat nobody the way they treated me. If you're good, you're gonna make it.

Me and Patsy got closer together all the time. She taught me a lot of things about show business, like how to go onto a stage and how to get off. She even bought me a lot of clothes. Many times when she bought something for herself, she would buy me the same thing. She gave me rhinestones—I thought they were real diamonds— and I still have the dresses she bought me, hanging in my closet. She gave me one pair of panties I wore for three years. They were holier than I am!

She even bought curtains and drapes for my house because I was too broke to buy them. And she offered to pay me to go on the road with her just to keep her company. She was a great human being and a great friend.

Patsy loved to cook, and she'd call me up all the time to come over and eat something. Or she would come over to our house and eat rabbit, when Doo shot some. That's the one thing she loved. Remembering nice things about her, it makes me mad when people say bad things about Patsy. One singer was quoted in some article last year as saying Patsy was "a beer drinker and a cusser, which she got from coming up in a hard life, but she was mostly a good-hearted person." Well, I never saw Patsy drink too much beer or cuss much more than an ordinary woman, but it was certainly true she was a warm-hearted person, and she ain't around to defend herself, so I'd rather remember the good part about her.

Patsy was a good old country girl from Winchester, Virginia. I didn't know it at the time, but her real name was Virginia Patterson Hensley. She started as a dancer but turned to singing, and she worked some mighty rough places. The first time people ever heard of her she was on *Arthur Godfrey's Talent Scouts* in 1957 singing this song "Walking after Midnight." She drove 'em wild with that song. Then she did songs like "Crazy," "She's Got You," "Faded Love," "Leaving," "On Your Mind," and "I Fall to Pieces," one after another. She was really like Hank Williams, the way she got this throb in her voice and really touched people's emotions.

I remember the last time I saw Patsy alive. It was in Nashville on a Thursday. She came over to my house to hang drapes. Now, that year she was named Top Female Singer, replacing Kitty Wells. At this ceremony she told me I would be named number one singer next year. I told her she was wrong, that she'd be number one for years to come. Now, imagine the Most Promising Female Singer and the Top Female Singer hanging drapes. Pretty wild bunch, wouldn't you say? Those drapes are now in Doolittle's office. I'm gonna put 'em in my museum that I'm putting in the mill back home.

Later that same Thursday night, I went over to Patsy's house because she had some tapes she wanted me to hear from a recording session. At that session she cut "Sweet Dreams."

I remember that while we listened to the tapes, Patsy embroidered a tablecloth. She did that to relax. Her little boy Randy was on a rocking horse, rocking very hard. I was worried that he'd fall off and get hurt, but Patsy said not to worry. That night we made plans to go shopping when she returned from doing the benefit show in Kansas City for some disc jockey who had gotten hurt in a wreck.

Just before I left her house about midnight, she said she had something for me. Then she gave me a great big box filled with clothes for me to take home. One thing in that box was a little, red, sexy shorty nightgown. She told me, "This is the sexiest thing I've ever had. Red is the color men like." I never did wear that nightgown, though. I'm gonna put that in my museum. (Maybe I just might wear it one of these days—just for my old man, of course. It's made out of two small Band-Aids and one a little bigger.)

I remember that before we said good-bye, we'd usually hug each other, but that night I was carrying that huge box. Patsy said. "Aren't you going to hug me?" I put down the box and hugged her. Then came the last words I would hear from her. She said, "Little gal, no matter what people say or do, no matter what happens, you and me are gonna stick together."

On Tuesday evening, March 5, 1963, Patsy, Hawkshaw Hawkins, Cowboy Copas, and Randy Hughes, the pilot, were flying home from the Kansas City benefit, in a twin-engine Comanche, when they ran into a storm near Dyersburg, near where I live today. On Wednesday morning I wondered why I didn't hear from Patsy. I was gonna call her up and say, "You lazy-head, why ain't you here?" Just then, I got a call from Patsy's booking agent, who told me she was dead. I said, "Baloney, her and me is going shopping." Then I realized it was true. The radio said her plane was missing, and finally they announced the news that there were no survivors.

That just about broke me up, to think that someone as good as that was gone. And I guess I was selfish enough to mourn almost as much for myself as for her. I was upset because who would I turn to? Patsy was like a mother and a sister to me. When she died, I just about gave up. I thought this was the end for me, too.

They brought four maroon hearses to carry the caskets; then the caskets were put in a large room. Each of the caskets had a picture of the artist on it. Just two days later, Jack Anglin was killed going to a memorial service for Patsy. Me and Doo also just missed being killed by a train at a crossing. We wondered what in the world was going on; it was such a sad, scary time.

The thing that kept me going was remembering how Patsy had told me she was gonna stick with me no matter what. I've always felt that Patsy was helping me with my career, even from beyond. I know that she tries to guide me. I feel she's here. You have to have ESP to feel it, but I know she's here. It wasn't but another year before I was named Top Female Singer, just like Patsy predicted.

I still think about Patsy a lot. I won't go anywhere near the place where the plane crashed. I named one of my twins after her. I've often thought about doing an album of her songs, but I never have because I know I'd start to cry. I've got all her albums and tapes. I think about the way she would hold out one arm, real ladylike, but I can't be like that. I'll imitate other singers sometimes. I started by imitating Kitty Wells, a real serious Christian lady who won't hardly joke around onstage. But there's something about Patsy I can't imitate, and I won't try. To me, Patsy was my best friend and I couldn't imitate her. It would hurt too much.

# 18

## My Kids

Little handprints on the wall,
Little footsteps in the hall,
Little arms that reach out for me in the night...
—*"One Little Reason," by Loretta Lynn*

Things got better for me after meeting Patsy. But I don't know if things got better for my kids. They were used to me being around to guide 'em, and now when they were growing up, I wasn't there.

Even today, with my four older kids in their twenties, I see signs that it wasn't good for me to leave 'em alone so much. They all live right close to our ranch, and I'm always getting involved in their troubles. Half the time I worry that I didn't know 'em well enough when they were young. The other half I worry that I'm too involved now. It's a pretty emotional subject with me—how I wasn't around when my kids needed me.

Sometimes when I get all worked up over their problems, Doo says we should just let the kids work it out for themselves. But when I'm home, I'm tempted to be an old mother hen. It's a funny deal. In country music, we're always singing about home and family. But because I was in country music, I had to neglect my home and family.

I look at Betty and Jack and Ernest and Cissy today, and I think of how I went out on the road. We had this dream about me making it in show business—and it's paid off, in money and other things. But in certain ways, I don't know.

At first, Doolittle stayed with the kids a lot. While we were still living in Washington, he'd cook their dinners and take 'em places like the drive-in movies. He's always been a good father with his kids. He taught 'em to survive and be independent. But when he joined me on the road, we left the kids, first with my brother, then with our mothers in Indiana.

When the kids came to Nashville, we left 'em with babysitters. Now, babysitters are all right, if you keep the same ones. But we didn't. We'd hire one babysitter for a month; then she'd quit or we'd fire her or something. It was hard on the kids and hard on me. I'd be in some motel room not knowing if the babies was eating right or going to school regular.

Betty Sue, the oldest—I think it bothered her the most. Me and her are real close to begin with—I've known her since I was fourteen. She was always such a bright, sensitive little girl, and sometimes these are the ones that suffer the most. Betty can remember those real old days when we were poor—how I made her bloomers out of cut-down burlap bags when she went to school for the first time.

When I started traveling, Betty was already in grade school. She didn't want to move to Nashville and she still talks in a Washington accent rather than a Southern accent. Sometimes she talks about moving back there, although she and her husband are doing real good in Tennessee.

I'd say the moving bothered her a lot. When I'd come

home from the road, I'd tell her to do one thing and she would do the opposite. She might tell you moving didn't bother her. But deep down inside, it did. When I was needed, I wasn't there. I came home from the road one time and Betty said she was getting married. She wasn't much older than I was when I got married. We tried to talk her out of it but she said, "You got married before you were fourteen." So what could we say? We knew she was gonna do it anyway, so what was the sense in arguing? It was just like me telling my mommy I was getting married. What could she do?

Betty was still young when she had two babies. Then she didn't have any more. The first baby was called Loretta Lynn, but everybody calls her Lynn now. The second is named Audrey. I treasure those two beautiful girls who made me a grandmother when I was twenty-nine.

Betty was in a pretty bad way after having the babies. She was supposed to take these shots, but sometimes she didn't have any money. I'd wake up in the middle of the night, dreaming about spanking Betty, and that would be a sign that Betty was sick. I'd call Gloria, the housekeeper, and she'd tell me Betty wasn't looking good. Or I'd call Betty and say, "You better go get a shot, and I'll pay the fifteen dollars." Other times I'd wake up dreaming about Betty Sue smiling, and I'd know she was all right.

Me and Betty Sue are really close, but we can get into it sometimes. She still likes to do opposite things, just to be mean. She's smart. People who visit my house always enjoy meeting Betty because she's so smart. She's got dark hair and a nice smile, and she's real pretty. But if I'm around—watch out! We can get into it pretty good.

It's all right for me to say these things because they're my kids. But if somebody else criticizes my kids, they'd better be careful. See, I know my kids' good points, too, and I ain't bashful about telling 'em.

Betty Sue is talented. She's a decorator and she's written three or four songs under the name of "Tracey Lee" that I've recorded. She's happily married to Paul Markworth, a real smart boy from up in Milwaukee who's been real good for Betty because he's considerate. He has a business in land management near Waverly, and she helps him. They're making good money, and it looks like a good future.

Jack Benny is my first son. He's real small, like Doolittle, and he even walks like Doo—with that cowboy shuffle, like he just got off a horse. In fact, Jack used to be a jockey when he was younger. He raced at a few tracks in Tennessee and even down south where they've got legal betting. But he's just a little too big now to be a jockey. He still rides in the rodeos around home—he even rides the bulls, which scares the daylights out of me.

Jack is kind of quiet. When he's got problems, his face gets kind of worked up, like Doolittle, but he don't talk about things very easy. When I see Jack is upset, it just tears me up inside, like I want to put my arms around him and comfort him. Of all my kids, he's the one I feel most sentimental about.

When Jack and his wife broke up, I just started bawling, because I love Pat like a sister. I wouldn't take sides because I love 'em both. Pat is from a nice family right over in Waverly. Jack got married before he got out of high school and then he joined the army for four years because his brother went into the marines, and Jack didn't want Ernest Ray to get anything on him. Jack got shipped to Korea, which didn't help his marriage. They had a girl, Lora Kay, and a boy, Jeffrey Allen, who is the apple of my eye. He looks and walks just like Jack and Doo. You should see the three of 'em walking side by side.

Jack just finished up the army at Fort Campbell, Kentucky. Some days he talks about taking off for California on his motorcycle. Other times he talks about going to veterinarian college because he loves animals.

Jack used to work on the ranch, but it was too much responsibility. We'd be on the road and he'd be having trouble with the help, so we had to let him give it up. Ernest Ray, our second boy, had the same problem. When he works on the ranch, we make sure to give him a separate job, where he won't bother the help. Ernest don't mind working hard and getting all dirty—when he wants to. When he doesn't, you can't make him do anything.

Ernest is the boy on all my religious albums. He's the most handsome boy you ever saw in your life, but is he ever mean! Ernest can tie you up with his little finger when he's sweet. He'll go over to old people and listen to 'em for hours, and they'll swear he's the sweetest boy they ever met. But he's the same boy that's always getting into car wrecks and stuff. He just hasn't grown up yet.

He's always been so beautiful. I never cut his brown curly hair until he was three years old. When we did it, I cried more than he did. Ernest liked being a baby. After we had Cissy, he used to swipe her bottles during the night. We'd get up in the morning and he'd be top-heavy from drinking three or four of her bottles.

When he was little, I put Ernest on my religious album because he had such a sweet face. He can sing and play the guitar real good. I even take him on trips with me, after warning my boys not to get him in trouble. But it turned out the joke was on me. When Ernest was around fourteen, we were on some long bus trip, and he was up front with the band. I got to wondering if my boys were protecting him. I went up front after a while and there was my band, rolling on the floor, laughing. I asked Don Ballinger what was so funny and he said,

"Mom, Ernest Ray told us a story that was dirtier than anything we know!"

I also told the boys to keep Ernest out of trouble when we got to the big cities. But it was no use. Ernest could find trouble if you tied him in chains.

But he could sure sell albums. He would tell the crowd, "Buy two Loretta Lynn albums from me—because I'm her son!" He'd come back to the bus with his hands loaded with dollars. He'd sell more than my whole band.

Ernest got married a few years ago to a sweet little girl named Cindy. They live at our place most of the time. We keep telling him he's got to get himself a life of his own, but he doesn't want to push himself. We told him we'd stop paying for all the things he bought, but he's too smart to believe us. I know he'd like to have his own car-repair shop—when he came back from the marines, he offered to fix Jack's motor. He swore to Jack that he'd worked in the marines' repair shop. So he fixed Jack's motor—then it blew up! Later Ernest admitted that his job was sweeping the floor at the repair shop. He's had a couple of motors blow up on him since then. Sometimes I see signs that Ernest is growing up a little. He's been singing in my show again recently, and some people say that boy has got a lot of talent. I think so—but I'm his mother. Anyway, I hope Ernest straightens out. It's like somebody told me about Tom Sawyer—Ernest might be president of the United States someday, if they don't hang him first.

Cissy is my fourth child. And if I had ten kids, I'd want 'em all to be like her. She's just so smart, but what's more important is she's so pleasant. I call her "The Waverly Newspaper" because I can talk to her for half an hour and catch up on all the news. People who visit the ranch feel like they've known Cissy all their lives.

I remember how upset I was when I got pregnant with

Cissy. The doctor out in Washington thought I didn't want that baby, so after delivery he put her right on my chest and said, "Here's your little girl." She wouldn't cry at first, and he was putting her in ice water, just to make her lungs work. Finally, he whipped her little behind so hard I was ready to get out of bed and whip *him*. I took one look at that little girl with the sandy-colored hair, and I was on her side for life.

Cissy has been a perfect child. She got good grades and finished high school and got a nice job with the water company in Waverly. Now she's married a boy named Gary, and they had their first child in 1975, named Harold Wayne.

Cissy was only nine when we had the twins—I'll tell more about them later—and I think she was a little jealous. Even today, she'll fuss with 'em and tell 'em she was really the youngest child. And they're so sassy they fuss right back at her. There's always something going on like that around the ranch.

Looking back, we tried to do the best we could with our kids. We didn't have much education, but one thing we could do was to teach 'em to work hard when they were young. After we got some money, we tried not to spoil 'em, but you know that's hard when you can afford good things. We still bought our clothes in the same stores as anyone else and they wore hand-me-downs, and they still do.

We never sent 'em to private school like some people do when they get rich. They went to public school. Sometimes they'd say, "So-and-so said we're rich; we shouldn't go to public school." And I'd say, "That's too bad—you're going to public school like everybody else." They wasn't no better than other kids. I kept their report cards, even to this day, to show they got mostly passing grades, as far as they went.

Still, I would have liked 'em to have more education than they did. Jack and Cissy graduated from high school and two didn't. I still think maybe Betty Sue will go to college someday, and maybe the other kids, too.

We still try to help the kids when we can, even though they've mostly grown up now. Maybe I try too hard—give 'em too much, because I wasn't around when they was growing up. If I could start over again, I would still go into show business. But if I could change just one thing, I would be with my children more.

# 19

# Performer

I don't know exactly when I'll be back this way
again,
'Cause the going's getting rougher every day...
—*"Blue-Eyed Kentucky Girl," by Bobby Harden*

While my kids were getting used to all them babysitters, I was out on the road, getting used to being
a singer. It was an exciting time for us, seeing our Decca
records start to sell, but I still had a lot to learn.

The Wilburns told me I couldn't just make records.
I had to get out and reach the fans. They set me up on a
tour in 1962, and I worked forty-two shows in twenty-
five days, at state fairs. Each show paid me twenty-five
dollars, and the Wilburns gave me another twenty-five. I
felt I was a millionaire. They also had me on their television show, which was seen all over the South. So I had to
get used to appearing before bigger crowds than I'd ever
seen before.

Then the Wilburns said they'd take me out with 'em,
doing clubs and auditoriums and stuff. Hap Peebles was
the promoter, out of Wichita, Kansas. They opened in

St. Louis—I wasn't supposed to be in that particular show, but they introduced me anyway. I was standing around looking like a mess, in curlers and traveling slacks, but I came out and said hello. The Wilburns were trying to see how I behaved onstage. I was still kind of nervous about making conversation.

They taught me a few jokes but they didn't like for me to just talk, because they were afraid of what I might say. Doyle used to tell me to just shut up and let him do the thinking.

I had some sorry times before I got things right. I had to learn to smile when I walked onstage, which wasn't always easy if the weather was terrible and I missed my babies, and especially if I was getting a migraine headache or stomach cramps.

Doolittle had to scold me to look happy. At first, he wouldn't let me wear any makeup onstage, but the Wilburns persuaded him—telling him I'd look better with it.

But makeup couldn't stop this heifer from being clumsy. I had some adventures up on that stage you wouldn't believe. The first time I ever wore panty hose, I bought 'em too big, not knowing they came in different sizes. I got onstage, and they slipped right down to my knees. I just kicked 'em off—what else could I do? Another time, I was playing my guitar and my bra strap broke. I was so uncomfortable I had to stop the show and go offstage and fix it.

Another time, I was wearing a tight homemade dress. I used to make dresses myself without a pattern, because I couldn't read too good. Anyway, this one was so tight that I fell down on the stage trying to walk. And to make things worse, I couldn't get up. I was wriggling in a circle, telling the band, "Help me, help me," but the audience and the band thought it was a joke. Finally, I got up by myself, but the people thought it was so funny the Wilburns wanted me to do it every show.

One night, I was more relaxed, and I did Mommy's little hoedown dance she used to do around the radio on Saturday night. Teddy said to me, "Loretta, that's a permanent part of your act."

"But I'll ruin my socks," I said.

Teddy said it was all right to ruin a pair of stockings every show if the audience enjoyed my dancing. And it was true. The audience used to laugh and applaud like crazy when I'd go into that squaw's dance. I don't do it too much anymore. Guess I'm getting old.

They were honestly trying to teach me things in those days. I didn't have much to wear, and I was performing in blue jeans, a fringed cowboy hat, and a pair of boots. We were in Salt Lake City, Utah, and it was cold outside. Teddy bought me some winter clothes—a thick car coat, the first overcoat I'd ever owned—and he also bought me a pair of golden slippers with high heels.

I said I wasn't going to wear 'em, but Teddy hid my boots just before show time, so I didn't have anything to do but go on with high heels. My first step, I felt like I was gonna fall on my face. I wobbled out there onstage, looking like I was drunk. I did a couple of songs, but it was no good. Finally, I kicked off my heels and felt more natural. I still do that today, even on television, and people tease me about it. But in the early days it was really necessary—I was afraid I'd fall.

I tried to learn how to walk in those clumsy shoes. When I got back to the hotel, I changed into my pedal pushers, tied up my hair, and put on them high heels. Then I went out in the hall to practice. But the carpet was thick, and I stumbled and fell down. Teddy heard something go "bump" and he ran to look.

"Everybody come here and look at Loretta," he

shouted. A big crowd of Wilburns and other people gathered in the hallway to watch me sprawled all over the floor. I was quite a sight.

Teddy and Doyle did teach me a lot of things—how to wave to the audience, how to get on and off stage, how to speak so people would understand me. But I felt like a little girl lots of times. I remember playing the Hollywood Bowl, around 1963, with Johnny Cash. There were so many thousands of fans out there, and I was used to playing Bill's Tavern, which held only three hundred people.

I was getting to be an old professional in lots of ways, handling them good old boys at the country fairs. You can picture 'em—husky boys in their bib overalls, boots still caked with manure. They may not have seen a woman in a dress since Christmas, and if you made your exit through the crowd, they'd show their appreciation by giving you a big old hug. They didn't mean anything by it, but they could break your ribs if they got too happy. I learned to reach out and pat 'em on the elbow. If you touched 'em first, they'd back off and treat you like a lady.

I've been pretty lucky. I don't sing sexy the way some of the girls do. I'd say about 99 percent of the men are gentlemen. But, boy oh boy, that other 1 percent!

I've had many a man pass notes up onstage saying they want to sleep with me. One time I glanced offstage and saw this guy exposing himself. I didn't dare look back for a long time, but the next time I looked he was gone. I hope the cops got him. Another time a guy threw his shorts up onstage. Fortunately, Dave Thornhill, my lead guitar, grabbed 'em quick and threw 'em behind the stage.

There are a few strange people that spoil it for everybody. Some fans try to grab my clothes for souvenirs, or snip off one of my curls, even my eyelashes—can you believe that? I've also had some real bad death threats, which I'll get into later. Anyway, I've got my bus driver, Jim Webb, who's around six feet four, to walk me from the bus to the stage and back again. I'm not trying to hide from my fans, just from that one nut in every crowd. I'd advise anybody with weird ideas to be careful. We country people can be as mean as we are nice.

I was learning from all my experiences, and I found myself getting booked all over the country. After a while, I'd get out onstage and start enjoying it, just smile and feel that people loved me. I can't explain what it is. I was always so shy, still am, really, but I found it easier to be natural on the stage.

Doolittle said he used to stand in the back of the theater and listen to people's comments. They said they didn't quite know how to take me, that I was half like a sister and half like a woman of the world. One man wrote he didn't know if he should pat me on the head or hug me.

I tried aiming my show more at the women, even though some of 'em got the wrong idea. One time I was playing this club in Baltimore and this old tank comes up to me and says, "So you're the woman that's in my husband's life. That's all I hear, before I go to bed, when I wake up in the morning, is Loretta Lynn. And I'm gonna break your neck."

I said, "Woman, I don't even know your husband. But if you touch me, I'm gonna kick the tar out of you." Before I got the chance, a bouncer threw her out of the club.

Most of the women liked me, though. They could see I was Loretta Lynn, a mother and a wife and a daughter, who had feelings just like other women. Sure, I wanted men to like me, but the women were something special. They'd come around the bus after the show and they'd ask to talk to me. They felt I had the answers to their problems because my life was just like theirs.

Of course, it was impossible to find time to talk to each one or to answer every letter that came along. I ain't Dear Abby with nine secretaries answering the mail. Besides, I had a few problems maybe *they* could have solved for me. Sometimes I think some people were disappointed when they met me and found out I wasn't any smarter or happier than they were. I'm proud and I've got my own ideas, but I ain't no better than nobody else. I've often wondered why I became so popular, and maybe that's the reason. I think I reach people because I'm with 'em, not apart from 'em. It's not the fancy clothes I wear, or the way I fix my hair, and it sure ain't my looks because I don't think I'm anything special. It's the way I talk to people. You can tell when you meet somebody—in their eyes, or the way they stand—if they think they're above you or below you.

After I was performing for a while, I got to like being with a crowd. I loved to get right down with 'em, with a long cord on my microphone, if I could. And if I was at a state fair or something, where they put you too far from the audience, I'd say, "This ain't the way I like it."

And if they couldn't hear me, if they was really from the country, they'd holler back, "We can't hear you." See, they knew I cared about 'em. I knew they saved their money for weeks to see my show. I've always had a feeling for people who didn't have anything. When I'm singing to them, I feel like I'm right at home.

Anyhow, I was getting more popular all the time. I went from being fourth on the Most Promising list in 1960 to Top Female Singer for 1964 in *Billboard* magazine. My first album, *Loretta Lynn Sings*, got to be number one in 1963. And I got invited back to the Grand Ole Opry for seventeen straight shows, which was a record for anybody who wasn't a member. Finally, they asked me to join, which was a big honor.

Since then, I've made hundreds of appearances on the Opry whenever I'm around Nashville on a Saturday. After I was in show business awhile, it was the only place where I'd get nervous. Just standing around backstage with all my heroes was enough to make me shaky. But it was a good family feeling, joking with all the stagehands.

That was in the old Opry building, the Ryman Auditorium downtown, which was too old and crowded for television shows and stuff but which felt like the good, old-time music halls. I was sorry when they decided to build Opryland out east of town and move the show to the new Opry building.

Since they've moved the show, I've got to admit that the new building is beautiful, with red brick and wood in a style to look like the old church building that the Ryman was. They've put in a section of the old Opry stage, right in the center of the new stage, for good luck. And they gave all of us members a present of one brick from the old Ryman, with our names printed in gold. The new building has modern dressing rooms and a huge backstage and lots of lights for television, and they're packing 'em in weekends, with three or four shows. But I don't get the same feeling from the new Opry. To me, it's just another new arena, just like the other cities have. When I go onstage at the new Opry, I ain't even nervous anymore.

# 20

# Songwriter

> Liquor and love, they just don't mix,
> Leave the bottle or me behind...
> — *"Don't Come Home A-Drinkin'*
> *(with Lovin' on Your Mind)," by*
> *Peggy Sue Wells and Loretta Lynn*

I don't know what it's like for a book writer or a doctor or a teacher as they work to get established in their jobs. But for a singer, you've got to continue to grow or else you're just like last night's corn bread—stale and dry.

I'd say material is 80 percent of a singer's career. You can have a great voice, but you'd also better have a new song that fits your style. And the best way is to write the songs yourself.

People forget that I'm a songwriter. They think of me as just a lady up on the stage, with a band backing her up. Well, let me tell you, I've sat in my room all night, scratching out most of my songs, going all the way back to those sorry little songs I wrote back in Washington.

People say I can't read or write, but what about "Coal

Miner's Daughter"? I wrote every line, just from things I remember from my childhood.

The way most of my songs got started was I'd hear a good line or make one up. When I get a good first line, I'll scribble it down on a piece of paper, hotel stationery, paper bag, or whatever, and slip it into my purse. Usually I write my songs at night. When I get 'em written down, I'm relaxed and I go to sleep. In the morning, I finish the song and try to find a tune for it, just starting with the first line and humming to myself. After I get the tune, I get somebody else to write down the notes for me because I still can't read music after all these years. But I don't think many country musicians are good at reading music. You go to one of our recording sessions and somebody will say, "Hey, how about doing it this way?" And he'll rip off a few notes on the guitar. And somebody else will say, "Oh, you mean like this?" And he'll rip off a few more notes. It's like they communicate with their own music language. Those studio musicians don't need written notes.

When I first started writing songs, Teddy Wilburn used to work with me, suggesting the next line or changing something. Since we've had that split-up, Teddy tells people he was to me like Fred Rose was to Hank Williams, only he didn't get any of the credit for it. Well, I don't know how Rose and Williams worked together because I never did meet Hank Williams. He was before my time.

I'll say this: Teddy Wilburn did work with me on lines for some of my songs. But they were *my* songs. And if he wants credit for a line here and there, why, I've worked with lots of other singers, giving 'em advice, changing tunes, writing a line, and I never took credit. That's just the way it goes. You're riding along in a bus somewhere and trying to work something out. You ask somebody you respect, "Hey, how does this sound?" And they give you a tip. But that don't make it their song. I don't plan to name names, but my friends know who I've helped on songs. And I don't want no credit for it.

Most of my songs were from the woman's point of view. In the old days, country music was directed at the men—truck-driving songs, easy women, cheating songs. I remember how excited I got back in 1952, the first time I heard Kitty Wells sing "It Wasn't God Who Made Honky Tonk Angels." That was the women's answer to that Hank Thompson record called "The Wild Side of Life." See, Kitty was presenting the woman's point of view, which is different from the man's. And I always remembered that when I started writing songs.

It certainly helped to have Kitty Wells and Patsy Cline come before me. The way I see it, the time was right for country music to get bigger. You think of some of the great artists in the Country Music Hall of Fame—Jimmie Rodgers, people like that. How many people really got to hear 'em in those days? They got on the Opry, and they had their fans, and they sold records, too. But it was like country music was a little club or something, a specialty.

But it seemed like the whole country was really ripe for country music in the 1960s, and I'm gonna tell you why: in my opinion, Ray Charles helped make country music more popular with more fans. Now I know what you're saying: Ray Charles is black, and he's a soul singer. That's right. And country music used to mean all white. But you think about it. How much difference is there between soul music and blues and some of our old-fashioned country songs? All of it is people letting their feelings out. Then Ray Charles took "our" songs and he gave a soul feeling to 'em. He made that song "I Can't Stop Loving You," and new people got the taste for country.

Ray Charles was a big man in show business. After hearing him, people were more prepared for Johnny Cash and Merle Haggard—and Loretta Lynn. When Charley Pride came along, sure, he had some problems being the first black country star. But he sang just like white men do—you listen to his records and he's not a soul singer. Well, Ray Charles made it easier for all of us to reach a bigger audience, and I don't feel he's ever gotten the credit he deserves from Nashville.

Personally, I like to listen to soul music. I love Ray Charles. I listen to Aretha Franklin once in a while. In fact, I try to do a little soul on each of my albums. You listen to "Blueberry Hill" on my *One's on the Way* album—I try to really let go. I'll bet you I've got as many black fans as Charley Pride. Of course, I'm Charley's biggest fan, so it balances out.

Still, I don't listen much to the radio or other people's records, because I don't want to be influenced by 'em. That's one thing I regret. People tell me about Joni Mitchell or Bob Dylan or the Beatles, and I've got to admit I don't know their work. I admire the good songwriters in country music—Kris Kristofferson and Tom T. Hall can tell a story better in one line than most of us can in five. And I think I've told a few stories in my songs, too. That song "Don't Come Home A-Drinkin'" got to be number one in the nation, and it was also the first album ever made by a woman singer that sold a million dollars.

I got lots of help in my recording sessions from Owen Bradley. If he would make a suggestion, he usually had a good reason. In the past five years, I've gotten more experienced about what's going to sell. So I don't clear my songs with Owen anymore. I just show up and record 'em.

The last time he didn't like a song was when I was singing "Wings upon Your Horns." He turned off all the recording knobs and hollered, "Hey, this can't go on the air like this. What's the matter with you?" See, he thought there was something dirty with the lyrics. I was singing "You're the first to ever make me..." and then I'd take a long pause and sing, "fall in love and then not take me..." Well, I didn't know "make" was another word for having sex. I told you, I'm real backward. That's just the way the words broke between the lines. I didn't plan it that way. Then Owen got all upset about using the word "horns." He thought it sounded dirty. And all I was trying to do was make a contrast between the devil's horns and the angel's wings. What's dirty about that?

I just hollered right back, "Turn that doggone thing back on. I ain't through yet." And it got to be the number one song of the year in *Cashbox*. We think pretty closely most of the time, though.

It was Owen that provided one of my big thrills in show business. Ernest Tubb, who recorded on Decca, was looking for a duet album, and he had his choice of women singers. Just on Decca alone he could have sung with Kitty Wells or Brenda Lee. But he chose me, after I'd had just a couple of hits. I remember Ernest chose me because, he said, I was an "honest country performer who sang with her heart and soul." It was a thrill to work with him, and I love him for all he's done for me. Ernest never tried to hog the songs. He'd just share the melody with me, without getting fancy, and I still think they're some of the best songs I ever did.

Nowadays I sing my duets with Conway Twitty, but I usually arrange for Ernest to make one tour with me each year. His boys are crazier than my boys are, and they pull some awful stunts. But when I get out onstage with Ernest, I feel like I'm still that little girl huddled on the floor in front of the Philco radio on Saturday night.

# 21

## We Bought the Whole Town

Flies are buzzin' everywhere; balin' hay or
rockin' chairs,
Supper's on, I'm almost there; it's back to the
country life for me...
— *"Back to the Country," by Tracey Lee*

Before I knew it, we were making more money than
we'd ever dreamed of. I went from twenty-five dollars a show up to fifty, to a hundred, and above. But I still
couldn't believe we had any money.

I still did my own canning and put food away for the
winter. I remember telling Grandpa Jones on the Opry
one time that I had a bunch of meat and vegetables salted
in my smokehouse because "you never know when this
show business is going to go kerflooey." Once you've
been poor, you always feel in the back of your mind that
you're going to be poor again.

And suddenly the records started to pay off. That
meant Doo could give up his job as a mechanic and take
more of an interest in my business.

We rented a little house in Madison, Tennessee, but

Doo always wanted his own ranch. I think he would have chucked the whole thing and moved back to Washington if we couldn't have a ranch. He must have spent six months looking before we finally found a forty-five-acre ranch out in Goodlettsville where he could start the rodeo he always wanted to run. We started to fix up the place for a family of four kids. Ha! We had a surprise coming.

After my first four children were born, the doctor fitted me with a diaphragm to stop having more. The Rh thing scared me, too. I didn't want to take a chance with another birth. But I guess you get careless when you're on the road, traveling as much as we did. Anyway, late in 1963, I discovered I was pregnant. I couldn't believe it at first, but the doctor told me it was true.

I suppose this sounds bad the way I say it, but I was unhappy at first. I was just starting to bring in some money, it was getting to be more fun all the time, and now it looked like my career was going to be interrupted or maybe even ended. Plus, I was sure my next baby was going to be affected by the Rh problem.

I remember bawling when I told the Johnson girls I was pregnant. They told me not to worry, that things would work out for the best. Doo seemed kind of pleased to see there was life in the old boy yet. I cried for nine months, worrying while they gave me shots to control the Rh thing.

Then we had another surprise. There were twins in my mommy's family, but nobody ever told me that they skip a generation. It was time for twins to pop up again. We had a young doctor and he seemed more surprised than we were when he told us he suspected there might be two.

One morning in August, I canned thirty-eight quarts of green beans. That evening I went to the hospital to deliver two of the prettiest little twins you ever saw, early the next morning, August 6, 1964—one of the best days of my life.

The young doctor had never delivered twins before, and when it was over, you couldn't tell who was the father the way Doo and the doc were shaking hands and congratulating each other.

I named one Patsy, after Patsy Cline, and the other one Peggy, after my oldest sister. They were as bright and happy as could be, and they've been a blessing on us ever since. They are my angels, my God-sent children. It's been a whole second life for me and Doo. Our first kids came when we didn't have any money, and no time to devote to them. I felt younger with the twins than I did when I was eighteen. Our two boys always said they wouldn't accept a baby if it was a girl. But when they saw those twins, Jack claimed Patsy and Ernest claimed Peggy. It's funny how their personalities matched just right.

We decided not to have any more kids after that, so Doolittle got his vasectomy. When they start coming in pairs, it's time to quit! But we were never sorry for a day after those babies were born. You know that record, "One's on the Way," where the mother is going crazy raising her babies? At the end of the song I say, "Gee, I hope it ain't twins again." Patsy and Peggy don't like the song for that reason. I guess that's why Dolly Parton is their favorite singer.

I knew I wanted to go back to singing again. Betty got married at this time, and the other kids were all busy in school. We had an older woman housekeeper, but she left when I had the twins because it was too much for her. Then we got fortunate and hired Gloria Land, who had two years of college. She's a religious lady who took real responsibility for the babies, and now it's almost like they're hers. She's not like a babysitter or a maid. She's really like a mother to them. She yells at 'em, and they yell at her, but she runs the house, and we all love her like a member of the family.

In fact, when I go home, I'm more like some favorite aunt that's visiting for a while, until the twins get used to me again. If I sit down next to Doolittle at the dinner table, they'll give me dirty looks until I move. They're closer to him because they see him all the time. They don't like me moving in on their father.

The twins don't believe I can cook, either. Gloria is a good cook—good, old-fashioned roasts with plenty of fresh vegetables. We don't eat real fancy—just put it on the table in the kitchen and everybody eats (after the twins say the blessing). But if I ask the twins if they want me to cook, you should see the panicked look on their faces. They won't eat my cooking, not even a sandwich or a hamburger or anything. What do they think I was doing the first eleven years I was married?

But when they were little, I was on the road. Doolittle can remember trying to wash the two of 'em at once in soapy water and being scared one of 'em was gonna slip out of his hands onto the bathroom floor. Finally he rigged up a little tub on the floor and covered the floor in towels. Later the doctor told him he wasn't supposed to use soap anyway but baby oil instead.

Another time, Peggy got a real high fever in the middle of the night, and over the telephone the doctor said to put her in ice water. Doo put her in a tub of cold water. But when the doctor got there, he yelled at Doolittle, "I meant *ice* water, dammit!" And he began tossing ice cubes in the water, so she wouldn't get brain damage from the fever. Doo said he was so shook he just jumped in his jeep and rode around the ranch until Doc said Peggy was all right. And meanwhile, I was on the road someplace.

I take them with me sometimes. They sleep in the back of the bus with me, when I open up the two queen-sized beds. They both talk in their sleep, just like me, and they're both kickers, too. But I like having them around me. They're both boy crazy. There's one friend who promises he's going to take them sight-seeing in New York City. All they want to know is, "Are there any boys in New York City?"

The babies are really funny. They have so much energy. Everybody says they see me in them. They're real talkative, always have an answer. They're identical twins, but you can tell 'em apart if you're real careful. Peggy stands real straight, and Patsy tends to slouch a little. Usually I can tell, but if I make a mistake, they're horrified. Doolittle can always tell them apart because he's around so much. It hurts me if I get it wrong. If I'm not sure, I'll say, "Hey, Twin, get over here." But that doesn't fool them. They'll pout on me. It's the same with strangers. One fellow tried to make conversation with 'em by saying, "When do you think I'll be able to tell you apart?" And one of 'em looked at him like he was really stupid and said in her Southern drawl, "Prob-ly never."

I went back to work and things kept getting better for us. Doo opened his rodeo and ran it on the ranch. When I was around, I'd be an attraction in the rodeo.

I never had ridden a horse until we got out to Washington, though I rode a mule in Kentucky. When Doo started the rodeo, I wasn't too crazy about the whole deal. One time Doo made me get up on the back of a horse and hold on to the saddle. But the horse reared, knocked me off, and tramped on me. I had to lie around in bed for a few days while the rodeo was going on at our farm. When the fans heard I was in bed, they trooped right into my room and started taking pictures. I was surprised some of 'em didn't ask me to show where I got hurt.

After we were on that ranch for a year or two, Doo wanted a working ranch as a good investment for our money. We talked about maybe moving back to Washington. We were never really part of Nashville's social scene like Minnie Pearl, the late Tex Ritter, and Roy Acuff, with big homes close to town and memberships in clubs and stuff. We were still just country people, and forty-five acres wasn't enough land for us.

One day we were riding down in Humphreys County, about sixty-five miles southwest of Nashville. We were looking at another place but we got lost on this little back road. All of a sudden, I saw this huge old house built on a hill overlooking a tiny town. It had these huge white columns in front, and to me it looked like the house Tara in the movie *Gone with the Wind*. I never pictured myself as Scarlett O'Hara, not hardly, but I could picture myself in that house. We were just parked down on the road, a hundred yards below this home, but I got all excited, jumping up and down on the front seat and telling Doo, "That's what I want! That's what I want!"

Doo said, "Well, hell's fire, Loretta, let's see if it's for sale before we go buying it."

Doo found out nobody had been living in it for the past twenty years. It belonged to the Anderson family, who owned the red mill across the creek, but the house was falling apart since the Andersons had moved away. They actually owned the whole town—Hurricane Mills—a company town, where the workers got paid in scrip, just like the old coal towns. Anyway, the new owners were looking to sell it—the whole package of 1,450 acres, some cattle and equipment, and the house—for $220,000. That was a lot more expensive than we'd figured on. We'd just signed a lifetime contract with Decca, and we tried to use that to get us a loan. Doo put down $10,000 of earnest money, and just four days before the deal was up, one bank accepted our contract and gave us the loan.

I was so excited. I took a tour of the place. It had three floors with winding staircases, front and back, and all kinds of extra buildings around it. There were high ceilings and a huge kitchen area, and of course, the old red mill, the post office, and the general store with a filling station across the creek belonged to us. I started making plans to decorate the house, and I went back on the road again, not knowing anything about the condition of the house. That I left up to Doo.

He never told me until years later, but that house was in a terrible state. We didn't really inspect it until we owned it, but when I went on the road, Doo started checking it out. He told me one day he crawled under the house and found it was almost completely eaten by rats and termites. The roof was bad. Doo once told a friend of ours, "I hate to admit it, but I laid under there for an hour, big tears in my eyes. I had a book of matches in my hand and I thought, 'Boy, the best thing I could do would be to set this old house on fire and build a new one.' But then I thought how much it meant to Loretta, how hard she worked on the road. So I thought, 'I'll just fix this son-of-a-gun up, even if it takes ten years and busts every bone in my body.' I put many a long day in that house. I guess if I'd ever burned down that house, I'd have never forgiven myself. Loretta has given so much of herself that I'm glad I fixed this place up."

That was our dream house. Doo used to drive out and work on the house while I was traveling with the Wilburns. Finally we moved in, early in 1967. Then we began discovering things.

First, somebody told us there used to be a slave pit on that land. That made me feel bad because, coming from the mountains, I never liked the idea of blacks being used for slaves. Second, somebody told us there was a Civil War battle at Fort Donelson, not too far away, and that there were nineteen Rebel soldiers killed and buried right on the property. We've since found Civil War bullets and little cannonballs. I'm real superstitious anyway, and I never liked the thought of them poor fellows lying under the ground.

It wasn't but a few years later that Ernest, my second son, woke up in the middle of the night and saw the ghost of a Rebel soldier standing at the foot of the bed. Ernest said he got so scared he just closed his eyes and didn't look for a long time. When he opened his eyes, the soldier was gone.

That was enough for me. I made up my mind never to spend a minute alone in that house. Even today, I insist on Doo or Gloria being there whenever I'm home. It got worse a few years ago, when I got interested in holding séances to try to speak to people who'd died. We were holding one in the house one time, and we got the table to move clear across the room. Another time it would move a little to give answers to questions. We were trying to raise up a spirit and the table spelled out that we were reaching a man named Anderson. We tried to talk to him, but he got mad and started shaking the table. If you have ever sat in a dark room and watched a table jump right off the floor and then fall down, breaking its legs, then you know how scared we were. The next day I learned that the original owner of the house, James Anderson, was buried right near the house. We never tried talking to him again.

Doolittle never let any of that stuff worry him. He bought another thousand acres—the timber rights had already been sold to a big corporation that was messing up the land. He was busy setting up the thing as a working ranch named the Double L. He set out cornfields and cattle pastures for three hundred head, fixed up the soil, and patched fences. It was a dream come true. He's put in around $150,000 more, but we've been offered a near million dollars for the property, so it was a good investment. Now we've sunk more money into the dude ranch we opened in 1975. It has space for around 180 trailers with a five-day minimum stay, including a Saturday tour of Nashville. We've got square dances, fishing, games, a recreation room, tennis court, laundry, bathrooms, and over 150 miles of horseback trails. Up to now it's taken up a lot of time and money, but we think it will be worth it in the long run. The only bad thing is all that traffic is on the county road right below our ranch. We've hired a guard for our house, but it's bound to be more crowded around Hurricane Mills than it was before we bought the town.

Doo really enjoys running the ranching end of it. He likes to work the land and restore things. The house was more my idea.

Me and Gloria started in the house by putting wallpaper up in the halls. We had some walls knocked down and the kitchen area opened up so that we have a large, country-style kitchen. The twins' bedroom is right off the kitchen area. We had to close in windows and the door, so we'd have enough room for their two white canopied beds. There's a back stairway from the twins' room that goes upstairs, but we keep it locked because you can guess what they'd be up to if we didn't. Doo recently had a large recreation room built near our pool, out in back of the house. It has a huge stone fireplace, and we keep the TV and stereo set out there. I bought Doo his own pool table for Christmas, and he keeps his gun collection locked up out there. Also, we put our old living room furniture out there. It's rugged and sturdy and suits the room. That meant I could buy a new set for the living room. Actually, it isn't new furniture at all. I found a beautiful old set of Victorian furniture, lamps and all. We don't use the living room much, because I'm on the road all the time, but it does look nice with its gold carpet and all. We use our recreation room for entertaining.

We had an interior decorator come in to help with our bedroom in the front of the house. It's a real fancy place, just like you see in magazines. It has a coral shag carpet, and the curtains and bedspread are printed in a big floral design, the same coral as the rug. We have a king-sized bed and even the headboard is covered in the same material. The nicest thing is a beautiful crystal chandelier that hangs from the tall ceiling. When we were knocking out walls, we had a bathroom added right off our bedroom.

The one thing we don't have in that fancy bedroom is a telephone. Doo has a thing about phones. He doesn't like 'em around. Until 1975, he wouldn't let us put an extension phone anywhere. Our only phone was right in the middle of the living room, so any calls we made were with everyone sitting around listening. It's what you'd call open conversation. It would be kind of frustrating when you'd be upstairs or out in the recreation room and you'd have to come all the way to the living room to answer the phone. Doo did string up a kind of private line to his little office in one of the outbuildings near the house. The only trouble is every time he used that phone, the one in the house went dead. When I asked for extra phones, he said he just doesn't like people talking on the phone. He wants me to rest, and I guess it's true I'd just keep on talking. Finally, in 1975 we got a couple of extensions put in, with buzzers to call out to the recreation room. We're getting real modern out at Hurricane Mills, folks.

In the hallway next to the living room, we had cabinets built to hold all the little china dolls, antiques, salt and pepper shakers, and Indian relics that people give me. I keep everything because you can never tell when somebody will visit the house and look for their gift. Gloria says the hardest part of me coming home for a day is when I unload all the food and presents my fans give me.

On the wall going up the winding stairway, we've got all forty-five of my albums framed in the order that I did 'em. There's some when I didn't use any makeup, before Doo finally let me. You can see me changing, album after album. It's really kind of weird to see.

I've got all kinds of souvenirs around the house—a bed Hank Williams owned, the cowboy hat Tex Ritter used to wear, my second rhythm guitar, some personal things Patsy Cline gave me. I have Roy Acuff's yo-yo, a suit from Hank Snow, a coat from Marty Robbins, Chet Atkins's golf hat, and a beautiful gown that my friend June Carter gave me. Someday I'm going to put 'em all into the museum I'm making out of the old red mill across our creek.

We left the high ceilings in the house, even a tin one in the family kitchen area, but they do make the house hard to heat. We've got modern heat and even air-conditioning, but because there's not any insulation in the walls, it really gets cold in the winter. Every room has its own fireplace, and let me tell you, we need 'em.

As soon as you walk out the door, there's liable to be three or four dogs and cats. I've got a pet ocelot in an out-building, and you can usually smell it. There're flies and birds and sometimes skunks and a snake or two.

Like I told you—we're country.

We don't have much artwork around the house. We do have a painting of Jesus that Loretta Johnson did. I'm real proud of it. It shows him suffering on the cross, with a real intense look of pain, and his muscles straining and the sweat pouring off him. She said she wanted to show he was a real man, suffering real pain. It's a real good painting.

We use the ranch for making our album covers and television specials. Mrs. Bobby Woods, who runs the general store across the creek, isn't going to forget the time an assistant from *The Dean Martin Show* came in and ordered thirty-four dollars' worth of baloney sandwiches. But she made 'em, spreading the bread all over the counters.

The problem is that I'm hardly at the ranch enough to enjoy it, and when I am home, I'm usually tired. My secretary does all my shopping and my manager sends me clothes when I need 'em on the road. So the only shopping I do is with the twins. I love to go to the five-and-ten-cent stores and the dollar stores, not the fancy stores. Me and my babies buy all kinds of junk. The only problem is, even in Waverly, folks follow me around the store, just staring at me. Maybe when I'm around more often, they'll get used to me as just another little old country girl looking for bargains.

When I'm home, Doo likes me to do outdoor stuff with him, like riding and boating—except that I'm scared of the water. One time in 1971, me and Doo went out in a motor-boat on the Buffalo River, near our ranch. I don't know how, but the boat overturned and I went under.

I couldn't swim, so I started going under—once, twice, then a third time. I knew I was drowning, but I wasn't really awake. Sometimes you wonder what it's like to know you're dying. Well, I knew it, and I wasn't scared. It was real peaceful, like floating away on a cloud. I remember thinking that Doo must have died, too, or else he would have gotten me.

But Doo wasn't drowned. He was searching all over

for me. Finally, he pushed up the edge of the boat and saw my hair floating in the water. He pulled me up and carried me over his head to shore. I was surprised to wake up and find him working over me. The water must have poured out of me for hours. I was just surprised to know I was still here.

I guess I should have been more nervous after it happened, but I wasn't. I didn't get nervous until Sunday night, when we were doing a show on the road. Suddenly, I had this horrible thought.

"Friends, this is Sunday, and I would have been buried today," I told the audience. And I told 'em about how I almost drowned.

Well, my knees started to shake so bad I couldn't remember my songs. My boys had to help me offstage.

I've stayed off the river since then, but last year we built this heated pool behind the house, and I made up my mind I would learn to swim. But one of the twins jumped on my back and pushed me into the deep end. They pulled me out, but I was more shook up that time than I was from the river. Now I stay in the shallow end of the pool.

Other things I like to do around the ranch? Plant flowers, go for a ride in Doo's jeep, maybe ride a horse. Or I just like to sit and talk with my kids. Or visit with company. There's always *somebody* visiting the house.

Like I said before, fans are all over the place when I'm home. They think nothing of walking right up to the door. If I play with the kids in the yard, there are fans coming up to take pictures or to talk. Somehow, my home doesn't seem like home anymore. I try to avoid going home for just a day if I've got time off between trips. It seems like the whole time is spent unpacking, getting laundry done, catching up on what's been done at the ranch. My kids come in and stay all day, and I'm glad to see 'em, but it gets hectic all squeezed into one day. It just don't seem like what we planned when we bought it. I don't know what's going to happen next. It's kind of silly for me to have business in Nashville and have to stay in a motel, but that's what I do. That's what I mean when I say being a success don't guarantee you happiness.

# 22

## Me and Doo

I guess you think I'm crazy,
But it keeps him here with me,
And I only see the things I wanna see...
—*"I Only See the Things I Wanna See," by*
*Loretta Lynn and Loudilla Johnson*

Buying that ranch was a good deal for us, but it also set up some problems for me and Doo.

First of all, the ranch has cost us so much money that I had to keep up a busy schedule. In country music, the only way people will keep buying your records is if you keep going back to their towns on personal tours. And while I was on the road all the time, wrecking my own health, Doolittle was pushing hard to fix up that ranch and watch the kids. That means we've got to be separated a lot of the time. You remember how our marriage got started, with us moving out to Washington State? Well, I still believe that was the best thing for us. If we'd stayed home, around our family and neighbors, we might never have stayed together. But being alone in Washington was good for us. Even though

Doo and I both had our faults, we grew closer together. You hear a lot of gossip in Nashville about me and Doolittle—heck, like I said before, you hear rumors about everybody in Nashville. This one is fooling around, that one likes both men and women, that one uses padded bras, that one's a drunk, that one lies about her age. I'd say the rumors flow more regular than the bourbon or the Cumberland River. But I'd like to put a stop to all the rumors and just talk about me and Doo for a minute.

I think it's honest to say I went into my marriage as a baby, didn't know nothing about getting along with a man. But I think I gave Doolittle my full love because that's the way I am—whatever I do, I plunge into it 100 percent.

In our scrapbook we've saved letters—all in my poor Kentucky handwriting—from me when I first went on the road, with me mighty lonely in some motel room, homesick and writing to Doolittle who was back working three jobs and watching four babies in Custer. I'd write, "Darling you no [that's how I spelled 'know'] I love you." Every other word in my letters was "darling" or "love." And that's how I felt. When you love a man, you love him all the way.

But I guess I always felt Doo was in charge of me, just like my daddy, because he knew better and was older. Maybe then I believed that a wife was her husband's property.

If we had stayed in Washington, we probably would have been too dog-tired to make new problems. Also, nobody would have cared about us, and we could have settled things in private. There's no privacy in country music, friends—I can tell you that. When you're having a little argument, it's all over town faster than you can say "Fist City."

Lots of times friends cause problems. Or people you think are your friends. Sure, Doolittle had himself a girl-friend or two in his day. I ain't saying he didn't—even if the truth hurts. But there were nights when he'd take a second shift at the welding shop, putting in six hours under the hood of a car, getting a hot welding torch in his face, and this friend of his would come to visit at our house and say to me, "Where's Mooney tonight? I didn't see him down at the shop." And all the time that "friend" was trying to get me to bed with him. That was the way he talked, trying to make me suspicious of my husband so I'd cheat, too. That stuff never worked with me, because frankly I just wasn't that interested. But it did get me mad at Doolittle. So he'd come home at mid-night all worn down from welding and I'd be sitting in the kitchen ready to jump on him. He'd look at me and say, "What did I do now?" And when he explained it, I'd know he was right. I'm a very jealous person because I believe in being faithful.

When we moved to Nashville, Doo let me know he wouldn't stand for me changing my values. I know that sounds like a double standard, but that's the way it is. I wasn't going to change anyway. All I know is there's no double standard in the eyes of God. It's just as bad for any man as it is for any woman.

My problem is that I'm too friendly. I adopt people. Whoever is singing with me at the time becomes a good friend of mine. Like Conway Twitty, my duet partner. Doo knows me and Conway are friends. I love people and I love to give a hug or a kiss now and then. I'm affec-tionate. But I don't get that excited over being around other men. It's mostly in their minds. I just mind my own business and stay out of trouble that way.

Still, once in a while some guy would get the wrong idea just because I'd call him at three in the morning.

I thought he was my friend so I'd call him. Heck, I call the Johnson girls at three in the morning, or I'll wake Lorene Allen, my secretary, at eight o'clock on Sunday morning, just to ask a question. So I don't mean nothing by it. But a few singers have gotten the idea that I was falling in love with 'em. And in Nashville, it isn't long before somebody will carry the rumor to your husband.

One time my tour was in Knoxville, and Doo heard some gossip about me and a singer. He drove all the way to Knoxville in a rage, but when he got to the hotel, he said, "I already felt like the damn fool I was." So he waited in my room until I got back from the show—alone, I might add. The next day he went home again. Really, he knows better. That's happened a few times.

Now, jealousy works two ways. I know that Doo gets lonely if his woman's not around. So if I'm on the road, I get all these visions of him having girlfriends back home. I'll get all worked up and call home at night—and find out that Doo fell asleep at eight o'clock, exhausted from working on the ranch all day. He barely had enough strength to take off his boots, the twins will tell me. So 90 percent of the stuff you hear about Doo ain't true, either.

Whatever you want to say about him, he's an outdoor man and a family man. He's not thinking up ways to get off to Las Vegas to play the card tables and drink champagne with showgirls. He couldn't care less. He'd rather be out setting feeders for his quail, or driving a bulldozer, or playing with his babies than living it up.

In fact, I wished he liked the travel better than he does. Since we quit the Wilburns, Doo has had to travel more with me. He's all right for a while, being cooped up in a motel room. And things run better when he's around. The schedule is better, the shows are better, everyone does their job. But after a few days, Doo gets this panicked look on his face. He can't let his feelings out the way I do, and he gets to feeling trapped on the road. He'll take a long walk from the motel, try to find some country road, and just enjoy the sound of the birds and the wind and the farm machines. But usually we're staying in one of those modern motels, surrounded by interstate highways and shopping centers, and there's no place to walk. I know it's hell on Doolittle.

And all those fans coming around. He's polite to them; he'll do favors for them, talk to them. But it's like a car engine overheating. It's painful to watch. The bad thing is Doo handles it by drinking. He don't like the boys to drink on the bus, but he'll have a cup of bourbon and just try to relax himself, or he'll hit the bottle in the afternoon just out of boredom, I think. And then we'll get into an argument, which maybe I'll start by criticizing him. Or he'll tell me I did something stupid in the show, which I don't like because I'm the performer. I've learned to live with it, but it hurts me when Doo drinks too much.

More than once, I've been up on a stage giving a show, or getting some award in Nashville, knowing that Doo was out sleeping in the bus. He knows it just tears me up inside and he says he's going to lick it by himself. I know if we could just slow down our pace a little, he'd be better, because Doo is a very capable, intelligent man.

Really, we're so entirely different it's a wonder we have stayed together. I think I need love and affection more than I need people telling me what to do. I just get all torn up by harsh words and violence. Like one time Doo got mad at a dog that was barking too much. So right in front of me, he just hit it once with a club and killed it. I just went to bed and stared at the ceiling for twenty-four hours, I felt so bad. I don't believe in force, unless you're really pushed. I think you can do things with kindness.

I don't like to be told what to do. I like to be asked. I don't think a man has the right to tell a woman what to do. He should say, "What do you think about this?" If somebody tells me what to do, I'll do just the opposite, just because I'm meaner than a snake in some ways. You ask Owen Bradley. I'm like that at a recording session. Tell me one thing, I'll do another. I never felt that one person owned another person. I think Doo feels the opposite. He feels he has the right to tell his wife what to do.

People who meet us get all nervous when they see us argue. Really, sometimes it looks bad. I'll get some notion in my head and maybe I won't even listen to him. Then he'll get annoyed and start talking to me like I'm stupid. Sometimes that leads to one of my headaches, and I'll just sleep for twelve or eighteen hours.

People who don't know me too well get all nervous about that. They worry about me "escaping" into sleeping too much, or getting too nervous. But I usually bounce back the next morning. I'll wake up and hear a redbird singing, or I'll have a funny line in my head, and I'll start joking around with Doolittle, and he'll see that I'm happy again, and he'll relax and take charge of the day's doings. Then the same people who got so worried the day before will tiptoe past our motel room, and there we'll be sitting around laughing like it never happened... until the next time.

People say, "You can't live like that forever." I say, look, we've stayed married this long; we must be doing something right. Sometimes people ask if we've ever gone for marriage counseling or guidance. Heck no. They don't know as much as I do about marriage. They weren't married as young as I was, I bet. I just believe you do what you can with yourself and hope for the best.

# 23

# The Hyden Widows

We talked about the pretty lady from the
Grand Ole Opry.
We talked about the money she was raising
for the kids...
— *"Trip to Hyden," by Tom T. Hall*

If there's one way me and Doolittle are alike, it's that
both of us are soft touches for a sad story. And believe
me, you hear a lot of them when you're on the top in
country music. Everybody expects you to do favors for
them, and it's hard to say no.

When we first got to the top in Nashville, me and
Doo would agree to almost any benefit for a good cause.
We were worn out until we hired David Skepner to be
our manager, because he knew his job was to say no and
protect us from ourselves.

You wouldn't believe some of the requests we get.
Like, we'll be driving down the highway in the bus and
some car will cut in front of us and make us stop. The
people say they've got a sick relative dying in some cabin
five miles off the road—and can we pay a visit? I've said

yes a few times, and Doolittle hides his face when his tears start to show.

But Doo has more sense than me. He says he catches me staring out the windows at all those pickers that wander into Nashville trying to get discovered. He swears I'd hire every one of 'em if he didn't put a stop to it.

We visit hospitals whenever we can. The best way to do it is to try and not think of all the problems that the people have. I was in the Walter Reed army hospital in Washington, and this young boy was in the cancer ward and he said, "I'll bet you don't remember me." The boy said it like he was sure that I wouldn't and he was all set to be disappointed. But I've got this memory for faces and it seemed like I knew him.

"Yes," I said, "it was in London, England, two years ago at that big stadium. You said hello to me."

And that boy got so excited he started crying. The doctor told him he didn't have long to live, but I told him, "Now, you just get better and then come and visit me at the ranch." Just by the way he cheered up for a while, I felt I did something real good for somebody.

It's the same way with charity. I would dig into my pocketbook and give away money all the time if they didn't stop me. I've done it. Somebody tells me a story and I just say, "Here, take whatever I've got." I know I can't do that forever, so now they've worked it out where we give a certain amount to charities like United Way. Whenever some group talks to me, I tell 'em to see my manager. That sounds cold, but it's the only way. And we give plenty. I know because we've helped build churches and given money to stop diseases, because I insist on it.

Doo keeps most of the letters away from me, but sometimes I get hold of one. We got a letter from a woman who said she had six kids and they were being evicted from their home and some had diseases. It was a real pitiful story. I was about to send 'em some money when Doo stopped me. Instead he called up the sheriff where that lady lives. The sheriff said that woman had six kids by six different men and that none of the kids had any diseases that he knew of. He also said they had a new car and a television on installments and that nobody was kicking them out. If it had been up to me, I'd have just sent the money.

I keep threatening to cut out all the extra appearances because I'm too tired. Pete Axthelm, who wrote such a nice story when I was on the cover of *Newsweek* magazine, remembers me saying, "No more benefits," until somebody reminded me that we had a benefit scheduled the following Monday.

"But that's for kids," I said. "That's different."

Which is true. How're you gonna turn down some poor kids?

Sometimes you can't help but get involved. At least I can't. My manager, David Skepner, told my writer this story, and it's true:

"Loretta had just returned to Nashville from a grueling six-week tour, and as usual, on her first day back, everybody within a hundred-mile radius was there to tell her their problems. She was scheduled to do a benefit performance that night and she could hardly keep her eyes open. She knew a number of the local 'squirrels' were trying to see her and she started to leave the bus to talk to them. We quietly tried to explain that she needed thirty minutes of rest rather than listening to everyone's problems. She looked at me with tired eyes that seemed to hold compassion for the whole world and said, 'Listen, when I die, I want God to put me in charge of all the people that nobody loves.'

"That is what makes Loretta Lynn, Loretta Lynn."

Well, that's mighty nice people feel that way about

me. I did say it and I meant it. And they can even put it on my tombstone when I die.

Sometimes it seems, though, the more I try to do good the more problems I have. I got into more trouble than you can imagine over that coal mine explosion at Hyden, Kentucky. There are still people down there that accuse me of lying, stealing, and cheating, when the truth is I put myself into the hospital because I just wore myself down with trying to make money to send their kids to college, to let 'em be somebody and stay away from the mines. But it didn't work out too good.

Everybody's told stories about me and Hyden, but I've never really told my side of it.

Hyden is a little town in Leslie County, Kentucky, about seventy-five miles from where I was born, but I never heard of it until December 30, 1970. Around noontime there was a terrific explosion at this mine on Hurricane Creek. That name caught my attention right away, because we live on Hurricane Creek down in Tennessee—but it's a completely different creek.

This mine was what they call a drift mine—just like my daddy used to work in—a tunnel straight back into the mountain. But it was one of those dogholes, a cheap, nonunion mine, whereas Daddy always worked for big companies.

There were thirty-nine men working on the shift that day. One of them was just heading toward the outside when the explosion blew him clear across the road, but he was safe. The explosion blew dust and timber across the holler, like a tornado. And right away, the news went out over the radio. I heard about it even though I was in a different state. I said a prayer for those men because I've seen how mine disasters are, and I knew the picture was bad. Whenever there's a disaster, the word gets out by telephone and radio, and by people yelling up their hollers. Within a few minutes, all the families of the miners were heading toward this narrow dirt road to the mine—women would just leave their cooking and their babies and start walking toward the mine to wait for the news. Nobody could go into the mine until the government inspectors got there, because there were all kinds of fumes. But even then, people knew it wasn't going to be too good.

They waited all evening, while the holler was crowded with official cars and trucks. People built bonfires, and the Red Cross gave out baloney sandwiches and coffee. The families huddled together while the press and other outsiders stood and waited. Some women cried and others just stared. The governor of Kentucky said something cold about how mining is a rough business and you've got to expect things like this sometimes... That was before they even found any bodies.

It started to snow around nine o'clock, and it got real miserable down in that holler. Then the rescue crews found some bodies and bundled 'em in pitiful canvas bags and brought them out by stretchers.

Well, it snowed all night, and all thirty-eight men were dead. In two feet of snow, they brought the bodies to the Hyden School and let the next of kin identify each man. This was right after Christmas—decorations were still up—and they were holding funerals. I saw pictures on television—houses all lit up, each with the casket in the front room and people praying. I've been to mountain funerals, and I could just hear the wailing. I saw one woman throw herself on the casket. She was about twenty-three years old and had a couple of babies. I remember my mommy and all the years she worried about my daddy. And I just sat in front of that television and bawled like a baby.

We followed that story for days. The mine officials

held a hearing and said the men were killed because somebody was probably using an illegal explosive that sets off sparks and probably touched off some dust. They still haven't settled it legally—the issue is still in the courts—but that's what was in the papers.

For me the thing that mattered was that thirty-eight men left 101 children behind. The insurance companies and the government people were trying to get those poor widows to sign all kinds of legal papers. And those women couldn't afford lawyers, so they were signing for payments that would get the company and the government off the hook. Meanwhile they had to bury their husbands and keep on living.

This just tore me up because these women were no different than my mommy would have been—or me, when I first married Doo. Those women weren't prepared for all this stuff because all that knowledge was in the heads of the men lawyers. So I decided I was gonna do something to help change things. The first thing was to visit Hyden. We went to the graveyards and I met the widows and I visited the mine. It was the saddest little mine, a little hole like a cave, no posts. All I kept saying was, "No wonder..."

I heard how Leslie County was one of the poorest counties in the whole United States, with a high birth rate and a high death rate. And the mines were the only way to make a living. Maybe the men did know what was going on in that mine, but if they or their wives had complained, they would have been out of a job and on welfare.

I decided I would help at a benefit show for the widows. But I didn't want the money to go just to lawyers or to get spent right away. I wanted the money to help people to break that way of living that keeps them poor and uneducated, that forces men to work in doghole mines and women to have too many babies and not know how to deal with lawyers and slippery little government officials.

Well, we organized this benefit for March 1, 1971, and we held it in Freedom Hall in Louisville, which can hold over fifteen thousand people. We got more than forty performers from Nashville. Over forty radio stations carried it.

I went around for a month beforehand, publicizing the benefit. I'd talk about it during my show; then I'd fly to Hollywood or New York and go on a talk show just to plug my benefit. I'd try to get the hosts of these shows to talk seriously about the sad life of a miner. It ain't easy being serious on these talk shows, if the hosts just want to make fun of your language or hear hillbilly stories. But I think I got my message across anyway.

People say I did it for publicity or something. Well, let me tell you, friends, I spent over $10,000 out of my own pocket just flying around between dates. And another thing, this was at the time when I was starting to break up with the Wilburns, and my health was starting to go on me.

Finally the night came. The Greyhound bus brought the families up from Hyden. Colonel Sanders, the real Colonel Sanders—he's from Kentucky himself—gave out free dinners.

The show wasn't organized as well as it should have been, because of Doyle Wilburn not being in good shape. The widows were seated off to the side somewhere. During the early part of the show, they actually threatened to walk out if they weren't treated better. It was all a misunderstanding, but David Skepner, who was working for Music Corporation of America at the time, had to do some fast work to make everyone happy. There was a lot of tension, but Doolittle got the show done with a lot of good country music and speeches and appeals for donations.

We heard that money came in from as far away as Canada, Sweden, and the Bahamas. One joker in Macon, Georgia, fancied himself a big steel executive and pledged one million dollars. Before we could check it out, somebody announced it over the microphone, and everybody went crazy. They were all figuring out the good things they could buy with a million dollars. But later it turned out the guy was just being funny at our expense, and we tried to explain to the widows that it was just a bad joke.

We also thought we were getting things for free that we weren't—for example, we had to pay to rent the hall. Then we found out there were unpaid funeral bills, and the attorneys figured they'd better clear them up first. Everyone thought we had over a million dollars, but our expenses ran higher than I would have liked. A few people charged us expenses for every phone call they made for months; meanwhile, I was paying for my own airplane trips. Anyway, when all the bills were paid, we still had around $91,000.

This money was in a trust fund to go for education for the widows and their children. But about a week later, we heard that some of the widows wanted their share of the money right away. Well, I could understand that: they had bills to pay and kids to feed. But that wasn't what we gave that benefit for. We wanted to do something special. We held out and didn't give 'em the money, but the widows kept asking for it. They'd call up my office or make a statement to the press that Loretta Lynn was taking their money. I know how they felt; they didn't do it for meanness. It just tore me up. It was hard to believe they'd turn on me.

They kept after my lawyers until finally, in 1972, my

lawyer advised me to split it up. You're gonna be driven crazy, he told me. He said I'd have to put up with it for the rest of my life.

Only one of those children received any education from the money. We split the money into thirty-eight equal shares of around $2,400, and that was it. I don't know what they did with the money. Since then I've heard some of 'em remarried, which is good, because nobody should be alone; and I've heard some of them ran into trouble in their little towns. They got to be known as the "rich widows" because of the insurance and benefits.

Anyway, I tried to do something at Hyden and I'm sorry we didn't succeed. But if any of these people from Hyden read this book, I hope you'll know I was on your side. I never thought I was better than you; I just wish we could have *done* better.

# 24

# The Truth about My Health

The way I let you treat me,
It's enough to make me sick ...
—*"What Makes Me Tick," by Loretta Lynn*

The deal with the Hyden show broke my health because it came at the time of the separation from the Wilburns. My health got so bad there were all kinds of rumors going about me.

One of the rumors was I was drinking too much, another rumor was I was having a nervous breakdown, another that I had cancer, and another that I was taking some kind of pills or dope. That's a pretty exciting combination for a girl to have, ain't it? The truth ain't as exciting, but at least it's the truth, and this is where I set the story straight.

The breakup with the Wilburns caused me to lose my appetite. I couldn't eat or sleep right. I started to lose weight during 1971 and people said I looked different. The Johnson girls were so afraid of me losing my spunk that they'd say anything just to get me riled up. Loretta Johnson would just tease me until I started rassling with her. Then she'd laugh like a maniac, because I was getting back to the mean old country girl she knew. But in truth, I was getting worn down.

I remember one time at the Disc Jockey Convention in 1971, when I stayed up all night giving interviews until I couldn't sit up straight. Around midnight, I was supposed to go to a club to get some kind of award. But I was so tired, and then some guy I knew reminded me it was time to go, and I started yelling at him in words I'm not about to repeat. I didn't realize I knew those words. But this guy wasn't aware of how bad I was feeling, and he started shouting back at me. I kept getting louder and louder, saying those words over and over again. They tell me that everybody was staring at me—I hardly knew what was coming off.

Now, I don't know what you'd call this feeling. Some people would say I was "overwrought" or "overtired." Some people would say I was on the edge of a nervous breakdown. I don't know what it was, but it wasn't good. And I suspect my health was the cause of most of it.

With my periods, always irregular, I'd get such bad cramps that it would be difficult for me to perform for three or four days. The older I got, the worse they became.

I've also had migraine headaches since I was around seventeen, but they got even worse around this time. Some people believe migraines are caused by tensions in your job or in your marriage. But I feel like mine are just a family weakness. I remember my daddy had 'em. He'd pace the floor just holding his head and sobbing. Now it was starting to catch up with me. I could feel this ache coming on, and unless I'd lie down and sleep, it would turn into this headache that would make me just pass out. Then I started passing out onstage.

Now, friends, if you really want to try something

unusual, try passing out in front of five thousand people. Fortunately, the boys in my band have learned to tell when it's coming. They just take me by the elbow and help me sit until it passes, or else they help me off the stage. One time I was off the stage about forty-five minutes and when I came back, Don Ballinger and the boys had done such a good job playing and joking that nobody cared whether I came back or not.

But what bothered me was hearing some fans afterward. "She must have been drunk," some fans said.

I couldn't believe it. I hardly ever drink, and there's a good reason. Have you ever known an Indian who could drink? My daddy, who was part Indian, couldn't drink, either. Give him one sip and he'd be just about drunk. My mommy had some homemade brandy once and went right to sleep. It's just a curse we Indians have. The most I can take is a sloe gin fizz once in a while, and never near a performance. I don't even take coffee, much less alcohol. None of it's good for you. I feel sorry for people who drink.

But can you believe it? They thought I was drunk. Now when I don't feel good, I make an announcement that I've got a migraine, but there're still people who don't believe it.

When I feel a migraine coming on, I just go crazy. I start crying or talking or banging my head against the wall or I cut my hair. A few months ago I just cut and cut and couldn't get it right and I got madder and madder until I finally gave up. If I hadn't stopped, I would have been as bald as a rock.

These migraines kept getting worse. I passed out in Calgary, Alberta, in Canada. Then backstage I said, "Let me go back to the hotel so I can die in peace." The doctor said he had migraines himself and sent me to the hospital. He gave me a shot to make me stop vomiting (that's one of the sure signs of migraine—nausea always either comes with it or follows it). After lying there twenty-five minutes, I was fine, but as soon as I stood up the whole room started turning on me. I lay down again and stayed for three hours. They let me out of the hospital and gave me medicine, which helped for a while. But it got to be a regular problem.

When me and the Wilburns got into a lawsuit over me leaving them, I couldn't sleep, even at home. One time my right index finger was all swollen, and I went to see a doctor in Nashville. I keeled over, right in his office. The doctor said I should go to the hospital but I told him I had to go on the road. Doo figured if I had to go to a hospital, it might as well be at home, so they put me in the hospital in Nashville and fed me through my veins for a week. When I left, they gave me nerve pills, but they didn't do me much good. I ended up in another hospital soon afterward. The reporters, the patients, and the nurses managed to find me anyway, even though I used another name.

I got over being exhausted, but in 1972 I had a checkup, and they discovered a tumor in my right breast. Now, that is always a rough thing for a woman to face, knowing it could be cancer. With Betty Ford and Happy Rockefeller both having a breast removed, it's been in the news, and of course Shirley Temple Black was one of the first women to make a public statement about it. But there wasn't much discussion about it in 1972, so I didn't know much. I was just plain scared they might have to do that to me, so I kept postponing the operation until they finally made me go into Baptist Memorial Hospital under a false name.

I was really worried because I had never been baptized, and I was afraid of what would happen to me if I died. It didn't help when the doctor said, "When you have an operation, your chances are from zero to death. And let me tell you, your chances are not zero." I was terrified until they told me the tumor was not malignant. But they also told me that while I was on the operating table my heart stopped for a second. It was a real depressing time for me.

They did a little plastic surgery after taking out the tumor and told me to be careful. But I kept getting blood poisoning and was all blue and swollen from the waist up. One side of me looked like Dolly Parton—noted for her country singing *and* her figure—but only from the infection, I'm afraid. So I was back in the hospital again. They drained out all the infection—and found another tumor, which they removed. They absolutely forbade me to sign any autographs for months and ordered me never to play the guitar again because it irritated where I just had surgery. I had worked my way up playing the rhythm guitar when some of those poor old bands didn't know B from G. But I was so happy they didn't have to remove my breast I did what they told me. I haven't played the guitar since.

But I did go back on the road again, probably too soon. I remember one time when I had one of those tumors removed: I think I still had the stitches in me; plus, they had been giving me shots until my rear end was black and blue. I went back on the road and joined the band in Colorado somewhere. I guess I looked terrible—I thought the band was gonna cry. But I did my shows, which were probably some of the worst I've ever done. I could hardly stand up; every time I bent my knees the way I do, my guitar man would have to put his hand under my elbow to help straighten me up. It was real pitiful.

I kept waiting for the bad times to end but they didn't. They found another tumor and had to check it out.

I spent more time in the hospital in 1972 than I did at home: I was in nine times.

But the headaches kept going into 1973 and 1974. I went to a brain man—a neurologist, I believe the word is. He sent me to a gynecologist, as if that would help. Then last year, I found out I had high blood pressure. It's supposed to be around 120, but mine was close to 160. That really scared me. That's what led to my daddy's stroke—high blood pressure. The doctors told me it would help to lay off all salt, so now I carry a special salt substitute. These days my blood pressure stays near normal most of the time.

But even so, the doctors say migraine is caused by some kind of pressure, something you try to push out of your mind. I guess it's understandable why I'd be getting headaches in my business, where there's so much tension all the time.

People are always giving me advice on how to help the migraines. The doctor told me not to take any more sugar. Someone else said to try acupuncture. Somebody else said to try black coffee. Other people tell me to try painkillers. I've always felt that aspirin wasn't good for me—made me feel woozy. But when I'd start feeling nervous before a show, when the migraines were coming on, I'd take a certain brand of aspirin, prescribed by my doctor, to get rid of the headache. I would either carry some with me or borrow one from somebody. Sometimes the pills would make the headaches go away, but I'd start feeling dizzy, or I'd seem to be confused or sleepy. That's probably when the rumors started about me being on some kind of dope.

I certainly wasn't taking aspirin to get high; I just wanted my headaches to go away. To tell you the truth, I've always been scared of dope. If somebody ever had dope around me, I think I'd be scared to death. I guess there are people everywhere, in show business, too, who take stuff to get high. But I don't need that.

Anyway, we finally found out what the problem was—the hard way. It happened early in 1975, when me and Conway were supposed to make a record. Me and Doo checked into the King of the Road Motel on a Monday morning. I was just getting over the flu, and I felt all achy and tired. Conway was smarter—he had gotten flu shots right away, on the road.

I didn't eat after breakfast on Monday, and the flu was still bothering me, so I took an aspirin. That night Doo said he was going out to get us some Chinese food, which we both love. But he didn't come back for a long, long while.

I found out later he was out partying with Faron Young.

I was still feeling bad, and worrying where Doolittle was, so I took another aspirin. Then I waited a couple of hours and took another one. When he finally came in around four o'clock in the morning, I was so mad and so nervous—I hadn't slept all night.

Tuesday morning I went to the doctor for a double shot for the flu and I finally got something to eat— a bowl of oats. But I still felt bad, so I took two more aspirins because I knew we had to go out and record. Altogether, I think I had taken nine pills in twenty-seven hours, which isn't *too* bad—unless you're allergic to 'em.

Anyway, as soon as I got into the motel room, I just passed out. Doo thought I was fooling around, but when he saw me hit the floor, he knew it was bad. I started going into convulsions, just rolling around on the floor. He called for the ambulance, and they carried me out of the motel on a stretcher. When I woke up, I was in the hospital.

They fed me through tubes and ran all kinds of tests on me. Finally my doctor came in and said, "The next time you feel like taking an aspirin, you might just as well take arsenic, because this brand of aspirin is just like poison to your system." So I was allergic to 'em and didn't know it. They kept me in the hospital until Friday, when I got back on the bus to hit the road. We did a bad show that night, but at least I showed up. I figured, if I'm gonna die, it might as well be on the stage.

I knew I had to get back to the show, because Doo hates for me to cancel out. He gets real nervous whenever I'm sick anyway. I once heard him say, "If there's one thing I can't stand, it's a sick woman." Well, maybe this woman won't be sick anymore.

I've learned my lesson. Now if I feel nervous, I just think happy thoughts or lie down. I feel 100 percent better now that I'm off aspirins. I can see how woozy it made me. Friends tell me I'm more clearheaded now than I've been in years.

I'm learning how to take care of myself. I used to waste away to under a hundred pounds during the year. But now the doctors have told me to keep eating. They say I have to eat a banana a day because my body doesn't produce enough potassium.

Also in 1974, my doctor prescribed water pills for my migraines. I take 'em for a week before my period, and they seem to take away most of the pressure in my system. Since October of 1974, I only had three migraines— that's more than a year. Before that, I was having 'em every three weeks, so maybe I'm starting to get answers to my problems.

I've really got to take it easy, though. I'm taking off the last ten days of every month. I've started sleeping better, not going outside the room except to perform. But it seems life is getting wound up into just performing and traveling and resting. I don't have the time or the energy I used to years ago. I think back on the busy, capable housewife I was when I was poor, and I ask myself, "Is it worth the price?" I'm not really sure.

# 25

# Mexico

There's wild red blood running through my
veins,
And I wish my skin was, too...
 —*"Red, White and Blue," by Loretta Lynn*

The real thing that saved my life this past couple of
years was buying a house in Mexico. Now, you ask,
what's a country girl from Kentucky doing with a house
in Mexico? But I'll tell you, I need to get completely away
from things. I think that's where I'll go when I retire.

We found this place a few years ago when me and
Doo took a vacation in a big camper. Now, that ain't
exactly my idea of a good vacation, not after being on
the road in a bus all year. But Doo, he was itching to
go someplace warm and do some fishing and just poke
around the way we used to do. I could understand that,
so I went along, just dreading more time with the wheels
turning under me. But it wasn't bad.

We headed down to the west coast of Mexico, around
Mazatlán, a big city, a beautiful city. We headed down
the coast some more—I'm not telling where—till we

found this little village, right on the ocean. The people there were part Indian, so I felt real comfortable with 'em, even though I couldn't speak Spanish and they couldn't speak much English. I think you can always get along with your hands and the way you smile and stuff. The people there were beautiful. Then we met this old fellow who looked like my granddaddy—a real dignified, smart Indian. He was a fishing guide and he collected old Indian pottery. He gave me some, wouldn't let me pay a penny for it. Then he showed us all around the countryside. All of a sudden we saw this piece of beachfront property for sale. I told Doo, "That's where I'd like to build a house, right there." Now, Doo liked it himself. So we talked business with the man and we made a deal. We leased it for around forty years, with the option for another forty. (The Mexican government doesn't allow Americans to buy as much land as they used to.) But we felt we could go ahead and build a house on the property, and we finished it by the end of 1972.

Now we've got this house with every room facing the ocean and a big swimming pool with a separate little house called a ramada. We go down there at Christmastime and stay. The first winter we stayed a month. The next year we stayed six weeks. I think this year I'd like to stay for three months. And if I could, I'd never leave.

Every day is just perfect. We get up and don't bother to dress fancy. Nobody knows who we are and nobody cares. We go down to the ocean and just play in the water. I've got some Mexican women who come in to help me. I tease 'em, and we try to rassle each other into the water. We laugh and argue like a bunch of idiots, but they do more work for me than anyone I could get in the States. We're just like a family. They know I'm no better than they are, just another Indian.

One time we were on the beach and there was one

Mooney Lynn
Custer Wash

VIA AIR MAIL
Special Delivery.

Clara Webb
33 E Water St
Wabash, Ind.

Custer Wash
4-24-60

Dear Clara
as you probly know
by now Loretta is on
tour she will stop on
see you sometime this
week so would you please
give her this letter for
me. We are all well
here hope this note find you
all the same
that afout all I have
the heart to write as
I miss Loretta so much

Your Son
Doo

My husband never was big on writing letters. When I was on the road promoting "Honky Tonk Girl," Doo stayed back in Custer with the kids. He sent this to me at Momma's. He didn't know how else to get it to me.

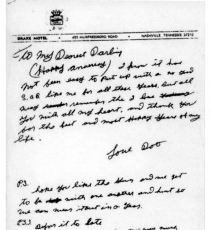

DRAKE MOTEL • 420 MURFREESBORO ROAD • NASHVILLE TENNESSEE 37210

*To My Dearest Darling*
*(Happy anniversary) I know it has not been easy to put up with a no good S.O.B. like me for all these years. But all I want you to remember the I love you with all my heart, and thank you for the best and most Happy years of my life.*

*Love Doo*

*P.S. hope you like the thing and we get to be with one another and hunt so we can mess about in a year.*

*P.S.S. before it to late*
*love you very much,*
*Doo*

Doo could be a real sweetheart when he wanted to be. He gave me this love note on our anniversary. When he died in 1996, I didn't know if I could go on. But I did.

I treasure this handmade card Doo made for me one Valentine's Day. He didn't much remember anniversaries and birthdays and such early on, but he got the hang of it.

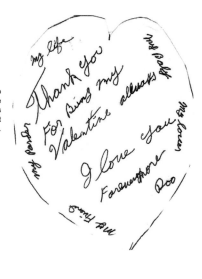

Conway and me were best friends and partners. He was real shy, which made him so fun to tease. He'd get me back by teasing me about my crush on Gregory Peck. He and David Skepner gave me this framed picture of Mr. Peck in 1971. A few years later I got to meet the man himself!

Tour buses weren't around when I got into the music business. We all packed into one car like a bunch of sardines. When I got my first tour bus, I was so happy! We put about a billion miles on that thing. I'm as comfortable sleeping in the back of my bus as I am just about anywhere on God's green earth.

I never was much of an office person. This was me messing around in 1968. I have my desk set up in my "writing room"— the laundry room at our house.

Being out on the road, I'd dream about getting home to my kitchen that Doo renovated in the house at Hurricane Mills. Crisco made me their spokesperson in 1979 and we filmed a lot of the Crisco commercials right there in that kitchen over the next decade.

Those who serve our country in the military are some of the finest folks in the world. I try to perform for them whenever I can. This picture was taken in 1976. I was real proud that they gave me this American flag.

We had too much fun at my birthday party in April 2019. They called it the All-Star Birthday Celebration Concert in Nashville's Bridgestone Arena. At the end, all the performers and me sang "Coal Miner's Daughter" together. There's no way we could have got all those people in one photo, so this will have to do. This shows me with my son Ernest, Tanya Tucker, Martina McBride, and my sister Crystal Gayle. Behind us you can see just a little bit of Darius Rucker, Alan Jackson, and Dennis Quaid. My wish came true that night when Keith Urban popped out of a huge birthday cake and sang "Happy Birthday" to me. I loved it so much that I asked them to bring me that cake. Now I have it in my museum in Hurricane Mills.

This is me and Doo in Branson, Missouri. At first we were happy. Then things got tough and he got so sick.

Me and Conway were a great team. I loved him so much. I still miss him every day.

The Honky Tonk Angels: me, Dolly Parton, and Tammy Wynette. Our album was released in 1993 and we sang "Silver Threads and Golden Needles" at the Country Music Awards that year.

Tim Cobb designed so many of my gorgeous gowns over the years. He made this one for me to wear on the *Van Lear Rose* album cover. I liked it so much I had him make me a pink version too. This picture was taken at the old house in East Nashville where we recorded that whole album.

Photo credit: Russ Harrington

I wore the pink dress for the "Portland, Oregon" music video with Jack White. We filmed in an old honky tonk in Memphis, Tennessee.

Photo credit: Russ Harrington

American guy in the waves and another on the beach. I said, "You sure got your britches wet." He said to his friend: "If this wasn't Mexico, I'd swear that was Loretta Lynn."

But the people don't care who I am. And my fans don't know where I am. It's the one place I can go to relax. So I ain't gonna tell nobody where it is.

We bring the babies down with us. They think they're getting a good deal by getting out of school. But Gloria, our housekeeper, comes down with 'em. She finds out all their work from their teacher and she makes 'em work every morning. They fight with her like mad. They come to me and I tell them to get back to Gloria before I whip 'em. So I make sure they get their work done.

I guess one of the things I like best about Mexico is the people. The Spanish and the Indians, they show their affections. I think it's bad when you can't. When a man says to his boy, "You shouldn't hug; you should be a man," I think it's a shame. Ever since Daddy died, I made it a point to show my feelings because I don't think I ever let Daddy know how much I loved him. Daddy was never able to see me as a performer, and he didn't have nothing. I wish I could have given him more. I was always able to show my affections but not as much until Daddy died. I guess that's why people follow me from show to show. Love is like a magnet.

We have a boat down there. Doo likes to go out and go real fast, but like I said before, I'm scared of the water and always have been. I believe I must have drowned in one of my earlier lives, and since I almost drowned in Tennessee, I've been real scared of water. Doo tells me I'm no fun because I won't let him go fast, but we do have a good time. We fish and eat all day long.

That's another reason Mexico is good for me. After my 1973 tour, I was down to about ninety pounds. It was disgraceful. I was wearing size-three dresses. None of my regular clothes fit. I was ashamed to let people see my arms and legs, I was so skinny. We got down to Mexico right after Christmas, and I could see Doo was worried about me. I was nervous, tense, underweight, and worried.

Doo, who is supposed to be this tough guy, was watching me to make sure I'd be all right. Well, the first morning we were there, I ate a huge breakfast of eggs, bacon, biscuits, and potatoes and whatever else there was. Then we went out to the beach. Around ten o'clock, I started dipping into the lunch basket, eating sandwiches and cookies and anything that was packed. By lunchtime I'd eaten somebody else's food. Then I ate a big supper, and in the evening I'd eat another snack. I'd just eat like a pig all day.

Well, I gained about one pound a day for almost a month. Doo said I was like a flower opening up. He said he could see the color coming back day by day. And it was true. I stayed a month more and canceled an appearance. When we had to go back to work again, I weighed 115 pounds. I was back up to a size five or seven again, and I didn't look like a ghost. The only time I felt sick was when I thought about going back. I'm telling you, I was born to be a housewife, not a singer.

During the work year, Doo is always pestering me to eat. Whenever I get nervous about some little problem, I just think about Mexico. I can't wait to get back there. I just let my hair hang long and stringy and don't care how I look. And that's the way I like it. I'm telling you, someday they're gonna be looking for me backstage and I ain't gonna be there. But I'm gonna pin up a note and it's gonna say, "*Buenas Noches.*"

# 26

# Entertainer of the Year

Why me, Lord, what have I ever done
To deserve even one of the pleasures I've
known? ...
      —*"Why Me?," by Kris Kristofferson*

Going out on my own was the best thing I ever could have done. I hate to put it in terms of money, but how else do you measure your value? When I left the Wilburns, I was getting around $2,500 to $3,000 per show. Now I get around $10,000 a show. I don't think I've improved that much as a performer, so it must be the people who are managing my business.

Doolittle has taken more interest in the management; plus, we've hired real professionals to do the work. Me and Conway Twitty have our own booking agency called United Talent. Jimmy Jay books us the best schedules in country music.

I've also got an office on Music Row, where Lorene Allen is the manager. She keeps me posted on all the news and writes some of my songs.

And I've gotten a lot of nice publicity since we started

working with a smart fellow named David Brokaw out in California. I always look forward to my trips to California to talk to him.

We've also got some interest in the Loretta Lynn clothing stores. We used to have a rodeo for ten years, but we got too busy and had to sell it. I know it broke Doo's heart—but now he's got the dude ranch on our property, with room for around 180 trailers. So that's keeping him busy.

I don't know if we really should have all these side businesses. Instead of just doing my own show, I'm worrying about whether it's raining on our dude ranch, or whether Kenny Starr, the young boy who sings in our show, will have a hit record. Plus, all my companies have given us a payroll of over $350,000 a year.

There've been times in the past when I took on extra dates just to pump money into one of our businesses. I used to play over 200 dates a year. Now I've cut it back to 125, mainly because my money is being handled better.

Things have been more organized since we hired David Skepner away from the Music Corporation of America. David is a college graduate from Beverly Hills, California, who's our business advisor. His job is to advise me and Doolittle what our choices are—and we make the decisions. Sometimes people get upset when he protects me from too much attention. I'll tease him by saying, "I know what people are saying—'There comes Loretta Lynn and her SOB.'"

David has cured me of carrying too much cash around with me. One time in New York City, I had $30,000 in cash in my pocketbook. I thought David would explode. He asked a policeman to escort us to the nearest bank, where we could convert the money into cashier's checks. David once told a reporter, "Loretta has no idea what she's worth. All she knows is that she has a good time every day and she gets well paid for it."

Well, I'm getting a little smarter than that. David has given me a lot more confidence about appearing on television. He's been able to book me on all the major shows and he always tells me, "Loretta, just act natural. Say whatever you think is right, and the people will accept it."

And that's what I've been doing, folks. I'll never forget the time I fell asleep on *The David Frost Show* while the queen of women's liberation was talking. It happened like this: I was back in the dressing room and this gal started cussing and arguing something terrible with a guy from a union. I didn't know this woman from Adam. She was running on about women's rights. I said something like, "Isn't it awful what you have to put up with in your own dressing room?" and she smarted off at me, and we were really going at it. Then I get on the show and they march her out—and I said, "Oh my God, it's *her*." It was that Betty Friedan. Anyhow, she starts talking about women's liberation. If I'm not interested in what somebody is saying, I let my mind wander. I must have closed my eyes for a few seconds because all of a sudden I hear David Frost say to me, "What do you think of that, Loretta?"

I guess I jumped a little bit and I said, "What?" like I was real startled. That made everyone in the audience laugh, but I didn't mean to be smart about it. I just wasn't listening, that's all.

Dinah Shore had me on her show. She's from Tennessee, and we always talk about biscuits and stuff. She's got the kind of show where if I mess up, we just laugh and go ahead with it. To me, that's what country is, too. And that's my idea of television.

I don't think television has country down right yet.

They've had me on variety shows, but there's always some guy from Los Angeles or New York running around behind those sunglasses telling us just where to stand. What you see on television is a bunch of poor old country boys and girls hunching up their shoulders and looking like they wished they were never born. Now, that's not country. I say, let us out there with our own bands, not those television bands with their saxophones and clarinets. If you just put me in front of that camera, I'd say, "Let 'er rip, Flip!" And we'd give 'em a good show. But television's not ready for us yet to be ourselves.

I'm still unhappy because we didn't get a national television show. They had me and George Lindsey— Goober—on the *Orange Blossom Special USA* on Thursday, November 15, 1973, right after *The Waltons*. They were going to see if I could be the first female country singer to have her own national show.

I've always said that if you want to be a success, you have to be yourself. Sure, you need writers, but you've got to take what they give you and turn it into *you*. I do my own shows, where I ain't afraid of saying what I think. But when I get on television, they're always passing those cards at you with those big words. Yes, I admit I have trouble reading those big words, but when I did that show, I was just myself. We just didn't get enough rating points to get the show. But you can't argue with them. I figure it will come up again sometime.

After I did the benefit for Hyden, I got a letter from then president Nixon. I thought that was nice of him. I thought about writing back to him to ask why they put Kelly in jail. I meant Lieutenant William Calley, the guy they convicted in the massacres of My Lai. I thought his name was Kelly. I don't know too much about it but it seemed strange they should pin everything on one little lieutenant. Maybe he did wrong, but there were a lot of other people who should have known better, too. Either everybody who was guilty should be put in jail or nobody should be put in jail.

Anyway, before I got a chance to write, I got invited to Washington myself, for a dinner. I mean, not just me, but around a thousand people who worked for the United Way in the United States and Canada. They were honoring Mrs. Nixon for her work in the charity. I made a commercial that raised enough money to put up a new building, so I got invited. Well, I figured as long as I was going to be singing there, I might as well speak my piece. When I got on the stage, I said, "Pat, I've been wanting to write a letter to tell Richard to let Kelly go. We brought Kelly home from Vietnam and put him in jail. Why don't we stop picking on just that one little man or else let him go?"

I could tell that shook some people up. But I didn't have time to think about it because I had to sing my song. I didn't think anything of it until I saw it the next day on the front page of the *Washington Post*. They acted like I did something bad calling her husband Richard.

The next day we flew to Chicago for a show, and this television announcer met me at the airport. He asked me why I addressed the president of the United States as "Richard." I said, "They called Jesus 'Jesus,' didn't they?" That guy took one look at me and started running. I never learned his name or I might have called him by his first name, too.

It seems funny that anyone would mind what I was saying. That's why I appreciate my fans; they accept me for being myself. The only bad publicity I've ever gotten was in my home state when some people said I should pay for paving the road up to Butcher Holler. But mostly I get good stories because I tell the truth. Whenever I get involved in anything, I get in touch with a columnist in

Nashville named Red O'Donnell. I call him up and tell him exactly what it's all about. I trust him to get the true facts out, whatever they are.

Since I struck out on my own, lots of different things have happened to me. Why, I was even in *Penthouse* magazine with all those naked women. I didn't know what kind of magazine it was. This reporter came in and said he was gonna do a story on me. Well, that was just fine with me.

Then one day we were sitting in the airport and I wandered over to see if they had the magazine. I took one look at the cover, and boy, was I shocked! I didn't know it was that kind of magazine. I wanted to see it but I was too bashful to buy it from the lady. So I got my bus driver, Jim Webb, to buy it. I was afraid maybe they caught me in some picture without my clothes on, except I'm so skinny they'd be out of luck. As far as I know, there's only one set of nude pictures of me in the world. They were taken by Doolittle when I was around sixteen. He had converted one of our rooms into a dark-room, and he got me to pose for him. We've talked about burning 'em, but we decided to keep 'em under lock and key. We take 'em out once in a while, just for a laugh. But *Penthouse* didn't get ahold of them, and their story was pretty nice.

By now, my career was really rolling along. I had little singing parts in four movies—*Forty Acre Feud*, *Music City U.S.A.*, *Nashville Rebel*, and *The Nashville Sound*— and I was the first woman country artist to receive a gold album for one million sales—for "Don't Come Home A-Drinkin' (with Lovin' on Your Mind)," which I wrote with my sister.

But I don't always write all my songs. Sometimes we get songs from fellows like Shel Silverstein. Now, he isn't what I'd call country. He's bald and he's got a beard and from what I hear he spends a lot of time at *Playboy* king Hugh Hefner's houses in Chicago and Los Angeles. Plus, he's got himself a houseboat out in Sausalito, California. But he knows how to write country songs. Johnny Cash's "A Boy Named Sue" is one of Shel's songs, and he wrote "One's on the Way." I recorded that one, and it turned out to be a smash. Shel also wrote "Hey, Loretta," which I didn't like because I don't care for songs about myself. He heard that I wasn't going to do it and flew in from Alaska. We finally put it on an album, but the disc jockeys demanded that we also make it a single. I got to like it—especially when it got to be number one.

But people got to know me best after I wrote my life story on that song "Coal Miner's Daughter." That really made me familiar to people—it gave me a title they could remember. And it told everybody that I could write about something else besides marriage problems.

I'm proud that other writers like that song. I'd always wanted to write a song about growing up, but I never believed anybody would care about it. One day I was sitting around the television studio at WSIX, waiting to rehearse a show. I figured this was a good time to work on a song. I went off to the dressing room and just wrote the first words that came into my head.

It started, "Well, I was borned a coal miner's daughter..." which was nothing but the truth. And I went on from there. I made up the melody at the same time, line by line, like I always do. It started out as a bluegrass thing, 'cause that's the way I was raised, with the guitar and the banjo just following along. Really, the way you hear it on the record is the way I imagined it.

I had a little trouble with the rhymes. I had to match up words like "holler" and "daughter" and "water." But after it was all done, the rhymes weren't so important.

In a couple of hours, I had nine of the best verses I

ever wrote. The next time I had a recording session, I did that song. But you know what? We kept it in the can for a year. I didn't believe anybody would buy a song just about me.

When they finally released it and had to cut three verses, like I said before, it just about broke my heart. One verse was about Mommy papering the walls with magazines, right above my head, with pictures of movie stars and such. Another was how the creek would rise every time it rained, and Daddy would have to cut logs across, so we could get downhill. The third was about hog-killing day in December, so we'd have fresh meat for Christmas. I can remember Mommy yelling, "back-bones and ribs," while Daddy was a-scraping the hair off the hog.

Well, they released that record around the start of 1971, and three weeks later somebody called up to say it was a smash. I said, "Ahhhh, come on," because I never believed it. But they made an album called *Coal Miner's Daughter* and it made me so popular it led to the biggest award of my life.

Everyone knows about the Oscars for the movies and the Emmys for television. Well, country music has its own awards. They give 'em out every October in Nashville, on national television, on the same week as the Grand Ole Opry's birthday. That's the week they have the big Disc Jockey Convention, when all those boys from around the country flock to Nashville to listen to all the musicians. It's all sponsored by the Country Music Association, which is a big collection of publishers, promoters, record companies, disc jockeys, writers—everybody in country music, really. Everybody has one vote and they go for the top singers, the top songs, the best duet of the year. But the biggest award of all is Entertainer of the Year.

The Entertainer of the Year Award goes to the performer who puts on the best shows on tour and on television, plus putting out good records. It's the best, really. For the first five years that award went to the men—Eddy Arnold, Glen Campbell, Johnny Cash, Merle Haggard, and Charley Pride—which was all right with me.

The way I see it, the men travel with bands and they put on a complete show. They have good women singers with 'em, plus extra male singers, plus maybe a comic or a musical act. But they are the stars. They get right out there and tell stories and run the whole show. But the women, the way it always was, just sing their songs and act more ladylike.

Now that's changing. You've got a lot of us with our own bands and leading our own shows. I give around two hours of a show every time I put my name on the program. I'll dance and tell jokes and let my boys play their instruments. And we give an extra-good show whenever I have Ernest Tubb, Cal Smith, or Conway Twitty on with me. So I feel like I'm an entertainer, just like the men.

Well, in 1972, I got nominated for Entertainer of the Year. I didn't care if I won it. I was just proud to be the first woman ever nominated. We always schedule ourselves into Nashville for that DJ convention, but this year it was especially important, because I wanted to be there for the awards. When we looked at our calendar, though, Doo realized he'd arranged to take a bunch of his friends out to Colorado to go hunting. Doo said he would cancel but I said, "Go ahead and go hunting," because I knew he'd rather be out in the woods than sitting indoors. I felt bad that he wasn't going to be there, but I understand what he needs to do.

When the night came, we put on our shiny outfits and went over to the old Ryman Auditorium. I was with

David Skepner, and we stood around backstage just hoping I'd win one of the other awards. That's some sight, all of us country bumpkins in our velvet and sequins and tuxedos, with the diamonds sparkling. I can remember when we were all wearing dungarees, with a little fringe on it—if we were fancy.

I was wearing a long green gown, which I had just bought. Since then, I stopped buying gowns in Nashville because I got tired of going to some big ceremony and seeing one of the other girls in the same exact dress. That happened once to me and Dottie West and it wasn't funny. Now, if I make it myself, it may look homemade, but at least it's not gonna look like anything else—you can bet on that.

Then they started giving out awards. First they gave me and Conway the award for Vocal Duo of the Year. Then they named me Female Vocalist of the Year, which I was pleased about. I won it the first year the award was presented, and Tammy Wynette won it three times after that, followed by Lynn Anderson. So I was glad to get it back.

They saved the biggest award for the end of the show, with Chet Atkins and Minnie Pearl presenting the Entertainer of the Year. When I heard 'em call out my name, I thought I was gonna flip. I was somewhere else the rest of the evening. I just kept saying, "I can't believe it; I can't believe it." People kept telling me they were glad I won.

I kept waiting for Doo to call that night, but he was out in this little tavern in Colorado, listening to the news on television. When they announced I won, he got so excited that he bought a round for everybody. Then he said he couldn't reach me on the telephone because a big bolt of lightning hit the wires.

People tried to make a big thing about Doo not being

there. I just made a joke about it by telling 'em, "Doo's out hunting—but I don't know what he's hunting." That's how I handle things usually, by making a joke out of it.

The next day, Doo got on a plane to Nashville. I was about worn out from being on the *TODAY* show before dawn. I was glad to see him, especially when he told me how proud he was. That's still the biggest award I can get.

I remember people asking me if I thought the women's liberation spirit had anything to do with my getting it. I told LaWayne Satterfield of *Music City News*, "You know better than that. The people did it and they didn't pick the best man or the best woman—they just picked the one they thought was the best. That's why I'm so proud."

But I will say this: I think it's good for people to realize that women can do things as good as a man. And I think show business is one of the places where that's true.

There're more women stars in Nashville all the time. They've got their own shows and their own buses, and they're proving they can do the job the same as a man. I get along with all the women singers, but especially Dolly Parton, who was voted Female Vocalist of the Year in 1975. We're good friends because we talk the same hillbilly language. Dolly is from Tennessee, and when we get going, nobody can understand us.

I love Dolly, and I understand why she wears all that fancy jewelry and makeup and piles her hair up the way she does. She once told me she was poor when she was a kid and now that she can afford pretty things, she said, "I'm gonna pile it all over me." And I say good for her.

Me and Dolly like to talk about the old days when we were poor. We can remember how the snow and rain used to blow through the cracks. One time Dolly asked me, "Remember when you had company coming, how you'd shoo the flies out the door with a towel, then slam the door real fast?" That's what it was like in those old cabins.

But whenever we talk like that around the new Opry, I get the feeling people are nervous. Hillbillies are going out of fashion in Nashville, I think.

I had some other wonderful honors following the Entertainer of the Year Award. I was named one of Tennessee's top five women, along with women in college and medicine and government and business. In the Gallup poll in 1973, I was listed as an honorable mention, after the world's ten most admired women. Golda Meir of Israel was first, so you could say I was in pretty good company.

I've won other big awards in music since then, too. In 1973, I got the Female Vocalist of the Year Award again, which gave some of my fans the idea that I owned the award. Well, friends, nobody owns nothing in this world. Even your breath is just loaned to you. There're a lot of good country singers around, and nothing goes on forever.

That was my feeling in 1974, when they moved the awards show over to the new Opry and Johnny Cash was the master of ceremonies. I was nominated for Female Vocalist of the Year and Entertainer of the Year. Sure, I wanted to win 'em, but I was so tired of working I would rather have been on the beach in Mexico.

I knew it wasn't going to be easy for me to win in 1974 because my own record company, MCA—it changed its name from Decca—had two women up for the same awards: myself and Olivia Newton-John. She's an English girl who grew up in Australia and never appeared in Nashville. But she had three hit records in 1974, and a lot of people were saying she was gonna win something.

Some of my fans were upset because they said she wasn't country. But her records had kind of a country sound to 'em, and they also sold big on the "pop" charts. I know MCA was glad to have her. It's like a restaurant. Some people like steak, some people like lobster, so you sell both. And if you got something new on the menu, you advertise it a little extra.

That didn't bother me any, but a couple of female singers were sitting around the dressing room on the night of the awards, griping 'cause Olivia Newton-John didn't even come to America for the awards. She was on tour in Spain somewhere. Well, all I could remember was me winning the top female singer's award in England four years in a row and how nice people were to me there. So I told the girls to cut it out. I hate to hear all that jealousy coming out.

Anyway, Olivia Newton-John did win the Top Female Vocalist Award. I don't think the applause was very big, and some of the Nashville people were still grumbling backstage.

Later they even organized something they called the Association of Country Entertainers to make sure country musicians get their fair share of awards. But I stayed neutral. I don't want to get involved in politics and jealousy. Besides, I never heard people complaining when Lynn Anderson's record "Rose Garden" crossed over into popular music sales, or when Tammy Wynette crossed over with "Stand by Your Man," or when Johnny Cash had a big record with "A Boy Named Sue."

See, it's like a double standard. If they were from Nashville, it was all right to win pop awards. But because Olivia Newton-John wasn't from Nashville, they didn't like her winning our awards. Well, I know that a lot of country fans—some of 'em my fans—have bought Olivia Newton-John's records, so she must have something going for her. I've got no complaints. Look, she walked off with the Grammy Award for 1974 pop music. When you're hot, you're hot—that's all.

Anyway, me and Conway did get the award for top country duo from the Country Music Association. And later I won the top female singer and top duet from the Academy of Country Music.

Besides, two nights later, I won the *Music City News* award for top female vocalist, and the fans vote in that one—not the big shots. They gave me that award at the United Talent show at midnight, at the Opry, and all the disc jockeys stood up and cheered. Conway got up onstage and said, "Who's this Oliver Newton-June anyhow?" I got so embarrassed I almost fell through the floor. I gave Conway a dirty look that said, "No more of that." But he was being funny—he likes Olivia, he told me.

I can remember Patsy Cline and Kitty Wells standing up for me when I came along. So Olivia Newton-John, when you come to Nashville, you give me a call, and I'll help you any way I can. There's room for all of us, honey.

# 27

## Death Threats

We all know what our enemies will do...
— *"Five Fingers Left," by Loretta Lynn*

There's another part of my career I ain't too happy about, and that is all the bad mail and telephone calls I get. It first hit a few years ago when I started winning all the awards. Then it seemed like every crazy person in the world was after me.

We're supposed to have this unlisted telephone number at home, but sometimes my fans get it anyway. I don't mind their calls too much. But when some nut calls up and says to leave $250,000 downtown, or else they'll cut off my son's head, now that's just plain bad manners, folks.

Or one of my babies would pick up the phone and there'd be some character on the other end saying something she couldn't understand. When those things started getting worse, we changed our number again, but people catch up with you.

I once asked my manager why I got this kind of stuff. He said other performers also get bad calls and he explained: "The same thing that makes you appeal to all the good fans also touches off some spark in the screwball. There's a few public figures who manage to stir up a lot of people, one way or the other, Loretta—and you just happen to be one of them."

That scares me, because I think of people like John and Robert Kennedy and George Wallace and Martin Luther King Jr., who get people stirred up. And all that stuff going on in Israel with the Arabs hijacking and scaring people to death. At the same time there was so much violence in the world, I had a whole rash of scary incidents.

There was one man who had robbed a couple of my western stores and then started traveling wherever we went. He would check into the same motel every night. At first, I didn't think nothing of it. I'd be sitting in the room with the shades open and I'd see this young boy with long golden hair. I said to Doo, "Now, he's a good fan." But it turns out the police were looking for him. And the police were traveling around with me, too, only I didn't know it.

One night in West Virginia, that fellow got a girl to come to me and say she wanted to show me some new songs. She seemed like she was drunk or on drugs or something. She no more than got into the room when the police busted in. They dragged her right out; they showed her no mercy. That night I was told that I was in danger; then three days later they caught him. I said I didn't want to hear nothing about it. He's in the pen now—I don't know where.

That's when I started to get nervous about these calls. One time I was on the road and a woman friend was traveling with me. I was taking a bath when I got a call and this man said he was five doors down from me. I didn't pay it any mind. I just hung up. But my friend got all riled and I had to calm her down. I was really scared even though I said I wasn't.

Just to calm her down, I said, "Well, I ain't afraid to go out in the hall." So I get dressed and open the door and there's this man standing there. I stared at him and tried to act brave, but all of a sudden my knees got weak and I jumped back in the room and closed the door. Who knows what he had in mind?

One night in Beckley, West Virginia, I was all alone in my room in my bus getting dressed for my show, when I looked out in the parking lot and saw this young kid. I could swear he was loading or unloading a pistol. I got scared to death. I didn't know what to do. Then he disappeared somewhere. The next thing I knew, I heard the bus door open. I had my room closed, so I couldn't see who it was, but I got scared that it was the boy with the pistol. Usually, when something goes wrong, I do the right thing, so I talked loud, like my husband was with me. I said, "Hey, Doo, turn down that television; I think I hear somebody on the bus." Well, I could hear the bus rocking as this guy walks outside. I never did see him again, but I was scared. I told my boys never to leave me alone on the bus again. So now there's always someone guarding me.

And I mean guarding me right. More than one of my people carries a pistol. Some people get all scared about being around pistols, but it doesn't bother me. Growing up in Kentucky, I got used to it. Doo carries a pistol around like I carry a pocketbook. It ain't that you're trying to be tough or anything; you're just trying to protect yourself. And we feel we need to. Doo even offered to get me a pistol, but I'm too softhearted, and I know my boys will protect me.

The worst place for a while was Oklahoma. Every time we went through, there was something. One time the newspapers got a call that was supposed to be my sister, Crystal Gayle, saying I was kidnapped. Well, that couldn't happen because she wasn't even on the trip. But the FBI had to check it out anyway. Another time there was a call saying I drowned in Mexico. Still another time, somebody said I would never get off the stage in Oklahoma City. The FBI got into that, too.

They checked everybody out, even my old man, Doo, who's got a permit to carry his pistol. But we got real tight with our plans. They took me off the bus outside of Oklahoma and sneaked me into another hotel, while the bus went to our regular place. But it didn't matter: we got to our room, and five minutes later some guy called on the hotel phone and said, "We found out where you are." Doo was standing by the door with his .38 out all night. The call had to come from the hotel because they won't let outside calls go to my room. I don't know how in the world they found me, but they did. We told the FBI, and they were all around me when I went to the show that night. I still get the shivers whenever we go to Oklahoma.

But it's not just Oklahoma. We got a bomb threat during the Disc Jockey Convention in Nashville one year. Somebody said the show was never gonna go on because they blamed me for breaking up Conway Twitty's marriage. Well, I didn't know about it until I got backstage. They cleared out the place and didn't find a bomb so they let the show go on. I was the last one to sing, and I said I was nervous. The stagehand said, "Don't get nervous, Loretta. Every other man backstage is an FBI agent." And when I looked, they all had their guns bulging inside their jackets. How I got through that show I'll never know.

The last scare we got was in a motel. I was in my suite working on some songs when I got a call. This man said he was a hired killer, paid five hundred dollars to knock me off. He said he had been following me for three days and that he wasn't gonna do it because he thought I was such a fantastic singer.

Finally the guy said, "I'm gonna tell them that I just couldn't get close to you. But you better be careful, because the next guy they send might not be a big country fan like me."

Well, I was half-scared and half-laughing at that line. I think the guy was putting on an act and just wanted attention, but I make it a point never to be alone.

When Doo ain't with me, I register in different names now. And I always have my boys in rooms all around me. I always keep my door locked, and my calls and fan mail are screened. I only see the good letters; the others are sent to the FBI. They're building up a file on these little deals. I also get connecting rooms with Jim Webb, my driver, or David Skepner, or any of the boys. And we keep these doors unlocked, so if I need help, they can just rush in. I feel better knowing that my boys are around me.

But for two whole years, I went onstage scared. I didn't know what was gonna happen, if someone was gonna put a bullet in me, or what. Every time somebody took a flashbulb picture of me, I had no way of knowing whether it was the end. I got more and more nervous and started talking about getting off the tour completely. But when I asked my manager, he said, "Loretta, you have two choices. You can find some place out in Montana somewhere, and you can dig a big hole, and you can hide and never perform again. Or you can just go out there and not think about it."

So that's what I did. I made up my mind not to worry about threats anymore. I just go out and sing.

# 28

# Baptized at Last

I believe above the storm the smallest prayer
Will still be heard.
I believe that Someone in the Great Somewhere
Hears every word...
     —*"I Believe," by Ervin Drake, Irvin Graham,*
        *Jimmy Shirl, and Al Stillman*

I don't know if I could have lived through the sickness and the death threats if I hadn't gotten stronger in my religion. When things were looking bad for me, I just put myself in the hands of Jesus and let Him do what was best for me.

I've always been religious in my own way. When I was growing up, if we could afford just one book in the house, it was the Bible. We'd go to church on Sunday and listen to Preacher Elzie Banks tell us about God and the devil. I believed it all, but for some reason I was never baptized. After I started in music, I got away from going to church and reading the Bible. I believe I was living the way God meant me to, but I wasn't giving God the right attention.

Coming from the mountains, I have kind of funny beliefs anyway—kind of a mixture of religion and superstition. I know people in the Church of Christ ain't supposed to believe in reincarnation and séances and stuff, but I guess I do. I'll probably get in trouble with the church for saying this, but I've often tried to make contact with people that have died, especially my daddy. I really feel like Daddy can hear me sing, even though he's dead. The Bible says nothing about that, does it? Anyway, that's one of my beliefs. I've always believed in a hereafter, even if I can't imagine what it's like. I guess nobody really knows what's gonna happen to us. I figure we just do our best and hope we get to heaven by the grace of God.

I've never believed that man was too sinful; if he was, God would have destroyed him, like he did Sodom and Gomorrah. I think it's up to a person to make their own life, good or bad. But I never considered getting baptized or making a strong stand about God until John Thornhill and I started talking about religion, even arguing sometimes.

John is the twin brother of Dave Thornhill, my lead guitar player, and they joined the band about the same time. John played the bass. He liked to drink and cuss like most of the boys when he first joined the band. He even owned his own airplane. His wife was real religious, but John kind of went his own way. Then he started flying with a preacher who said to him one day, "John, I think it's about time you got baptized."

Nobody is sure what convinced John, but he agreed to get baptized. The next morning, real early, he called up his twin brother and said, "Guess what?" Dave thought it must be something real serious to call so early in the morning, but John said, "I just got baptized." That kind of surprised everybody.

After that, John was a different person. He carried his Bible study books with him on the bus, and he'd read and pray whenever he got the chance. He was a born-again Christian, and they're the strongest kind.

It was kind of strange for the other boys. John stopped drinking and staying out late, and if the boys would see a pretty girl outside the bus, John wouldn't even go to the window to look. I think the boys were not sure how to take this new side of John, but he just did what he felt was best.

On Saturday night, John would go out and buy some grape juice and he'd offer to have Communion on Sunday. I was interested in what he was thinking about, so I started studying with him. We'd say a prayer and have Communion and then we'd study the Bible together. And he'd be telling me I should get further in my studies.

I got pretty familiar with parts of the Bible. It's my favorite book. There's sadness, happiness, foolishness, wisdom, anything you want to feel in the Bible. But the most important thing, for me, is the story about the Jews and how they were God's chosen people, and how Jesus came to earth for all of us. That's what I believe. But even with all the studying, I didn't feel like getting baptized.

That went on for about a year, while I was getting sick so much. One time, when I was in the hospital, John came to visit me. I didn't think I was ever gonna come out of that hospital alive. John said, "If you believe, then you should be baptized, just to say you're a Christian."

I was still resisting it, you know, when I went back on the road again. But one night me and John were having an argument in the back of the bus.

I said, "I'm going to heaven. I don't drink or black-guard or run around, so I know I'm going to heaven."

And John said, "Loretta, unless you get baptized in Jesus's name, it's not enough."

We were still arguing while I flipped through the Bible, looking for a place to read. You know how it is sometimes—you flip over the pages and suddenly your eye catches something. Well, that book just flew open to James 2:26, where it says, "For as the body without the spirit is dead, so faith without works is dead also."

To me, that meant it wasn't enough to behave yourself, to do good things. You really had to stand up and show your faith, to be counted as a believer in Christ.

I didn't say anything at the time to John. But in the back of my mind, I decided I was going to get baptized sometime. Then I landed in the hospital another time, in 1972, and that's when I made up my mind. As soon as I got out, I told my daughter-in-law, Pat, that I was ready. She's got an uncle, Dr. Joe McClure, who used to be a preacher until he decided people needed a doctor even more. But he still preaches some. I called him one morning and said I wanted to get baptized before I went back on the road. He told us to come over at three in the afternoon and he'd do it.

I was real nervous because the Bible says you have to be immersed, and like I've said so many times, I'm scared to death of the water. But it was a very private thing—just the preacher and his wife and my daughter-in-law. Nobody from my family volunteered to go with me, but I didn't mind. The Bible says you've got to walk this lonesome valley by yourself. They dunked me in this special tank at the church, and we said the prayers, and I became a baptized Christian. I felt stronger right away, too. Like I was given new strength by Jesus to go about my work. I went back on the road that night again. I didn't tell anybody for a day, until I told John Thornhill.

I've tried to keep up with my religion since then. I can't get to church most Sundays because of my traveling but I'll read the Bible whenever I can. I want to make another religious album someday, but it will have to be without instruments. The Church of Christ feels you should make music in your hearts, but they're against instruments for religious music.

The people in the church are good people, trying to live as close to apostles as they can. Sometimes they ask me to do a benefit or do something else. I'm proud to be a member of their church, and I just hope they understand my interest in things like reincarnation and séances.

Of course, I respect other people's religions. I think if you're living right with God, you can beat temptations. It really makes no difference to me what church you go to. We're all working for the same Man, trying to get to the same Place.

Early in 1974, John Thornhill announced he was quitting my band to study religion. He got a job in a factory in Nashville and he was real happy to be home every night with his wife and children. I know they're happier, too. It's a rough deal for a family man to be traveling, and I respected John's decision.

I think it was hard for Dave and the other boys to understand, though. They had all come up the hard way, just like John, and they couldn't see giving it up just when he was starting to make good money. But everybody respected John's decision. I guess you could say I'm the one who got left out on the deal. Since then, I haven't had anybody to study the Bible with.

I don't know if people are surprised to hear my religious views or not. I try not to make a big issue out of religion while I'm working because I know everybody's got their own point of view.

In 1974, there was a big fuss when a bunch of people were celebrating Jesus outside the Opry. They were asked to keep moving and Skeeter Davis got mad at the policemen for that. As a result, she got suspended from the Grand Ole Opry, which really hurt her.

The way I feel about some of the Jesus people is this: I was walking out of the Opry one night and I was in a hurry. This girl stopped me and she kept asking, "Do you know Jesus? Do you know Jesus?" And she kept preaching to me right on the street. Well, I told her I knew Jesus since I was knee-high, and I walked right on. Sure, I know Jesus. Anybody that wants to can know Jesus. I don't want to criticize Skeeter, because she's got a right to her views. The Bible says you should let your light shine but I don't think it should shine so bright it upsets other people.

It's not for me to tell another person what to believe because like I said, I respect other religions, too. Growing up in Butcher Holler, we didn't have any prejudices. We hardly knew any Catholics, and the Jews were written all over the Bible as God's chosen people, but I never knew any Jews until I got into show business. Since then, I've met a lot and found them to be real smart and good workers. A lot of the people in my organization are Jewish, and I learn a lot from them. I never knew that many Jews don't eat pork, out of religious belief, until we had a barbecue one time and one of my friends said they didn't eat pork. Now we're real careful, me and Doo, about offending anybody about that.

The way I feel about it, I'm proud to know Jewish people. Don't forget: Jesus was a Jew. I never knew much about their history until a few years ago. When I was first married, Doolittle told me about the war in Europe, where he served. But it just didn't sink in what went on over there.

Then, after my songs got pretty popular, we made a big tour of Europe. They offered to take us sightseeing in Germany, and I went along. I thought it was a beautiful country and the people all worked hard. I was enjoying myself real well until they took us to a camp they said was a prison during the war.

This guide, a German, was taking us around. He talked about ashes and bones being buried there. He showed us a big stove he said they had put Jews in. I just couldn't believe it. I said, "You did *what*?"

He told me the Germans marched the Jews in there and burned 'em. I got out of there as fast as I could. I don't like to feel hatred for anybody, and I was feeling hatred over what the Germans did. I just didn't understand it, and I haven't been back to Germany since. The place I want to go to is Israel. Doo and me have talked about that a lot. We were gonna go a few years ago, but they had all that trouble and we didn't want to get caught in a skyjacking or nothing. But we'll go there soon. That's one of my big ambitions.

Really, all kinds of prejudice bother me. I've heard more than enough color prejudice from other people, but I don't have it. I'm always happy when black people come to my shows or ask for my autograph. At the motel in Nashville they all know me. I'm very comfortable with blacks—maybe because I'm part Cherokee and we understand each other. I don't know.

I don't like to talk too much about things where you're going to get one side or the other unhappy. It's like politics. I've got strong opinions on a lot of things I don't talk about. You come out for one side, the other side won't like you. And anyway, my music has no politics.

Politicians are always asking me to support 'em, and I've had lots of politicians on both sides be real nice to me; there're some that I count as my friends. But I ain't gonna endorse 'em because that would make the other side mad at me. What party am I? Well, let's put it this way. My daddy was a Republican because that's what people are up in the mountains. But that don't mean I have to be. What party was Franklin Delano Roosevelt in? See, there's good on both sides.

George Wallace called me up and wanted me to do a fund-raising show for him. I said politics and music mix about as well as liquor and love. George McGovern came to one of my shows and talked to Doolittle. He even led the applause when we finished our show with "God Bless America Again."

That song now is a perfect example of what I mean. Bobby Bare and Boyce Hawkins wrote it back in the 1960s when we had all that trouble about the war in Vietnam, and then in 1970 college kids were killed by the National Guard at Kent State, and then there were beatings in Chicago. It looked like this country was really breaking up. Well, that song is about some person with not too much education who just can't figure out what's going on. So all he can say is, "Wash her pretty face, dry her eyes, and then God bless America again."

Now some people thought that song was in favor of the government and against the long-haired people. But I'm still singing that song today, and we've had a vice president and then a president of the United States both quit office when they were accused of things.

And I still don't understand what's going on—I feel like it's about time for honest people to start running this country. And I don't care what party. Just get somebody that will feed the poor people and forget about these wars. I wasn't for Vietnam. When I told that to the hippie newspaper in Atlanta, *The Great Speckled Bird*, all my people got nervous. Both my sons were in the service in Asia, and they said there was dope and everything. It was a big waste.

Anyway, things still ain't rosy today. You just go out

in your cities and look at the back streets. There's so much poverty in this country—Doolittle's had hundreds of men asking for just any kind of job on the ranch. I'm waiting for a politician who'll help the people. Then maybe I'll support him. Or her.

# 29

# Confessions of a Bug

I'm glad that Raquel Welch just signed a million-dollar pact,
And Debbie's out in Vegas, working up a brand-new act...
—*"One's on the Way," by Shel Silverstein*

My friends in Nashville say if I wasn't an artist, I'd be spending all my days as a bug—you know, one of those fans who are always bugging famous personalities. Just let me loose in Hollywood, and I'd go crazy. I'll introduce myself to anybody, ask for his autograph, just stand around and gawk. I'm terrible. I even embarrass myself.

You saw me on that Grammy television show, right? I was so excited being in Hollywood I came on screaming, "Here I am; if anybody wants to make me a star, here I am!" Then I forgot to read the names of the singers nominated for the award. I lose my mind when I get out there.

I remember the first celebrity I ever saw: Remember "Hoss," that big guy on *Bonanza*—Dan Blocker?

Me and Doo were pushing my record down in Texas or Oklahoma somewhere and we saw him. I just stood in the crowd and got his autograph—told him I was a singer. He was a real nice fellow. I was real sorry when I heard about him dying.

Well, I ain't changed any since then. I was doing a television show in Hollywood a few years ago when I found out Flip Wilson was in the next studio. "Flip Wilson!" I said. "Point me where I can find Geraldine, 'cause I want to get some tips from her." I found Flip in the wardrobe department, and he was real nice. He said he knew who I was. Later he dressed up like Geraldine and came over to the Dean Martin set and said he wanted to give Loretta Lynn some tips. I laughed so hard. Now we're good friends, and whenever I do a television show, I want him to be on with me.

There's only one famous man I've ever had a problem with. I ain't gonna say who, because he's an important man on television. I ran into him at NBC one time and said, "Hi, I'm Loretta Lynn." Well, he looked at me like I was delivering the garbage and he gave me a real fish handshake and then turned away. I don't know if he knew who I was, but it didn't matter. I wouldn't treat anybody that cold.

But I've had some real thrills in my life, too. Like my favorite actor has always been Gregory Peck. I've seen him in everything he's ever done—*To Kill a Mockingbird* and *Duel in the Sun* are my favorites. To me, Gregory Peck is everything—he's handsome, he's smart, he's polite to people, he's brave. I've always had admiration for that man, so when I got to Hollywood a few years ago, I kept telling David Skepner I wanted to see Gregory Peck. The people at MCA said they would arrange it, and finally they did it for my birthday. They said I was going for an interview, but instead they took me right into his office. He just raised up out of that chair like a good ole country boy that'd been behind a plow all his life. I knew it was Gregory Peck the minute I saw him— big man, black hair, all man. He was like country, so down-to-earth. He looked exactly like he does in all his movies.

He and Doolittle started talking about farming. For almost an hour they talked about horses and cattle and stuff. And me? I just sat there with my mouth open and looked at him. Finally, I found my tongue. I said he looked Indian, what with those high cheekbones. And I was telling him about parts of his movies that he forgot. Like *David and Bathsheba*, with Susan Hayward. To me, that's one of the greatest movies I've ever seen. Now when I want to see it, I've got a copy in my recreation room.

When we were finished talking, I got a big picture of him. That one's hanging in my bedroom, and I've got one in my pocketbook, too. Doolittle didn't mind—he just put up a picture of Dolly Parton. Anyway, I'm still dreaming about doing a movie with Gregory Peck as the producer. It would be terrific.

There was a television movie I was supposed to be in, playing a woman who was a mother by the age of fourteen. Sound familiar? It would have been about immigrants traveling across the country. I liked the idea, but we couldn't work it into my schedule. We were booked six months ahead, and they called me three weeks before the filming was to start. Television is funny that way. It's too bad. I could have played that as myself and wouldn't have needed any acting lessons. I've got to act natural— can't be nothing but myself.

It's like when they had me on *The Dean Martin Show*. Now, that was a mess. I was rehearsing all week and never saw Dean Martin. He's got this stand-in who rehearses all week. Then Dean Martin comes in for the show, and you've got to push him into his place because he hasn't rehearsed. Anyway, they wanted me to sit in Dean Martin's lap at the end of a scene. I said no, I wasn't raised to sit in other men's laps, not even for television. I don't sit in Doolittle's lap in public; it's just bad manners. All these Hollywood people were looking at me like I was crazy. I didn't care. I know what's right and wrong and I wasn't sitting on Dean Martin's lap. Finally they said I didn't have to, which was a good thing, because there was no way I was going to.

The next day the producer sent me a dozen roses and said he wanted to meet the woman who wouldn't sit on Dean Martin's lap. I guess they're not gonna forget that too soon. But I did the same thing on Dinah Shore's show. The producer wanted me to model with a silver cigarette holder. I said I didn't smoke and wasn't going to model any holder.

But I love being around show business. I've met so many stars: Vic Damone—he followed me on a show one time and we both messed up our lyrics. Lorne Greene—I ran into him in the restaurant at the Sheraton Universal Hotel. He had beautiful gray hair, said he knew my records. Louis Armstrong—we talked about doing an album called *Loretta Sings the Blues*, but he said he wasn't strong enough to record at that time. He died two months after that. Of course, Dinah Shore—she's my special friend, always giving me good advice. And Mike Douglas—the minute I walk into his studio, I feel at home. He understands my Butcher Holler ways and he just lets me be Loretta. I like a person who don't make fun of your accent or your upbringing. That happened to me with one talk show one time. I told the guy after the show I wasn't going to be back with him. And I didn't for a long time. I heard he got some bad mail about it.

But most of the people have been great. My twins are bugs just like me. They want to meet Gregory Peck. And you know what? When I got the top vocalist award in 1972, they weren't excited for me—they were excited because they got to see Charley Pride. Now they're asking me if I really know Dolly Parton. I figure that must be Doolittle's influence.

# 30

## On the Road

I hear her voice, in the morning hours she
calls me;
The radio reminds me of my home far away;
Driving down the road I get a feeling
That I should have been home yesterday—
yesterday...
—*"Take Me Home, Country Roads," by
John Denver, Bill Danoff, and Taffy Nivert*

Now that I've told you just about everything in my
life, maybe it's time to take you along with me for a
few days, so you'll see all about my "glamorous" life as
a country singer. Usually the way that works, people get
all excited about traveling in my bus. But after a day and
a half they start asking, "Hey, where can I catch a plane
out of here?"

Our schedule is a bunch of one-night stands. It isn't
good business to sit in one place too long. You figure all
your fans are gonna make an effort to see you one night.
But there may not be enough for two nights. Plus, I'd
rather keep moving than stay in one town. It makes the

time go faster. You stay in one place for a week and you swear you've been there a month. But the traveling can get pretty rough, too.

Let's take a weekend in May, the first weekend when my writer, George, was traveling with us. After a couple of days with my boys and me, George didn't know which end was up.

We were in the middle of a long tour. We try to make the dates as close as possible, in a straight line, but we can't always do it. When you get a good offer in Toronto on a Thursday night, you take it. That's why we have the bus, so we don't have to depend on airplanes. We can go a thousand miles between shows if we have to. On this trip, we'd gone from West Virginia to Toronto and back into Ohio again. I had this migraine headache, and my doctor had just told me my blood pressure was up. So I was a little scared and got to thinking about giving up this business, and I was missing my twins, like I do, as this weekend started.

Friday, May 5, Cincinnati, Ohio: It's four o'clock in the afternoon and I'm trying to take a nap in my hotel room. We've been driving all night from Toronto and I'm exhausted. I just took a nice, long bath and I'd love to sleep some more, but my fans are running up and down the hallways, giggling and banging on doors. We try to keep our hotel a secret, but it's not hard to spot our big bus with my name on the side. The hotel's not supposed to give out our room numbers, but the fans find out somehow. Bless 'em, I love 'em all, but I wish they wouldn't disturb me and my boys when we're trying to sleep.

At times like this, I really feel sorry for Jim Webb. He's been with me a couple of years now. He used to drive for Continental Trailways, but he never had a schedule like this. He's expected to drive all night, though Dave

Thornhill, my lead guitar man, takes over on long hauls like last night. Jim is trying to sleep in the next room, and they're banging on his door.

There's no sense trying to sleep. I look out the window, at the interstate highway over the river into Kentucky. The bridge is jammed with mountain people heading home for the weekend. I start thinking about the hollers in May, how they're just bursting with green leaves. Then I remember the old Depression days, and I decide I ain't so homesick after all.

Jim Webb gives up sleeping, too. He bangs on my door and wanders in—he's a big boy, around six foot four, from Laurel, Mississippi. His hair is styled just like Elvis Presley's. Jim is a very important part of my tour. In addition to driving the bus, he takes all the telephone calls and makes travel arrangements. I depend on him, particularly when Doo's not around, like now.

"Did you eat yet?" Jim says. That's one of his jobs—to make sure I remember to eat. We're always worried about keeping my weight up, so he orders me a steak and baked potato with string beans and salad and pie and ice cream. He watches over me until I finish eating. Then it's time to leave for the show. I just wear my regular travel slacks and go down to the bus.

That bus is important to us. We sleep in it and I do all my dressing in it. We found it was better to have a bus with a dressing room, instead of counting on using whatever they give us at the auditoriums. Sometimes they've got good rooms, and sometimes just a bathroom without even a mirror. But we've always got the bus.

We got our first bus in 1967, after my babies were born. It was better than traveling by car with Doolittle or Jay Lee driving. Now it's like a second home. Truck drivers see my name on the bus and wave as they go past. Last year when there were gasoline shortages and the truckers went on strike, people were shooting out windows on trucks. But we didn't have any trouble. In fact, that crazy Tom T. Hall had bought my old bus with the sign "Loretta Lynn" still on the front, and he didn't have no trouble, either.

Our bus cost around $147,000 to fix up. I designed it myself. It's regulation length. The front is for the driver and has couches for sitting. The upholstery is purple velvet, and there's a violet-patterned carpet and a ceiling of white leatherette. There are some little gold tassels and stuff to give it a fancy feeling. The boys say it looks like a hearse. Up front we've got a little refrigerator, a television set, and a tape deck, plus a table where the boys can play cards. Just recently we installed a microwave oven for cooking hamburgers and stuff. In the middle there're eight bunks. The back part is for me.

The boys all crowd into the bus at 5 p.m. It's the middle of the rush hour and we just squeeze our way across town. People line up on the sidewalks, waiting for city buses, and point their fingers at us. My boys wave back at the pretty girls.

"Now, boys, behave yourselves. You got two shows tonight," I tell 'em.

"Ain't no harm in looking, Mom," says Don Ballinger in the little-boy voice he uses onstage when I scold him.

We get lost for a minute, as all the musicians give Jim different directions to the Taft Theatre. But Jim finds the place finally despite their help, and he maneuvers the bus halfway up on the curb, right next to the stage door. The boys start loading all their instruments and sound equipment onto the stage. Then they run a test, to make sure everything sounds right. Then they get into their stage uniforms. Tonight they're wearing their brown suits that I designed for 'em. They've got an hour before the show to sell albums and pictures in the lobby.

The boys share some of the profits from selling the souvenirs. Ken Riley, the tall drummer who used to be a tap dancer, is in charge of dividing the money. They call him "Bread Man" on account of money being called "bread" in my boys' language. I feel real comfortable seeing my boys working around the bus. Those boys are just like a family to me. I remember one time, when I was having all those death threats, my dentist came to visit me at the bus. I looked out the window and saw my boys had him backed up against a wall. I said, "Boys, what in the world are you doing? That's my dentist." But they didn't know. They were just a little jumpy.

Most people say, "The band would kill for Loretta," and I guess that's true. When I see 'em get an award, like *Music City News* voting 'em the top band last year, I'm as happy as they are.

I've had my band since I started breaking up with the Wilburns. Before that, I'd have to play with the house band wherever I went. If the band was good, I'd sound fine. But if it was bad, I'd get real nervous and couldn't sing at all. One night the house band took off in one key and I took off in another. They were just a sorry little country band—steel guitar, bass, and fiddle. I told Doolittle, "Either I'm getting a band or I'm quitting." So he got me a band.

I never told this story before, but I almost got an all-girl band. You don't see too many women in country music. Sure, there're the big stars, but all the bands and studio musicians are men, just about. And you know there're women around that can play just as good as men. I used to have Leona Williams playing bass in my band and singing harmony. She's one of the best musicians in Nashville, and now she's out trying to make it on her own. I bet she does, too.

I was going to hold tryouts for women and call 'em

"The Lynnettes." But people started saying you can't have a traveling girl band—if you had one incident, people would start gossiping about it. It was that old double standard again. If a man goes out on a date, people smile and say, "Well, that's how men are." But if some woman goes out on a date, people say, "She's a loose woman." And it wouldn't be good for business if that kind of stuff got started. So we hired an all-man band, and I ain't been sorry to this date because I love my boys. But an all-girl band would have been fantastic.

Right away, my band made my act better. I always knew what music they were playing, and if I started to get sick, they could keep the show going.

It's not hard to find great musicians in Nashville. It's the truth—the streets are packed with 'em. But I've got a certain kind of boy I like to hire—somebody who's worked in the factories up north. They can appreciate being in my band a little more after working the shifts in the factories.

You take a boy like my lead guitar, Dave Thornhill. His daddy was a real coal miner in Kentucky, and then they moved up to Ohio, where he worked in a factory. On the weekends, he'd play in country music places and dream about going to Nashville. Finally, he chucked his job and moved to Nashville—broke, without a penny. He heard that I was looking to hire a guitar man, so he tried out.

I remember at the tryout, he looked familiar to me. I said, "Ain't I seen you before?" And he said he used to back me up whenever I played in Columbus, Ohio. So I knew he could play my music. I listened to a few notes and told him to be on the bus with his bags packed in half an hour. Dave ain't been off my bus since.

Dave is an important part of the show. He watches me real careful and makes sure the band is following me. If

I break time or something, he breaks time right with me. He's real proud of being my lead guitar man.

My boys get paid a straight salary, fifty-two weeks a year. Plus, they get six or eight weeks off after Christmas when I go to Mexico, and time off when I'm in Nashville. The only deal is they have to be ready to go with me whenever we have a show. Most of 'em live in Nashville now. They bring their wives and kids around, and we get to know each other. I think a man works steadier when he's got a good family.

Now the bus is nearly empty, except for a fellow from my record company. We talk business for a few minutes. Then Cal Smith gets on. Cal is one of the best singers in the business, and he's been making this tour, along with Ernest Tubb and his band. Cal is from Oklahoma, and he used to be the front man for Ernest, so he's having a great time with his old buddies.

"Where you been?" I ask him.

"On Ernest's bus," Cal says. He's one of these people you can never tell if he's joking or serious.

"What you been doing?" I ask.

"Getting interviewed," Cal says.

I decide not to ask him the details. It's probably better I don't know. Cal has been egging Ernest's band and my band into all kinds of crazy stunts. Lately he's been imitating the Wilburn Brothers, something he knows I don't like. He'll get onstage and talk with his hands up in the air—drives me crazy. Now he's got my whole band doing it behind my back.

Last week my boys put Ernest's bus up on jacks and it took 'em an hour to get it off. But Ernest's boys paid us back. They've got this bus driver named Hoot who looks just like Gomer Pyle and talks like him, too. Me and Ernest are supposed to sing our big record, "Sweet Thang." Well, last week they sent Hoot out in Ernest's clothes, about three sizes too big. Hoot starts moving his lips and his hands, while Ernest was singing offstage. The audience thought it was hilarious but I was going crazy. The whole bunch of 'em is nuts.

Luckily, there're a few normal people left in the world—I think. About 6:30 p.m., two of my fan-club presidents from Kentucky, Jean Powers and Martha McConnell, come pecking on my door. I give 'em a big hug and we talk about the old mountain days—they both grew up in eastern Kentucky—and the fan-club activity. They put out a newsletter, plugging all my new records. Whenever I get near Kentucky, they come visit me. I've got a rule that I only let fan-club presidents on the bus. That avoids a lot of hard feelings. I just can't let everybody on—the insurance company won't let us.

Around 7 p.m., Jim Webb pops in the bus and says Ernest's show is just beginning. That means I've got about an hour to get ready. Martha and Jean are welcome to stay, but I've got to go in the back of the bus and work some miracles.

The back of the bus is about twelve feet long and six feet wide. That's where I spend half my life, it seems. I've got two purple couches that open into one king-sized bed when Doolittle is around. Far in the back, I've got a Hollywood vanity and sink and makeup table. There're bright fluorescent bulbs lighting everything up. I sit on a high-back swivel makeup chair that's white with purple trim.

On the other side, there's a closet holding over a hundred dresses. I make some, and some are shipped by Barbara Smith, who works in my office and is a close friend. She does most of my shopping for me in Nashville so I never have to go into a store. She knows my size and what I like to wear. If I don't like 'em, I just send 'em back. My dresses are size three or five, depending what time of year it is. After Mexico, I'm size five, or even seven. Late in the year, I'm down to size three.

I spend half an hour at the vanity, just making up. A writer named Carol Offen once asked me why I got dressed up so fancy in these days when a lot of women are wearing blue jeans and letting their hair just hang. I said that's all right for other women, but I think my fans expect me to look a certain way. It's part of my personality onstage. Also, I enjoy seeing me change from Loretta, the gal in jeans, to Loretta, the woman in the long gown. It's a little like seeing one of the Hollywood stars appear before my own eyes. I guess my mommy should never have let me sit looking at pictures of movie stars when I was a baby.

But lately I've been cutting down on all the phony stuff. I'm tired of all that work, pretending I'm something I ain't. I'm tired of the rollers and the creams, the eyelash curlers, the lipsticks, the powder. I still use hot curlers to get my hair curly; then I spray it. I must use a truckload of it every year. I used to wear a fall made out of Korean hair, after some fans cut off my curls with a pocketknife. But the hairpiece was giving me a headache, so I gave it up this year. I don't wear false eyelashes anymore. Too many fans were pulling them off. From now on, what you see is what I've got.

I keep fussing in front of the mirror, curl by curl. It still ain't right, but there's Jim Webb knocking at the door.

"Five minutes, Mom," he says. Then he takes my arm and we rush off the bus, through a stage door, and we're backstage. I take one look around me—same old theater, just like always, a few familiar faces backstage. Then I hear the announcer say, "Ladies and gentlemen, the first lady of country music, Miss Loretta Lynn." And I see a spotlight out there, and I wobble out in my high-heel shoes, as clumsy as ever. Dave Thornhill kicks over the first notes to "Coal Miner's Daughter" and we're off.

We've been starting with the same four or five songs—"Coal Miner's Daughter," "Your Squaw Is on the War-path," "Help Me Make It through the Night," "Me and Bobby McGee," and "You Ain't Woman Enough to Take My Man."

It's always the same songs, and sometimes people ask me if I get tired of singing 'em. Yes, I do. At first it's good, but you go for years and you really get tired of 'em. But people want to hear your hit songs, so you've got to.

After the opening songs, I introduce my band. I never know what they're going to do next. After we're on the road awhile, our biggest kick is making each other laugh. After it gets real bad, I'll say, "Boys, you'd better pay your way in tomorrow, because you ain't per-forming for the audience tonight." But I'm as bad as they are.

It's real dangerous when you've got a man like Don Ballinger around. Don's my "front man"—the one with the big smile who warms up the audience at the start of the show. He's always telling the audience how bad he's paid, or he pretends he's scouting for pretty girls in the crowd. He's got his good points, though. When I'm not feeling well, he'll start clowning around until I've got my strength back.

Tonight he starts talking about the girls he saw from the bus.

"There was a bunch of tanks," Don says. "Real big ones. Sherman tanks."

I put my hand in front of my face. Only one way to hush that boy up—that's to sing. So we sing a few num-bers; then I introduce my other musicians. Gene Dunlap, our Louisiana piano man, sings in that deep "country soul" voice, just like a white Ray Charles. Then it's time for me and Ernest to sing "Sweet Thang."

You never know what's gonna happen. But fortunately, there's no stunt this time. And it ain't Hoot, Ernest's bus driver, walking onstage, but it's really Ernest. Thank goodness, because this is still one of my favorite songs.

Now we're getting toward the end. I do "They Don't Make 'Em Like My Daddy." But while I'm singing, I see my boys doing that Wilburn bit, talking with their hands again. That makes me so mad I feel like walking off the stage. But of course, I finish the song and then "Love Is the Foundation" and, finally, "One's on the Way." But I don't do any requests and I don't do "God Bless America Again." I just nod to Dave Thornhill that I'm finished, and they play the little hoedown number while I go offstage, still angry at them for teasing me like they did. Ever since I broke with the Wilburns, I don't like to see any of their mannerisms. My boys just do it for meanness.

Jim Webb takes my arm and escorts me back into the bus. I start slamming things around my bedroom while Martha and Jean ask me what's wrong; and I tell them.

"They just do it for a joke," Martha says.

"Well, it makes me mad," I say.

"Don't let it show," Jean says. "That just makes it worse."

We just sit there for a while, until Cal Smith comes on the bus. He knows I'm mad, but he can't resist teasing me.

"What's the matter, Clytha June?" he asks me. That's his nickname for me—meaning I'm all country.

"When are you going back with Ernest Tubb?" I say.

But I can't stay mad at anybody for long. In a few minutes, some of the boys are drinking a soda and talking with us, and it's all forgotten. We do the second show at 9:30, and it's 1 a.m. before we get back to the motel. Did you ever try to get a good sandwich at 1 a.m. in Cincinnati? They may have some great restaurants, but that late-sandwich bit can't be done, folks. I end up eating a cold cheeseburger, and it makes me queasy all night long.

Saturday, May 6: My stomach still hurts. I don't order any breakfast, just lie in bed feeling miserable. The bus is leaving at noon, and I just wait until Jim Webb tells me to get packed. We get in the bus and take off. Me and George sit in the back and talk. I keep the shades drawn as we roll on along the interstate highway. Like I said before, I've seen the roads too much in my life.

About three o'clock, we stop in front of another motel. If you ask me, it looks just like the one we left.

"Where are we?" I ask.

"Columbus, Ohio," somebody says.

I never gave any thought to it, but the boys must be happy this trip. Most of 'em have family around Columbus, particularly Don Ballinger and Chuck Flynn, the new bass player. I look out the window and there's Chuck with his kids. It's probably the first time he's seen 'em since he joined our show a month ago. I get to thinking about Doo and my twins back at the ranch, and I get kind of homesick.

Up in my motel room, I order a big lunch of liver and potatoes, salad, milk, and pie. Ever since the doctor told me I've got high blood pressure, I've been trying to build up my iron. I turn on the television set, but I fall asleep until it's time for the show.

We take the bus out to the auditorium, and I'm still half-asleep. But I wake up fast when I see my cousin Marie. Oh my gosh, I forgot. We're in Columbus, Ohio. Half the time I clear forget what town we're in! Marie's closer to me than a sister. Her husband died early this year, and I ain't seen her or talked to her since. I motion for Jim to open the door for her, and she comes in.

We look at each other, and I can see how broken up she is. We give each other a big hug and a kiss. She's trembling like she's freezing.

"I'm nervous," Marie says. "I can't sleep none yet."

"I'm sorry I couldn't get to the funeral," I say. "I told Mommy to send flowers."

"She did," Marie says. "It's been rough. Every time my little grandchildren ask, 'Where's Grandpa?' I just fall apart."

We go to the back of the bus. Marie takes a Valium, hoping it will calm her down. She and Charles had their problems, like all married couples, but he was a nice feller. It's gonna be tough on Marie, I think to myself. She offers to fix my hair, so I lean back and relax. The Valium calms her down a little bit and she does a good job with my hair. We talk about the old days, back in Butcher Holler, and then it's time for me to do the show—only one show tonight.

I get out onstage and there's a different feeling tonight—more sparks. It's Saturday night and people are out for a good time, or something. Plus, most of our boys have friends and family in the audience, and they're giving it their best.

After our first five songs, I stop the show and introduce Chuck Flynn, who replaced John Thornhill on the bass. Chuck walks to the microphone and says in that slow, country style of his, "I come from Mount Vernon, Ohio, just up the road a piece. My fan club was gonna give me a parade, but one got sick, and the other had to work."

About fifty people cheer for Chuck. He's real popular up here. That makes Don Ballinger start pouting like a baby, wanting his attention. I remember I saw his wife,

Nancy, offstage somewhere. She's a pretty gal who's raised four kids and has a regular job and puts up with Don. I figure, what the heck, it's family night, so I call Nancy out onstage.

Can you believe this? Here's this pretty woman walking out onstage and you know what Don calls her? "The Tank." He looks her up and down as she walks toward us.

"It's sad how much she's aged since the last time I saw her," Don says.

I give Don a shove and tell him to stop smarting off. Now you see why I'm on the women's side. We get on with the music and finish up good. Afterward, I decide I feel well enough to sign autographs. I sit at a table and sign, while the fans line up. Some of 'em just stare when they get close while others ask questions.

"Do you know so-and-so from Paintsville?" somebody asks.

"How are the twins?"

"Is that your real hair?"

While I'm signing, I catch a glimpse of an old friend of mine from Van Lear—Audrey Blevins Honaker. She was one of the coal-camp girls who works in a supermarket in Columbus now. When I got started in show business, she used to have me over to her house and she'd fix chicken and dumplings and corn bread and pinto beans—my favorite meal. But lately it seems like my schedule is too tight and we never see each other.

"Did you get the food?" Audrey asks.

I don't remember any food.

"The pie and cookies I put on the bus," Audrey says.

I never saw 'em, but I tell her I did.

"They were terrific," I say. Hmmm. My boys must have eaten 'em.

"Next time, you come out to the house," Audrey says.

I promise I will, and keep signing. Seven hundred autographs later, I go back to the bus and I find the boys have saved me half of Audrey's strawberry pie and a few peanut butter cookies. Me and Marie eat and talk in the back of the bus until the boys have loaded their equipment. I give Marie another big hug—her starting to tremble again, me not knowing what I can do or say that will really help my cousin. We hold hands for a minute, and then she leaves the bus.

The bus goes back to the motel. All the boys are invited out to Frontier Ranch, where they used to play. I just go up to my room and try to find a Gregory Peck movie on television, then stay awake until three o'clock, just tossing and talking to myself, and thinking about my babies and Marie and my headaches. And finally I fall asleep.

Sunday, May 7: It's raining ugly out. Just a mean, gray day, and I don't feel like getting up for nothing. But Jim Webb knocks on my door and tells me we've got to leave by nine. You mean it ain't nine yet? I stumble around, throw my clothes on, grab my little red overnight bag, and we take the elevator down. There're some of my fans in the lobby. Take a good look, fans—now you're seeing the real Loretta Lynn. Ain't she something?

I climb right back in my bed on the bus and sleep until eleven o'clock. Then I freshen myself up and visit the front of the bus. Somebody tells me we're playing a four o'clock show in Toledo, Ohio. That's fine with me. Nothing I can do about it anyway. Just go up there and sing.

I enjoy sitting up front with my boys. We talk about our problems and I'll give 'em advice. I've even lent 'em money when they need it, though Doo says I shouldn't get so close to the boys. But I can't help it. When you're living in the same bus with people you like, you can't help but get interested in them.

We've only got a couple of rules about the boys. Doo says they're not supposed to bring more than two beers apiece onto the bus. Usually, they follow the rules, but once in a while they'll slip. I'll start crying and then they'll bring me ice cream and presents, so I can't stay mad at 'em.

Just recently I decided they were blackguarding too much, so I set up fines. A dollar a cuss. Right now they're arguing whether certain words are cusses. Bob Hempker, my steel guitar player, and Ken Riley, the drummer, are talking it over with Don Ballinger. I know they're just being real foxy. This just gives 'em the chance to say the words over and over again. So I decide to settle things.

*Me:* What's the problem?

*Ken:* Kenny Starr said, "By God," and that's cussing.

*Bob:* It ain't cussing. God's name is in the Bible.

*Don:* Yeah, but you can't say, "By God." That's cussing.

*Me:* That's right. Where is that little devil?

*Ken:* He's asleep in his bunk.

*Me:* Well, I'm gonna fine him three dollars right out of his paycheck. Then we'll put it in the piggy bank.

*Don:* Mom, you're running one of those company stores. Next thing you know, you'll be paying us in scrip, like in the coal camps. It's almost that bad now.

*Me:* You hush up, Don Ballinger. I'm the boss here. I'll fine you for sassing the boss.

*Don:* Sassing's not a crime.
*Me:* On my bus it is.

Anyway, that's the way it goes for the next hour, just arguing about fines for the fun of it. There's already fifty dollars
in there, mostly from Jim Webb and Cal Smith. When
the tour is over, we'll throw a party or something—if the
boys don't get the money when I'm not looking. I don't
know how Jim Webb finds time to cuss. He's so busy
driving the bus and making conversation on our citizens
band radio. He's always talking to truck drivers about
"Smokey the Bear." I thought maybe Jim was just interested in stopping forest fires, but it turns out Smokey is
the nickname for the state troopers. They didn't used to
bother us, but since the interstates dropped their speed
to fifty-five, they've been a problem. You ain't supposed
to give messages about state troopers on the radio. That's
why they talk about bears so much.

We pull into Toledo around noon. The boys are all
starving. There's a big diner, but it's packed with folks
coming from church. We usually like McDonald's and
avoid Howard Johnson's. But this time we see a fish-
and-chips place that looks empty. The reason it's empty
is because they don't open until the stroke of noon. The
boys go out, around nine of 'em, and breathe heavy on
the clean glass doors, until the women get disgusted
with 'em and open the restaurant. The boys know I
can't go into restaurants because my fans would sur-
round us and wouldn't let us eat. So they bring some
fried fish back into my room as we drive to the auditorium. It's a beautiful new place out in the country. You
don't even see Toledo. I'm thinking of getting more sleep
but there's a reporter from the Toledo newspaper who
wants an interview. I always like to meet writers because
they've been nice to me over the years. This man is

named Seymour Rothman. He acts like he don't know too much about country music, asking me simple questions like do I enjoy one-night stands, how do I write my songs—stuff I've answered a thousand times before. I can see Jim Webb and Cal Smith laughing at the questions. They start to clown around, pretending to play poker and stuff. But the man is so nice I answer all his questions. Then his photographer wants to take a picture of me out on the lawn. It's country music, see, so they want to get some green grass. All right. Only it's dropped to around forty degrees, there's this vicious wind blowing, and the rain is starting to feel like wet snow on my cheeks. The photographer keeps clicking away and my hair is blowing all over the lot.

"You're gonna make me look like a mess," I complain.

"Just one more," the photographer says. That's what they all say.

Finally we're done. We go back in the bus while I thaw out. I'm convinced that article is going to be a disaster. (Six weeks later, Seymour Rothman writes a cover article for his paper's Sunday magazine. The picture of me is beautiful—and the article goes into all the main points of my career. A real nice job. I should have known he was a professional. The only thing that makes me mad is he guessed too high on my age.)

Anyway, we do two shows in Toledo. In between, they feed us a nice chicken dinner in the backstage cafeteria. This is a first-class operation here. We're all exhausted from the long trip. After the second show, we drive back to Columbus.

The bus needs some fixing at the home garage, so we're going to stay in Columbus for a few off days, then head to Canada and upstate New York. I'm looking forward to nothing but resting. It may not sound too exciting—three days off in Columbus—but it means sleep. I probably should fly home to the ranch and see my babies, but by the time I got there, it would be time to start packing again. So I'm just gonna sleep. We get back to the motel in Columbus, and there're no Gregory Peck movies on the television set tonight, either. So it's just me and the four walls.

# 31

## What's Next?

And love is the foundation we lean on,
All you need is love to ease your mind...
—*"Love Is the Foundation," by William C. Hall*

This is my life today, my "glamorous" life. Sometimes I ask myself, How long is this gonna go on? My twins are always asking, "Mommy, when are you going to stay home?" And my doctor tries to cut down my travel time because of my migraines and high blood pressure.

I hear people in Nashville gossip that I'm gonna wear myself out. But other singers keep traveling until they're fifty or sixty. Look at Ernest Tubb. He's learned not to wear himself down. He just does what he needs to do, and he's still going.

But you can't be halfway in this business. If you don't meet the fans, you lose all you've got. And I love people and I love to sing—that's what keeps me going. But when we get to the point where we don't need another penny, I'd have to think about it. I've done everything there is in this business. Maybe there's something else I could do that would help people more.

A lot of people say I'd really miss show business if I quit. Well, I'd miss some of it. But I never realized it would be like this when I started—all this traveling. Now it's the only life I know.

I've never developed any other activities over the years—don't play cards anymore, don't read much, don't play tennis. I was never on a golf course in my life until Ernest Tubb dragged me out to watch him play in 1974. I told him I'd rather watch baseball, where you can see the ball. So I guess I won't take up golf when I retire. Really, I don't know what I'd do with myself. Wash dishes? Heck, we just got ourselves a dishwasher last year.

Maybe I could spend more time with the kids. The twins are gonna need me around as they get into being teenagers. I want them to graduate from high school and maybe go on to college. I believe in education and wish I had a better one. Maybe I could help my older kids, too, on account of not being around when they were growing. They've got kids of their own now. I could be a real grandmother—babysit and stuff like that. But I don't feel like a grandmother. And don't tell me Doo is a grandfather—who wants to be married to a grandfather?

It's been almost fifteen years since me and Doolittle had what I'd call a normal life, if we ever were normal, that is. I sometimes wonder what it would be like if I stayed home. We argue like crazy when I stay home for a day or two. It's really kind of funny. I've worked all my life and now I'm in a spot where men tell me how to run my business, and when I go home, other people tell me how to run my home.

But all that is changing. I'm not the bashful little girl I was fifteen years ago, when my only dream was a comfortable house for my family. In those days, if Doolittle disappeared for a day or two, I just accepted it. I got mad—but I accepted it. I'm different today. I refuse to be pushed around anymore.

I know how lucky I've been. I wouldn't have dared to ask God for all that He's given me. I'm just grateful for the benefits my family has enjoyed. I didn't do it. I couldn't have done it on my own. I thank God every day for what I have.

I told you I don't go to church regular. But I pray for answers to my problems. Am I doing God's wishes by performing the same songs, over and over again, until I'm fifty or sixty? Am I living the way I was meant to live?

Some people would be afraid to ask themselves those questions. Well, I'm not afraid. I want more out of life than I've gotten—and I want to give more, too. I'd love to travel more to other countries, particularly the Holy Land. I'd love to work more with the American Indians, my people.

It's like I said at the beginning of the book. I feel things starting to change in me again. I'm starting to dress more modern. I'm watching how the young people are looking for answers. I'm putting my life in God's hands, nobody else's. So that's where the book ends, folks. I can't give you the entire Loretta Lynn story, because I'm positive there's more to come.

You just watch.

## What Came Next

---

# Forty More Years
# with Loretta Lynn

# 32

# The View from the Mountain Top

Well my daddy worked down in the dark coal
mine
Shovelin' that coal one shovel at a time
Never made a lot money didn't have much
But we're high on life and rich in love…
 —*"High on a Mountain Top," by*
 *Loretta Lynn and Patsy Lynn Russell*

Go for your dreams!" People say that all the time, especially when they want fame and fortune. They think
it'll be sunshine and cherry pie 24/7.

Folks, that's a load of bull.

When *Coal Miner's Daughter* came out in 1976, I was
on top. I had hit records. I'd been named the first ever
female CMA Entertainer of the Year. I had my own band.
I traveled in a tour bus that was custom-made for the band
and me. Me and Doo even owned a whole town!

Let me tell you something. I'd have traded it all to just
be normal.

I never wanted to be rich or famous. Growing up in
Kentucky we were poor as dirt and livin' in the backwoods.

That's the way it was. We didn't know any different. I never thought of leaving that little place. Then came Doo. I loved him enough to leave my family and everything I knew behind. Four babies later, Doo put a guitar in my hands and got me onstage. That's how it all got started. Not me chasing a dream. Just lovin' a man, and a lot of years of hard work. And a few lucky breaks.

That's how I got to the top. You'd think I'd stop there to rest and enjoy the view. But folks, I didn't. I couldn't. I'd worked my tail end off to make it in the music business. By all accounts I'd made it. But still I was struggling. Seemed like the more successful I was, the harder I had to work.

The death and kidnapping threats kept coming. My people kept them from me, but I wasn't blind. The FBI folks would be backstage with their guns bulging under their jackets. That made me feel mighty restless and anxious.

Most of the time I was as nervous as a cat in a room full of rocking chairs.

My health wasn't good. I worried plenty about whether my body might give out. My migraine headaches could come outta nowhere, like my daddy's used to. The boys in my band watched me, wondering if I might pass out while I was onstage. That happened more than I care to recall. Kind of crazy, ain't it? I was in and out of hospitals with surgeries and then blood poisoning. The way they poked and prodded me I felt like a dang pincushion.

People thought I was living the dream.

Some dream.

Doo loved me through all that. And I loved him. Once in a while I'd beg him and he'd agree to come out on the road to take care of me. Trouble was when he came, he'd find something to get mad about. Or I would. We'd drive each other about half crazy.

Doolittle, smart as he was, spent our money just as fast as we could bring it in. It got so aggravating that I got what you might call a hair trigger. Since Doo was the closest to me, I took a lot of that out on him. Mostly I'd just fuss and then he'd yell. We could fight like dogs. I'm not proud of it. 'Course Doo never got a hit in that I didn't get two back at him.

When I was on the road, all I could think about was getting back home. I'd hear my twins on the other end of the phone and my heart would break in a thousand pieces. All I wanted was to be with my family again. Then I'd get home and me and Doo would get to fussing, and boy, I couldn't wait to leave. People said me and Doo were headed for divorce.

How did we stay together? I just kept writing. I kept making music. People say I sang what women were thinking and feeling. If that's true, good. All I know is I wrote what I felt. I wasn't trying to make a statement or fight for women's rights. I was fighting for me. And for my family.

# 33

## Locking Horns

If you don't want to go to Fist City
You better detour around my town
'Cause I'll grab you by the hair of the head
And I'll lift you off the ground...
— *"Fist City," by Loretta Lynn*

When they gave me the CMA's Entertainer of the Year Award in 1972, I was the first woman to win it. That got me started thinking. Why wasn't I getting paid the same as the men? I worked harder than most and somehow I was earning less. My manager wouldn't push for higher fees. That burned me up. Finally, I couldn't take it anymore. Doo and I agreed. I needed new management. Only trouble was the Wilburns were my managers. They were like family. I was all worked up, but I didn't have the guts to fire them. So, Doo did what he always did. He did what I couldn't. Doo called Teddy to break the news. I left the room, so I don't know what all was said. I went to my bedroom and cried until Doo came in to tell me it was done.

That's how it all started. We locked horns and got

stuck. Soon we were fighting through the lawyers. It was ugly. I felt in my heart it was the right thing for my career, but it hurt all the same. We stayed that way for about ten years.

If you think folks in Nashville were on my side, think again. The music business folks didn't like it one bit. I was rocking the boat. It ticked them off. It was rare for artists to push back, especially female artists. And it was still pretty much a boys' club. I didn't care. It wasn't right. Once I pushed back on them boys, they pushed back, too.

Some say, "Loretta helped topple the powers! No more lifetime contracts! She paved the way for female artists." Well, I didn't do any of that to be a trailblazer. And I sure didn't mean to hurt nobody. I just got to where I couldn't stand being pushed around anymore.

My lawyers had their hands full watching out for me, especially when we were writing *Coal Miner's Daughter* and making the film. Anything I might say about the Wilburns, good or bad, could be used in the lawsuit. They told me not to talk about the Wilburns. That's how life is sometimes—you do the best you can with what you've got. I hated leaving them out, but I had to.

That's all over now. Enough time has gone by. It's time to set the record straight. Here's what you need to know. The Wilburn Brothers, Teddy and Doyle, were a huge part of my life. It hurt me to watch the movie of my life and not see them in it, because they were main characters. More than that, they were family. When we broke up, it was like somebody died. That's how much I grieved. My heart broke about anytime I thought of them boys.

# 34

# My Work Husband (Conway Twitty)

If I've made someone smile
Or just one life worthwhile
Who's gonna miss me when I'm gone
If there's one thing I've done
I'd like to know I've left someone
Who's gonna miss me when I'm gone

Who's gonna miss me tell me
Who's gonna miss me Lordy
Who's gonna miss me when I'm gone...
—*"Who's Gonna Miss Me?," by Loretta Lynn*

When Doo came home all those years ago in Washington State with a guitar instead of a wedding band like I'd wanted, it changed my life. Sometimes I wish he'd have got me the ring, to tell the truth, but he didn't get me a real wedding ring until after we moved to Nashville. Don't get me wrong—I'd have kept on singing, just for me and my babies, but I'd have had a wedding ring to show for it.

Doo had other plans. I got into the music business

because of him. We were a package deal. He believed in me. But it was just me out there performing, just me traveling and doing appearances. Doo pushed me out on the stage; then he was free to go do whatever it was he'd do.

Conway Twitty was a different kind of partner. He was one of the best things that ever happened to me.

Conway was a pop singer to start with. I'd hear him on the radio back when I was still living in a shack in Washington State. I loved his singing. He sounded like Elvis in a way. Maybe that's because he'd recorded with Elvis Presley and Sam Phillips at Sun Studio in Memphis. All I knew was I liked him. I hung his poster on the wall of our bedroom. You'd think Doo wouldn't like that, but he didn't care.

One day I came into Owen's studio at Bradley's Barn. He said, "You told me you love Conway Twitty. What would you think of meeting him?"

I broke out in the biggest grin. "I'd love it!" I said. "'Course I'd probably never get the chance."

Owen said, "Well, Loretta, how about just turn around." I did and there was Conway! He was right there in the studio. I about fainted. Once I got my feet back under me, we got to talking and we became good friends.

Soon we went to England for a package tour—me, Conway, Tex Ritter, and Bill Anderson. Doo came with us. Doo and Conway really hit it off. Conway was real low-key. He wasn't a big talker. He'd just listen. Doo would tell the biggest stories. He loved to make Conway laugh. You could hear him laugh for miles.

Even though Doo and Conway hit it off, Conway's wife, Mickey, wouldn't have much to do with me. She wouldn't talk to me on that trip to England. I never did think much of her after that. Maybe she didn't like me being Conway's singing partner. But it wasn't weird for Doo. He loved Conway. And Conway loved Doo.

He kinda took the pressure off. I felt more comfortable working with him. To this day I still get nervous before a show. Having Conway with me made me braver, stronger. He was someone I could kinda lean into.

Me and Conway had such a good connection that rumors flew that we were having an affair. Some people even said we were married. Friends, that's baloney. We sang about love and breakups because that is a lot of what country music is. We were both married and in love with somebody else. That's probably why me and Conway never did have any problems. When you have romance, you have problems.

Me and Conway brought out the best in each other. He was shy and conservative. I used to be shy but by the time we were singing partners, I'd got to where I'd say about anything to anybody. It was fun to tease Conway. One time I had this short jumpsuit stage outfit made. I wore it under a long, ruffled skirt. It was perfect for "Coal Miner's Daughter." Me and Conway had a number together right after that and when he came out, I pulled the tear-away skirt off with just that little short pantsuit underneath. Boy, Conway got so red! I just laughed. The audience loved it. Me and the band had a good time messin' with Conway.

We had a really special partnership. Our voices worked so good together. Our first hit was "After the Fire Is Gone" in 1971. That was our first number one. It went straight to the top and stayed there. When we got Vocal Duo of the Year in 1972, I thought I'd about died and gone to heaven. Then we got it the next year, too! Can you believe we got that award four years in a row? Altogether we had twelve top-ten hits and twenty-two industry awards.

Doo never was jealous, not for a minute. He trusted Conway. Those two loved each other like brothers. It was Doo that found "Louisiana Woman, Mississippi Man" in 1973 for us. He said, "Conway, I've found y'all's next big hit." We played it for him and Conway turned to me and said, "Damned if he hasn't found it." We had a big time with it.

We were friends forever after that.

Conway and me and Doo were a good team. After me and the Wilburns broke up in 1971, Conway and me started our own talent agency. We named it United Talent. We kept performing and recording separately and we'd keep coming back together over the years, too. We kept on singing and working together till the day he died. Strange thing was me and Doo were with him that day.

# 35

## True Love

I lie here all alone
In my bed of memories...
— *"Miss Being Mrs.," by Loretta Lynn and
Phillip John Russell*

Me and Doo moved out to Branson, Missouri, in the early '90s to try and settle down a little. It seemed like that way I wouldn't have to travel so much. More and more, Branson had lots of tourists coming to see music acts. I'd been traveling for so long that I kinda liked the idea of letting audiences come to us for a change.

We bought a theater for me to perform in and a home where Doo could hunt and fish, relax a little. I thought it'd be good for us. Doo had been sick. He was losing his battle with diabetes. He'd gotten sober for a while, but he started drinking again after our oldest son, Jack Benny, died in 1984.

Doo loved it at first. We'd found the prettiest little house by the lake. Doo got a new boat and was all excited about fishing.

To make it work, I had to do two shows a day, five

days a week. Before long the schedule started to wear us both down—me for all the going and Doo for all the missing me. I had to leave early to get to the theater for the show and was stuck there until late at night. It was a mess.

Branson didn't work out like I hoped. It wasn't restful at all. I felt stuck though. My whole band had moved with us and so had our kids Ernest Ray, Peggy, and Betty Sue and her husband. They were depending on me.

Doo knew I was having a hard time. He worried about me and I worried about him.

Doo's health was really suffering. He had to take insulin shots or he'd get real sick. He'd get dizzy all the time. He couldn't hardly catch his breath. Finally, I convinced him to go to the doctor. He had to have a triple bypass. I canceled all my shows. The kids came and we stayed with Doo right next door to the hospital. I was right by his side.

All our lives together Doo was so strong and proud. Right then he was so tender, so sweet. I don't think he was scared so much as he just didn't want to leave me. Lord knows I wasn't ready to lose him.

When Doo made it through surgery okay, I promised him we'd get him back on his feet. We'd go back to Hurricane Mills. He missed home something fierce. We held hands and talked about me taking time off. Maybe we'd visit Washington State again. We could go back to the old haunts where we used to go.

All of a sudden, somebody came in and told us Conway Twitty was in the emergency room. What was Conway doing there? Doo looked at me, just as surprised as could be. I told Doo I'd go find out what was going on. Finally, I found Conway's sweet wife, Dee. They'd been married for several years and we got along real well.

Dee told me what had happened. Conway had been

out on tour and after his show in Branson he'd planned to visit Doo and me in the hospital. After the show he'd collapsed on his tour bus. They rushed him to the very hospital where Doo was laid up. So I sat there with his wife and kept telling her that everything would be okay.

But it wasn't okay. He was brought into the hospital with an aneurysm in his stomach. He had a massive heart attack while they were operating on him.

That was June 5, 1993. My heart broke in about a thousand pieces.

I'd have liked to go to sleep then for about ten years. I'd never felt so tired. But I couldn't sleep. I had to go tell Doo.

When I told Doo about our friend, he looked about as sad as I'd ever seen him. I just laid my head on him and cried. I prayed I wouldn't have to say good-bye to Doo, too. Not yet.

Doo stayed with me. But the battle wasn't over. He was in that Branson hospital a month. When they released him, the doctors said he didn't have long left. That was it for me. I sold everything in Branson, laid off the band and almost everyone who worked for me. I stopped touring. I wanted to spend all the time I could with my Doo. I took him home to our house in Hurricane Mills and stayed close to his side until the day I held him while he breathed his last and passed over.

That was August 22, 1996.

After all these years, I can still feel Doo with me some nights when I'm lying in my bed. Or I'll turn a corner and feel him like he's standing close. There's reminders of him everywhere I look. Anyone will tell you that man could be a rascal, but he'll always be an angel to me.

# 36

# Angels

I'm dreaming of your sweet kiss
Oh, how you loved on me
I can almost feel you with me
Here in this blue moonlight
Oh, I miss being Mrs. tonight…
*"Miss Being Mrs.," by Loretta Lynn and*
*Phillip John Russell*

I'd outlived my best friend, Patsy, two children, my singing and business partner, and the love of my life. Plus, a legal battle with my second family, the Wilburns. All that was enough to kill me. Somehow, I kept on living. I guess the good Lord had more for me to do. I wasn't recording as much, though. Me and Owen Bradley had worked together so long. He was like a father to me, really, so when he passed, I was a little lost.

Then Dolly Parton called me up. Dolly's been my friend since we were young singers in Nashville. She was on *The Porter Wagoner Show* and I was on with the Wilburn Brothers. We've been friends forever. I'd do about anything for her and she'd do the same for me. I call

Dolly my mountain sister because we grew up a hundred and fifty miles from each other. We grew up the same. Dolly had an idea for an album together with our friend Tammy Wynette. It didn't take much arm-twisting to get me to say yes.

It was fun recording *Honky Tonk Angels* with Dolly and Tammy. We'd known each other for so long already by then. Being in the studio together felt easy, like being with family. We all love Kitty Wells, so we decided to record "It Wasn't God Who Made Honky Tonk Angels" as a trio. We had ourselves a good time. And our album was a hit. It went gold. I'm real proud of that. I didn't really think about it at the time but three women recording a hit album together was new and different.

# 37

## Sloe Gin Fizz (Jack White)

> I lost my heart, it didn't take no time
> But that ain't all, I lost my mind in Oregon...
> —*"Portland, Oregon," by Loretta Lynn*
> *and Jack White*

Through it all I kept writing songs. It's how I made sense of what was going on. When I felt something building up inside, I'd grab some paper and start writing. I'd scribble out lyrics on the back of a receipt or just any old piece of paper. Most of the time I kept them in my laundry room, but you could find bits of songs all over my house—in the kitchen, in drawers, and everywhere. Without Owen encouraging me to record my own songs, I didn't do much with what I wrote. I tucked those scraps away and recorded other people's songs for a while.

Then Jack White came into my life. The White Stripes recorded a live version of my song "Rated 'X.'" It wasn't country at all, but it was good. It had a real strong, raw feeling to it. I could tell Jack White had a ball singing it. I hadn't heard of them before that, but when the White Stripes released a record called *White Blood Cells*, they dedicated it to me. They sent me a copy of that album with a letter. That was real nice of them, I thought. I listened to it and I was surprised. It wasn't country at all, but I could tell they were real talented. Something about it felt like when me and the boys used to play back in Washington State. I liked it.

My manager, Nancy, set it up for Jack and Meg to visit me out at my house at Hurricane Mills. I fixed chicken and dumplings and homemade bread. We had a good time. Jack said, "This is the best bread I ever tasted." I gave him a loaf and a stick of butter to take home. I gave Meg one of my stage dresses to wear when she performs. She loved it.

I'd been saying to my daughter Patsy that I wanted to get back in the studio to make another album. We started going through the house, gathering up my old songs to find some new stuff to record. That's when Nancy called and asked if I wanted to do a show in New York with Jack and Meg. I said sure. Why not? So, I went up and did a show with them. I told Jack that I was wanting to record again. He said he'd like to produce me. I said yes right away. I knew Jack would do a good job.

So, Jack came to Nashville. Jack was like Owen. He wanted me to record my own songs in my own words. He asked me if I had any written. 'Course I had, like, fifty. I brought a bunch in, all in a file marked "Songs." They were from all during my career—scraps of paper. Some were just titles and others were whole songs I'd been working on over the years. When Jack saw how many I had, he was surprised. He picked some out for us to record. We demoed eight songs all in one day to get a feel for them. He hired the musicians and did the arrangements.

We recorded in this old house on Basket Bell Street

in East Nashville. We'd do about a song or two a day. Jack worried he was working me to death. He kept checkin' on me, asking, "Am I wearing you out?" I told him it wasn't nothing for me. Besides, we were doing something different. Something good. While we were working, sometimes I'd take hold of Jack's hand and say, "This is really going to shake them up, Jack."

Together we made one of my favorite country records of my career. He's a smart cookie. He is so smart in a way that I ain't, and I'm smart in a way he ain't. So together, it's good. We had such a nice time. That album came out in 2004—*Van Lear Rose* for the title track I'd wrote about my mommy.

"Miss Being Mrs." is one of my favorites. I wrote it about missing Doo. It hurts my heart to sing. It was good to get that off my chest. Kinda bittersweet. We sure had good times making that record. I am real glad we did it. Some people didn't like it. Country radio wouldn't play it. They thought I was going too rock 'n' roll. But it's not. It's as country as anything I ever cut. Maybe more. We got two Grammys for it, too: Best Country Album and Best Country Collaboration for the song called "Portland, Oregon."

"Portland, Oregon" was a song I started back around 1974. I had a little crush on one of our United Artists singers named Cal Smith. Now, I never did fool around on Doo, but if I had, it'd have been with Cal. He wasn't hard to look at; plus, me and him liked to cut up. The boys would always drink and carry on, but me—I hardly ever went to the bars. One day Ernest Tubb and Cal talked me into going out to watch them play golf. But we had fun. That day me and Cal worked up a plan. We went to the hotel bar that night where the guys in the band were. We made a big show of holding hands and cooing over each other. We had a bet about how long it'd take for word to get back to Doo. I never drank so I asked Cal what to order. Then I said real loud, "I'll have me a sloe gin fizz!" Every head turned. We laughed 'cause we knew the rumors were flying already!

I liked that sloe gin fizz. After just one I was feeling tipsy and thought I'd order another. "The bar's about to close, hon," Cal said. So I hollered to the waitress to bring me one for the road. We headed out, Cal walking me back to my room, with the boys in the band following behind to make sure I got back safely. Then I went in and scribbled down the start to a song that began, "Portland, Oregon, and sloe gin fizz / if that ain't love, then tell me what is." The rest is history. We won a Grammy for that one and a Grammy for the album.

# 38

# Fake News

Stay with me, a little bit longer
Stay with me, if you can
Stay with me, a little bit longer
Ain't no time to go, darlin'…
—*"Ain't No Time to Go," by Loretta Lynn and*
*Patsy Lynn Russell*

I f I'd have had an affair with Cal Smith or anybody else, you can bet it would have been all over the news. Stories like that sell magazines and newspapers, whether they're true or not. Maybe there's a little bit of truth in them but you gotta take most of that so-called news as pure entertainment. My fans care about me and they care what happens to me, so they put my face on the cover of a magazine with a headline about me being in trouble— that gets the cash register to ringing. Ten years ago, I bought a magazine that said I was dead. Well, then who bought the dang thing?

I used to always get *Star* magazine. That was a good one. They were always good to me. My friend Jeane Dixon was *Star* magazine's psychic. I met Jeane in 1981, and we stayed friends till she passed. After we met that first time, she sent me a letter. She told me things that showed she had the gift. My momma had the sight. I have it, too. I just don't always want to see.

What you have to remember is the news is just people talking. I don't think a thing about it anymore, unless they show a picture of me I don't like. Truth is I worry if they're *not* writing about me! If that happens, I probably will be dead. Ha!

You'll still see me in the news plenty. I stirred up a bunch of talk not long ago when I did an interview with my friend Martina McBride. I told her I think country music is dead. Listen, folks, nobody loves country music more than I do. It makes me sad when country music isn't on the radio anymore. They'd be better off playing real country. Real country music is pure. It's simple. It's real. When a song ain't real, how's it supposed to get anybody through anything? They try to play music that crosses over, whatever that means. That's not country.

My friends got together for a celebration at Bridgestone Arena for my eighty-eighth birthday—now, that was country! All them artists are country—Garth, Trisha, Tanya, Darius, Keith, Miranda. Any one of them could've played their own songs and that would've been a country show. They sang all my biggest hits and a few of their own. The Highwomen played that night: Brandi Carlile, Natalie Hemby, Maren Morris, and Amanda Shires. If country radio stations have a lick of sense, they'll play the hell out of those girls' new record. They sang Kitty Wells's "It Wasn't God Who Made Honky Tonk Angels." Right then I closed my eyes and I was backstage at the Ryman with Kitty singing that song live on the Grand Ole Opry. Then I went back further, to Washington State, when I was hearing Kitty's song playing on the radio. To the first time I had a little pocket money of my own from picking strawberries. My heart got so full. So full it felt like it might break.

See, that's what I mean. When you hear country music, you know it. Country music takes me right back to those strawberry fields. Or further back, to that little house in the holler where Momma sang to me.

Country will always take you back. And it'll always feel like home, no matter what.

# Acknowledgments

# Reading Group Guide

## Discussion Questions

1. Loretta says being poor helped her become the person she is, and that she wouldn't go back and change how she was raised. How do you think it prepared her? Do you think your upbringing prepared you for the life you have now? Is there anything you wish your parents had done differently?

2. Loretta gives Doolittle credit for her career. Why do you think his support was so essential? Do you have anyone in your life that similarly helps and encourages you? How do you think your life would be different without them?

3. Doolittle told Loretta that "you make your own luck." How is that true in their lives? Do you find it to be true in your own?

4. Loretta claims that country music is popular with ordinary people because it covers real-life issues. Do you agree with her assessment? Are there any other genres of music that do this?

5. Patsy Cline and Loretta seem to have gotten close quickly and, although the friendship was short, it has clearly had a lasting impact on Loretta. Why do you think that was the case? If you've had similarly influential friendships, how have they impacted you?

6. When Loretta started writing songs, she wanted to make sure they were from a woman's point of view. Why do you think that was important to her? What effect do you think that had on the country music industry?

7. Loretta says she wouldn't let Nashville change her values. How do you think she managed to stay grounded while her star rose, despite the somewhat corrupting influence of the music industry?

8. Loretta would've traded all her fame and fortune to live a regular life. Do you think her tradeoffs were worth it? Would you ever want to be famous?

9. Several new chapters are included in this edition. Does it seem like Loretta's perspective on her life and career have changed? Are there moments from your youth that you look back upon differently now?

10. Loretta writes about living through some important losses in this book. What do you think kept her going? What has kept you strong through trying times?

# About the Author

**LORETTA LYNN** is an American country music singer-songwriter whose groundbreaking career spans almost sixty years. With more than forty-five million albums sold worldwide, multiple gold albums, and numerous awards and accolades, Loretta is the most awarded female country recording artist and the only female ACM Artist of the Decade.